# First Steps in SAP S/4HANA® Controlling

**Second Edition**

Ashish Sampat
Tom King

## Thank you for purchasing this book from Espresso Tutorials!

Like a cup of espresso coffee, Espresso Tutorials SAP books are concise and effective. We know that your time is valuable and we deliver information in a succinct and straightforward manner. It only takes our readers a short amount of time to consume SAP concepts. Our books are well recognized in the industry for leveraging tutorial-style instruction and videos to show you step by step how to successfully work with SAP.

Check out our YouTube channel to watch our videos at *https://www.youtube.com/user/EspressoTutorials*.

If you are interested in SAP Finance and Controlling, please join us at *https://forum.espresso-tutorials.com/* to get your SAP questions answered and contribute to discussions.

## Related titles from Espresso Tutorials:

- Stefan Eifler, Christoph Theis:
  **Value Flows into SAP® Margin Analysis (CO-PA) in S/4HANA®**
  *http://5497.espresso-tutorials.com*
- Tom King:
  **A Practical Guide to Manufacturing Variances in SAP S/4HANA®**
  *http://5646.espresso-tutorials.com*
- Nora Voigt:
  **Practical Guide to SAP S/4HANA® Controlling**
  *https://es-tu.de/uXasR*
- John Pringle:
  **Practical Guide to SAP® Profit Center Accounting**—Second Edition
  *https://es-tu.de/cYNZ*
- Tanya Duncan:
  **Practical Guide to SAP CO-PC (Product Cost Controlling) in SAP S/4HANA®—2nd edition**
  *https://es-tu.de/6wHx7q*
- Janet Salmon:
  **First Steps in SAP S/4HANA® Universal Parallel Accounting**
  *https://es-tu.de/AbGDJ*

Ashish Sampat, Tom King
**First Steps in SAP S/4HANA® Controlling**—Second Edition

**ISBN**: 978-3-960124-61-0

**Editor**: Karen Schoch

**Cover Design**: Olesia Donchenko

**Cover Photo**: iStockphoto.com | Gulcin Ragiboglu No. 1282893334

**Interior Book Design**: Johann-Christian Hanke



2nd Edition 2025, Gleichen



URL: *www.espresso-tutorials.com*



**Feedback**
We greatly appreciate any feedback you may have concerning this book. Please send your feedback via email to: *info@espresso-tutorials.com*.

# Table of Contents

# Acknowledgements


## Ashish Sampat:

A number of years back, a colleague introduced me to a book called "The Goal: A Process of Ongoing Improvement" by Eliyahu M. Goldratt. This best-selling business novel explained the theory of constraints in an easy-to-understand format. I was awed by the simple explanation of a very complex topic. I read the book several times and my admiration for the author grew each time.

Recently, while I was providing an overview of a client's SAP design to a fellow consultant, he suddenly asked me if I was going to write a book about SAP. I was taken aback for a moment and thought to myself, well, that's not a bad idea, and so I decided I would wait for the right opportunity to take up such a project.

Opportunity knocked on the door when the Espresso Tutorials' team reached out regarding a potential book project. There are very few books that deal with SAP Controlling and we thought that readers could benefit from a guide to this topic. While working on the outline for this book, I was inspired by the format used in "The Goal", which was written in the style of a compelling business novel.

This new, revised edition of "First Steps in SAP Controlling" is seen through the eyes of Alex—a finance professional who is learning his new job as a plant cost analyst at Global Confectioners, Inc.

I want to thank my co-author Tom King, who provided S/4HANA and Fiori inputs for the fresh look of this second edition. I am grateful to the team at Espresso Tutorials—particularly Martin Munzel, Joerg Siebert, Alice Adams for giving me an opportunity to write this book; and Karen Schoch, who painstakingly and patiently edited the book while continuously encouraging me to incorporate formatting and content suggestions.

I also want to thank my family, friends, colleagues, and fellow SAP consultants for providing continuous encouragement and support while I wrote this book. Particularly my wife, Meenal, and our children, Megha and Jash, who were supportive of me spending time completing the manuscript.

I enjoyed writing this book and I hope that you enjoy reading it.

## Tom King:

I also want to express my thanks to Ashish, Martin, and Alice for asking me to join this project and to help update this wonderful First Steps book to incorporate the realm of S/4HANA. It has been great working with the Espresso team. I am also honored to be working with Ashish, whom I met several years ago when he was presenting at a conference. I have always been impressed by his ability to distill complex topics into easily understandable concepts. I can only hope that my contributions to this book have fallen in line with his style to make this edition as successful as the original.

# Preface

The integrated nature of SAP business software becomes easier to comprehend when one understands the intricacies of SAP Controlling. This book is intended for beginners who would like to get an overview of the SAP Controlling module.

This book is set against the backdrop of Global Confectioners, Inc. (GCI), a fictional chocolate manufacturing company with its manufacturing facility in Chocotown. You will be taken through several day-in-the-life scenarios of various key functions: plant finance, manufacturing, inventory control, and information systems. Seen through the eyes of Alex, who is learning his new job as Plant Cost Analyst at GCI Chocotown, you will be introduced to SAP Controlling concepts with different examples drawn from this setting. Alex learns something new every day with the help of his manager, as well as his colleagues at GCI.

This book explains some of the complex SAP Controlling concepts using a case study approach. Characters in the plot interact through dialogue and questions, and concepts are explained using examples relating to issues that the team is dealing with.

This book is an ideal read for anyone who wants to understand the SAP Controlling module and its integration with other modules. Whether you are new to an organization using SAP business software, a member of an SAP implementation team, or are a finance professional who simply wants to learn about SAP business software, this book aims to provide answers to many of your questions. Additionally, screenshots are provided with examples, so that you can effectively visualize the data flow.

One of the issues that we had to deal with when updating the book from the older ECC environment to S/4HANA was the user interface. Due to the methodology that SAP has used to update finance to the Universal Journal approach, not all of the classic controlling functions have been migrated to the new database structures and Fiori interface. This particularly affects cost-center planning and the excellent cost center reports that were a main feature of the Cost Center Accounting module. Fortunately, the old Controlling database structure remains compatible with the Universal Journal concept, and a majority of the older SAP GUI (graphical user interface) transactions are still useable in S/4HANA. SAP has provided a method of executing GUI transactions from Fiori tiles by using SAP GUI for HTML

(WebGUI), and many of the older transactions have been delivered as Fiori tiles. Some important transactions were not included in this, so throughout the text we have identified when transactions have to be used instead of Fiori tiles. If a function can be executed from a Fiori tile, then we reference that tile. If only a GUI transaction is available to perform a specific function, we identify the transaction and the standard menu path to access that transaction. We also added Chapter 13 to discuss this topic and provide information on how new Fiori tiles can be created in order to execute the GUI transactions that were not delivered with the system.

---

We have added a few icons to highlight important information. These include:

**Tips**

Tips highlight information that provides more details about the subject being described and/or additional background information.

**Examples**

Examples help illustrate a topic better by relating it to real world scenarios.

**! Attention**

Attention notices highlight information that you should be aware of when you go through the examples in this book on your own.

Finally, a note concerning the copyright: all screenshots printed in this book are the copyright of SAP SE. All rights are reserved by SAP SE. Copyright pertains to all SAP images in this publication. For the sake of simplicity, we do not mention this specifically underneath every screenshot.

# 1 The characters—who's who at GCI?

**Global Confectioners, Inc. (GCI) is a fictional organization that manufactures chocolates and other confectionery products. Throughout this book, we use GCI as a case study to walk through real-life scenarios where SAP Controlling is used at a manufacturing facility. Like any other manufacturing organization, GCI has a finance controller (sometimes also referred as cost controller, or simply a controller), a manufacturing manager, an inventory controller, and onsite IT support staff. Our main protagonist is Alex, a plant cost analyst who has recently joined GCI. Alex has never used SAP software before and is an ideal candidate to take this journey with you, our readers.**

## 1.1 Alex—Plant cost analyst at GCI

"Welcome to Global Confectioners, Inc.," announced Iris, the human resources manager, as she greeted Alex on his first day at the company. Alex had met Iris during the recruitment process and was somewhat familiar with her.

Alex was excited to start his new job as the Plant Cost Analyst for GCI at their manufacturing facility in Chocotown. For the previous two years, Alex had worked for Fork-o-Lift Works (FLW) in a similar role. The difference between the two companies is that FLW is in the discrete manufacturing industry, whereas GCI is in a process-based industry. Alex was eager to learn more about this industry and looked forward to new career challenges.

Alex joined FLW fresh out of college. The previous two years had been full of on-the-job learning. A plant cost analyst is not necessarily a number cruncher, but it is important that that person understands the systems and financial business processes used in the organization. People are an integral part of processes and systems, and it is important to know not only who's who, but also who does what.

"First, let's go through some HR documentation and then I'll introduce you to your manager, Bob," Iris said. Luckily, Alex remembered to bring all the required documents to complete the paperwork. Everything looked pretty similar to the paperwork he completed at FLW—just a different company name and logo. "Hopefully things will get more interesting from here", Alex thought to himself.

"Okay, Alex, now that the paperwork is done, why don't I walk you over to Bob's office and he'll take over from there," Iris said. Once they arrived at Bob's office, Iris told him, "Please don't hesitate to contact me if you have any issues or concerns."

"Sure, thank you," Alex said.

## 1.2 Bob—Plant controller and Alex's manager at GCI

"I'm so glad you're here!" said Bob. "We're so happy that we found a bright person like you to join our team."

Alex took notes as Bob explained the department structure and Alex's roles and responsibilities.

"Soon, we'll be starting our annual budget planning process, and I want you to know the ins and outs of last year's budget. Here's the file that your predecessor, Kevin, prepared. Please go over it and let me know what questions you have." Bob pointed to a bulky binder. "Have you worked with SAP software before?" Bob asked.

"No," Alex responded, "we had a home-grown system at my previous company, but I've heard a lot about SAP from other friends and colleagues who've worked with SAP systems, and I'm excited to learn more about it."

"Don't worry," Bob said. "Read through this training manual that our IT team put together. There's a lot of interesting information here. It'll provide a good overview of the system setup. Going over this material should keep you busy for the next three or four days. In the meantime, we'll arrange for you to get access to the system."

Alex was curious and wondered what kind of training manual took three or four days to read through. He hoped it was detailed, with examples, otherwise he could easily lose interest.

Bob continued, "We've recently been having some issues with our monthly process order reporting. The numbers that we report do not match the numbers from the manufacturing team. I want you to get involved with this issue as soon as you can. Another area of immediate focus for you will be to address the inventory valuation questions that the inventory control folks have."

Alex replied, "Sure, I'll do my best."

"Come on, let me introduce you to the team." Bob stood up and walked towards the door.

Alex could smell cocoa as soon as they entered the manufacturing floor where chocolate was being produced. He looked forward to meeting the team.

## 1.3 Carl—Manufacturing manager at GCI

"Alex, meet Carl. He's responsible for manufacturing and will be your first point of contact for any questions you have in terms of production. Carl, Alex is replacing Kevin and will handle your costing-related queries."

"Welcome, Alex. It's nice to meet you. I'm looking forward to working with you." Carl shook hands with Alex.

Bob turned to Carl and said, "I haven't looked at your question yet about the process order variances from yesterday, but I'll get back to you asap."

"No worries, Bob, I understand," Carl said. "Because we're adding a new line next month I'm going to be tied up for the next few weeks, so I won't have much time to address the routine queries myself, but we'll figure it out. In fact, I have a meeting now with a couple of vendors, so I need to head off. I'll see you folks later." Carl exited his office and Alex and Bob stepped out as well.

## 1.4 Dave—Inventory controller at GCI

"This is our receiving and raw material storage area," Bob explained. "As you can see, this is the starting point for our plant's operations. I'd like to introduce you to Dave who's responsible for this area."

Alex took a visual survey of all the drums, pallets, bins, and racks around him.

"Dave, I want you to meet Alex—he just joined today as our new plant cost analyst," Bob said.

"Oh yeah, in Kevin's place, right?" Dave said. "We've been expecting you. Welcome to GCI. My team and I were actually looking at an inventory report earlier and had a couple of questions on the valuation. Maybe once you settle in and familiarize yourself you can help us out with that. In the meantime, I'll have to pick Bob's brain."

## 1.5 Erin—Finance IT support at GCI

"Alex, all the people you've met so far today are all cross-functional team members," Bob said. "However, the person who I'm going to introduce you to next is kind of an extension of our finance function."

"Erin, this is Alex. He just joined my team today. I've asked him to go through our Finance Training Manual, which I know you had a hand in developing. Alex, this is Erin, she is very knowledgeable on our overall SAP system setup, particularly in the areas of finance and costing. I consider Erin a great asset to our IT support organization. She's often my go-to person and I bet she'll be yours too."

"Uh oh!," exclaimed Erin. "You exaggerate a lot, Bob. Welcome, Alex. I'm looking forward to working with you. As Bob said, please go over the training material and let me know what questions you have."

"Nice meeting you, thanks for your help," Alex said.

"What a day", Alex thought to himself, "I have to get up to speed quickly and help the team address all of these questions".

# 2 Controlling—what exactly are we trying to control?

*"He who controls others may be powerful,*
*but he who has mastered himself is mightier still."*
—Lao Tzu

**The term "control" can be defined as the process of channeling efforts in a particular direction, towards a particular goal. It also includes course correction, as necessary, to reach the defined goal. In the context of this book, "control" refers to cost controlling, particularly in SAP Enterprise Resource Planning (ERP). In this chapter, we look at the modules and functional areas which are typically used in a manufacturing organization that uses SAP software as its system of record.**

## 2.1 Overview of controlling

Alex sat down and opened the Finance Training Manual. He was keen to learn about the SAP software. Alex started reading. The manual provided an overview of the SAP software system and how GCI recognized the value in streamlining processes by implementing SAP. Several pages provided step-by-step instructions on how to log into the SAP system. Alex would have to wait until he got access to GCI's system in order to try the steps out himself, but he could review the training manual until then.

The manual went into further detail on the various modules in SAP. Alex started taking notes.

### 2.1.1 SAP modules

#### Materials Management (MM)

In addition to procuring materials for the organization via a purchase order, the *Materials Management (MM)* module also deals with the movement of materials within and between various departments. MM supplies raw materials and other components for production. Once products are produced, the software enables materials to be stocked in the warehouse, ready to ship when needed. The SAP software (usually) records a financial transaction when goods are moved into/within/outside the organization. Vendors submit invoices and are paid at a later date—depending on the payment terms—thereby completing the *procure-to-pay* cycle. Alex remembered that they called it a *source-to-pay* cycle at FLW.

### Production Planning (PP)

*Production Planning (PP)* through the materials requirement planning (MRP) functionality uses information from sales orders, demand forecasting, and available inventory to create a production/procurement plan. The SAP PP module tracks the production of semi-finished and finished materials and makes them ready for the next level of consumption or shipment. In doing so, the SAP system calculates numbers for reports using the valuation of manufacturing components supplied by MM, the valuation of the internal labor and machine hours consumed in manufacturing, and overhead costs not directly associated with the manufacturing process. Here too, a financial transaction is recorded when goods are moved into/within/outside the production department. Alex could relate this to the shop-floor execution cycle at FLW.

### Sales and Distribution (SD)

The *Sales and Distribution (SD)* module tracks the activity from the start of a customer inquiry and converts it into a sales order, which is later followed up by a shipment. A sales invoice is then generated. The cycle ends when the customer makes a payment (FLW called it the *order-to-cash* cycle). Alex did not expect a financial transaction to be generated during the inquiry and sales order stages, but he could quickly relate to the shipment, billing, and payment steps, and the transactions carried out at each stage.

### Financial Accounting (FI) and Controlling (CO)

Now that Alex had a good understanding of supply chain functionality and how it mapped to the MM, PP, and SD modules, Alex understood how these transactions were recorded in the finance module. Every time there is a goods movement or a transaction with financial implications, the SAP software immediately records the financial transaction. The transaction is then typically entered into the general ledger (GL), as well as accounts receivable (AR) and accounts payable (AP). Each of the transactions records profit center information and provides further details for reporting.

It all made logical sense to Alex, but he was not able to understand what role the SAP Controlling module played in the structure. The Finance Training Manual went on to say that the *SAP Controlling (CO)* module was all about recording transactions internally within the organization. It dealt with cost center accounting (CCA), overhead cost management (OCM), activity-based costing (ABC), product costing (PC), and margin analysis, also known as profitability analysis (PA)—all of which support internal reporting requirements. Additionally, project systems (PS) enable tracking of a capital project and its eventual conversion to a fixed asset in the asset accounting (AA) module. Both FI and CO are integral parts of the *record-to-report* or *accounting-to-report* cycles. FLW called this process *finance-to-report*. A different name, but the same concept.

## 2.2 The link with FI

**"FI is all about data capture and external reporting, whereas CO is all about internal reporting"**—this was highlighted in the manual in big, bold font. Alex could relate this to his previous experience when it came to legal entity reporting and submitting reports to external agencies. He had to prepare a trial balance, a balance sheet, and an income statement, along with various other reports such as cash flow statements, accounting policy, and other statutory statements, as per his previous employer's requirements and the legal requirements.

Non-financial information, such as production volume, is not recorded in trial balance. However, it can be an important statistic that could be required for reporting performance to management. This means that there should be something that records information over and above what is required for external (legal) reporting. Is this called *controlling*?

**The difference between FI and CO**

Financial Accounting (FI) is all about data capture and external reporting, whereas Controlling (CO) is all about internal reporting. FI and CO complement each other to a great extent. SAP software is an integrated system, and all financial transactions are captured in Financial Accounting. Controlling supports internal reporting requirements.

"Why not have one single module and call it financials or reporting, or something like that?", Alex wondered. He continued reading.

If Alex wanted to perform some sort of an allocation of costs for sending costs from one cost center to another, FI could handle it. However, it would be too cumbersome to enter that type of allocation every time a source transaction occurs. GCI's software was programmed to perform the allocations at month-end.

Okay, Alex thought, GCI must use controlling as part of month-end closing processes.

Month-end closing has many tasks in addition to cost allocation. For example, depreciation calculation occurs in asset accounting (AA), foreign currency valuation and accrual postings in the GL. Bank reconciliation also takes place in the banking and treasury (TR) modules, etc.—all of these tasks are handled in FI. CO passes the work-in-progress (WIP) number to FI via the product costing module and enables the capture of certain costs in further detail. For example, depreciation costs, which can be captured at cost-center level, enable costs to be broken down into where they are incurred. FI can be compared to a big river that brings data in from all of the tributaries (modules) and then facilitates internal reporting via CO and external reporting via FI.

Alex noted that FI and CO complement each other to a great extent, but they might not be able to survive on their own because they are so dependent on each other. He thought he now understood the crux of the link between the two modules. He was eager to learn more about FI and CO.

## 2.3 Links with other SAP modules

The Finance Training Manual covered additional interesting links between various modules and controlling. There are links between the PP, SD, and the MM modules, but Alex was most interested in the links between supply chain functionality and the FI and CO modules, since that was going to be the main focus of his job.

### 2.3.1 MM and CO-PC

Standard costs of procured materials are calculated at the beginning of the period in Product Cost Controlling (CO-PC). The standard cost is then used to valuate inventory, as well as record goods movements during the month in MM.

### 2.3.2 MM and FI-GL + FI-AP + CO-PC

The actual price on the purchase order (from MM) and on the invoice receipt from the vendor (from Accounts Payable FI-AP) is recorded. FI-GL tracks purchase price variances in accounting compared to the standard price of the material (part of CO-PC).

### 2.3.3 PP and CO-PC

Raw material costs are derived using quantities from the *bill of material (BOM)* multiplied by the raw material procurement price. Conversion costs are derived using activity quantities from routing multiplied by the predetermined activity rate. BOM and routing/recipe (a recipe contains the steps to manufacture a product) are part of the PP module. Production and process orders record costs during the lifecycle of the orders and enable WIP/variance calculations at month end.

### 2.3.4 PP and CO-ABC

Production/process orders use activity types that are confirmed during production to record labor and machine hours. They use predetermined activity rates through the *Activity-Based Costing (CO-ABC)* component.

### 2.3.5 MM and FI + CO-PC

Supply purchases are directly expensed to a cost center. Raw materials are inventoried to the balance sheet. Consumption of raw materials is recorded on orders.

### 2.3.6 MM and FI-AA

Capital equipment purchases are recorded to an asset or capital project—part of *Asset Accounting (FI-AA)*.

### 2.3.7 SD and FI-GL + FI-AR + CO-PA

Customer sales are recorded in FI-GL and *Accounts Receivable (FI-AR)* at the time the customer is billed. Additionally, margin analysis/*Controlling–Profitability Analysis (CO-PA)* captures this information in multidimensional reporting known as characteristics and value fields.

### 2.3.8 SD and CO-CCA/CO-OM

Samples shipped to customers can be charged to a specific cost center using *Cost Center Accounting (CO-CCA)*, and internal orders can be charged using Overhead Cost Controlling (CO-OM), for future tracking and reporting purposes.

The training manual went on to explain that **"The MRP controller and financial controller are the two most powerful functions in an SAP environment"**:

- The MRP controller decides what to produce and when to produce it.
- The financial controller keeps track of all of the costs and variances in the plant.

However, all of this depends on demand. It is assumed that demand for the product will remain constant.

**Roles—MRP controller and financial controller**

The MRP controller and financial controller are often regarded as two key roles in any organization that uses SAP business software.

Alex remembered reading about how a manufacturing facility needs to ensure that it produces a good quality product at optimal inventory levels, while keeping a close eye on the costs. He realized that CO would help him achieve this task in his role at GCI as long as he used the available tools effectively and made sure that the processes were adhered to.

# 3 Controlling organization structure—all in the family

*"I cannot trust a man to control others who cannot control himself."*

—Robert E. Lee

**Every organization has various departments or functions that are responsible for implementing strategic plans, converting them into action, and managing day-to-day operations. This type of functional/departmental structure exists in the business system as well. This chapter provides an overview of the controlling organization structure in SAP business software.**

Alex continued to read through the Finance Training Manual and came across a chapter on organizational structure. There was a diagram illustrating the overall organizational structure at GCI (see Figure 3.1).

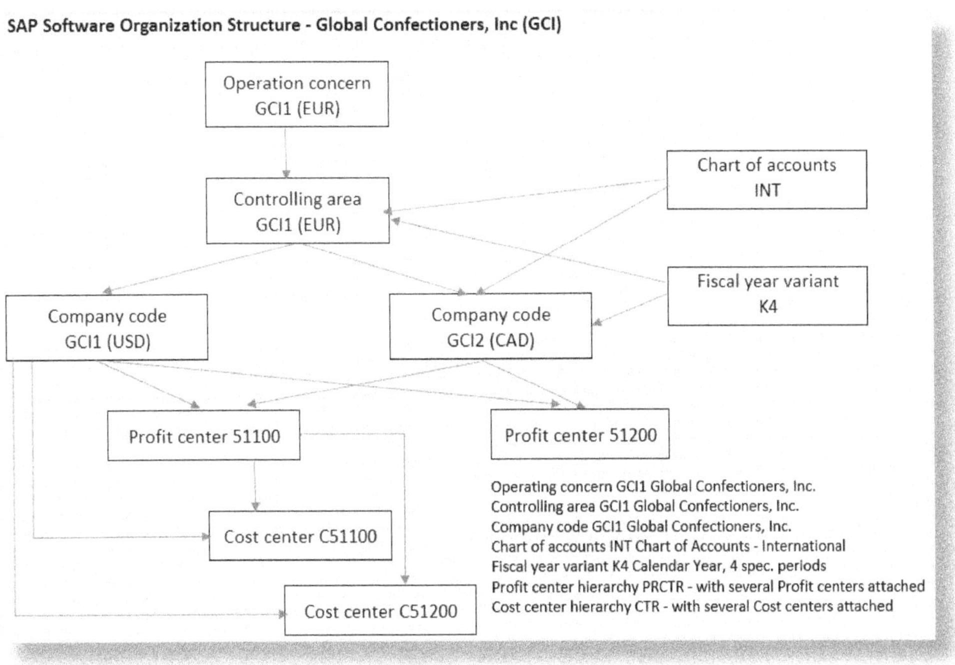


*Figure 3.1: GCI SAP software organizational structure*

The training manual went on to further explain the importance of the SAP software organization structure.

The *SAP software organization structure* is fundamental to the overall structure in which master data and transaction data is defined in SAP. It is essentially the backbone of the system. Accurate design and setup of the software organization structure is a critical step in SAP implementation—it is extremely difficult to change the structure once it has been designed and configured, and transaction data has been posted.

An SAP software organization structure reflects a business's own organizational structure, reporting requirements, and processes in the SAP system

An enterprise's organizational structure is mapped to the SAP system organization structure. This is done at the early stages of SAP implementation projects. The idea is to ensure that all business processes will be able to function smoothly, not only from a transactional processing perspective, but also for internal and external reporting.

A company code is defined based on legal entities. Because GCI has more than one legal entity, multiple company codes (e.g., GCI1, GCI2, etc.) have been defined in order to facilitate external reporting. However, there is only one controlling area, which enables consolidation for internal reporting.

## 3.1 Chart of accounts

The *chart of accounts* is a list of general ledger accounts. Accounts are broadly categorized into assets and liabilities, and then into more granular detail as required by the organization. SAP is an integrated system, and all transactions are recorded in the financials with GL accounts enabling data capture. The chart of accounts provides a structure for recording the transactions, which enables an accurate depiction of the overall financial and operational health of the organization.

The chart of accounts can be used across multiple company codes and provides a common definition across all companies. Additionally, it streamlines the consolidation of a company's financial books across multiple legal entities.

Being a global company, GCI adopted an *international (INT) chart of accounts* that enables assets, liabilities, income, and expenses to be captured as per international accounting standards.

The chart of accounts is maintained using configuration transaction OB13 (see Figure 3.2). The menu path is: TOOLS • CUSTOMIZING • IMG • SPRO EXECUTE PROJECT • FINANCIAL ACCOUNTING • FINANCIAL ACCOUNTING GLOBAL SETTINGS • MASTER DATA • GL ACCOUNTS • PREPARATIONS • EDIT CHART OF ACCOUNTS LIST.

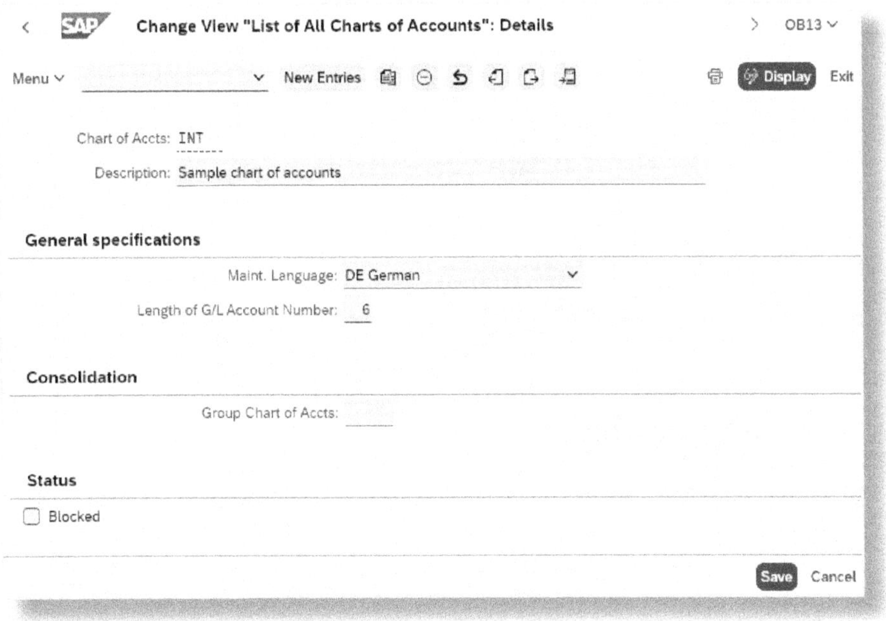


*Figure 3.2: OB13—Chart of accounts*

## 3.2 Fiscal year variant

A *fiscal year variant* defines an organization's financial and reporting fiscal calendar. GCI, like most companies, uses a calendar month as the reporting calendar and has adopted fiscal year variant K4. Four periods allow for optional additional buckets for quarterly/annual financial reporting. Fiscal year variant configuration is maintained via transaction OB29 (see Figure 3.3).

The menu path is: TOOLS • CUSTOMIZING • IMG • SPRO EXECUTE PROJECT • FINANCIAL ACCOUNTING • FINANCIAL ACCOUNTING GLOBAL SETTINGS • LEDGERS • FISCAL YEAR AND POSTING PERIODS • MAINTAIN FISCAL YEAR VARIANT.

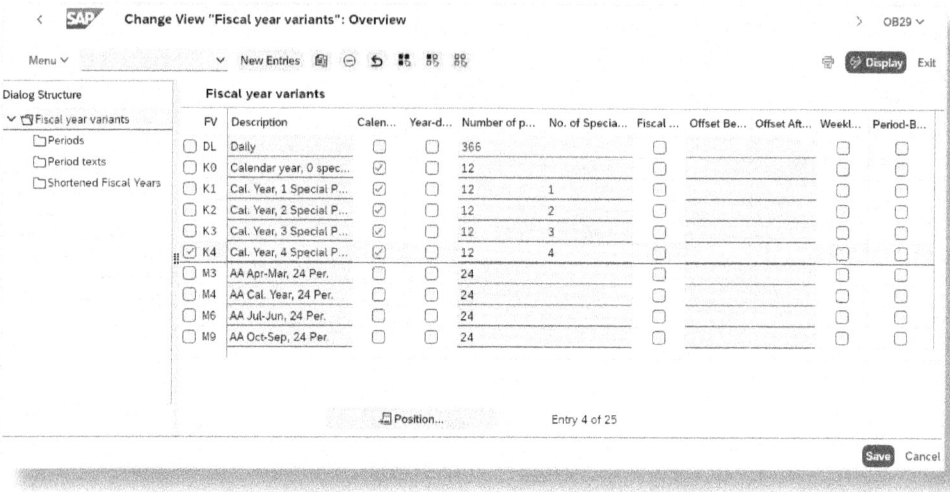


*Figure 3.3: OB29—Fiscal year variant*

## 3.3 Operating concern

An *operating concern* refers to an enterprise, with respect to profitability analysis. It is the highest organization structure element in SAP Controlling. It is possible to assign multiple controlling areas to one operating concern.

At GCI, there is one controlling area, assigned to a single operating concern. Operating concerns are maintained using configuration transaction KEA0 (see Figure 3.4).

The menu path is: TOOLS • CUSTOMIZING • IMG • SPRO EXECUTE PROJECT • CONTROLLING • PROFITABILITY ANALYSIS • STRUCTURES • DEFINE OPERATING CONCERN • MAINTAIN OPERATING CONCERN.

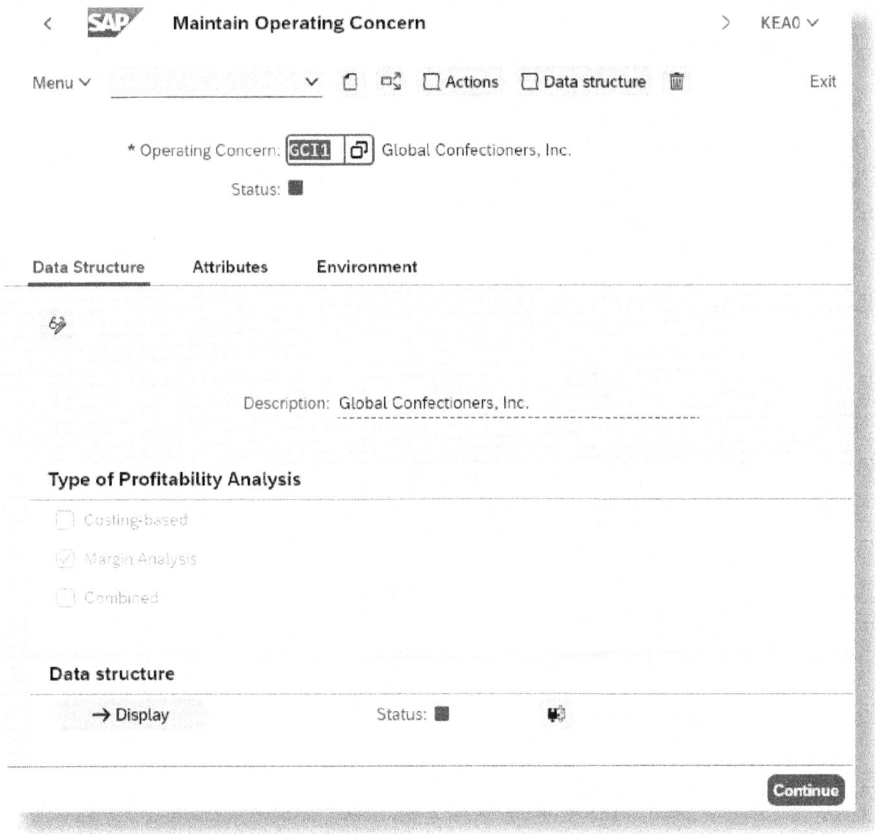


*Figure 3.4: KEA0 —Operating concern/Controlling area*

## 3.4 Controlling area

The *controlling area* captures and records costs and revenue across the organization, primarily from an internal reporting point of view. It also provides a cross-company view of the organization.

The controlling area enables the allocation of costs across cost centers within the same controlling area.

In order to be assigned to the same controlling area, all relevant company codes must have the same chart of accounts and fiscal year variant. Although the currency can differ across company codes, the controlling area has a unique currency in which all transactions are recorded.

It is possible to create multiple controlling areas, but it is not possible to allocate costs across multiple controlling areas systematically. One could, of course, post journal entries with different company codes which, in turn, would post to the respective controlling areas. However, this type of allocation is not possible using allocations in the CO module. In addition, consolidated management reporting capabilities would be lost (e.g., operating expense reporting and other profit and loss (P&L) management reporting).

Configuration of the controlling area is executed using transaction OKKP, as shown in Figure 3.5.

The menu path is: TOOLS • CUSTOMIZING • IMG • SPRO EXECUTE PROJECT • CONTROLLING • GENERAL CONTROLLING • ORGANIZATION • MAINTAIN CONTROLLING AREA.

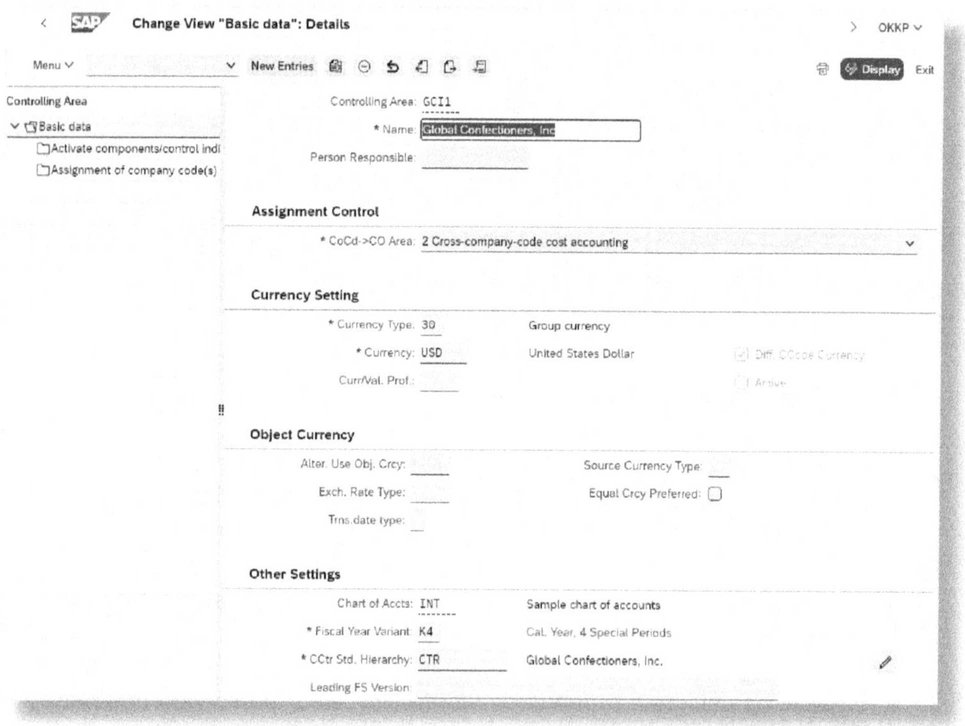


*Figure 3.5: OKKP—Controlling area*

## 3.5 Company code

A *company code* is the smallest organizational unit for which a complete set of self-contained accounts can be created or external reporting.

A company code represents a legal entity for external reporting. It records all relevant transactions and generates all supporting documents for the legally required financial statements, such as the balance sheet and P&L statement. Company codes are set up using configuration transaction OX02 and are maintained using configuration transaction OBY6, as shown in Figure 3.6.

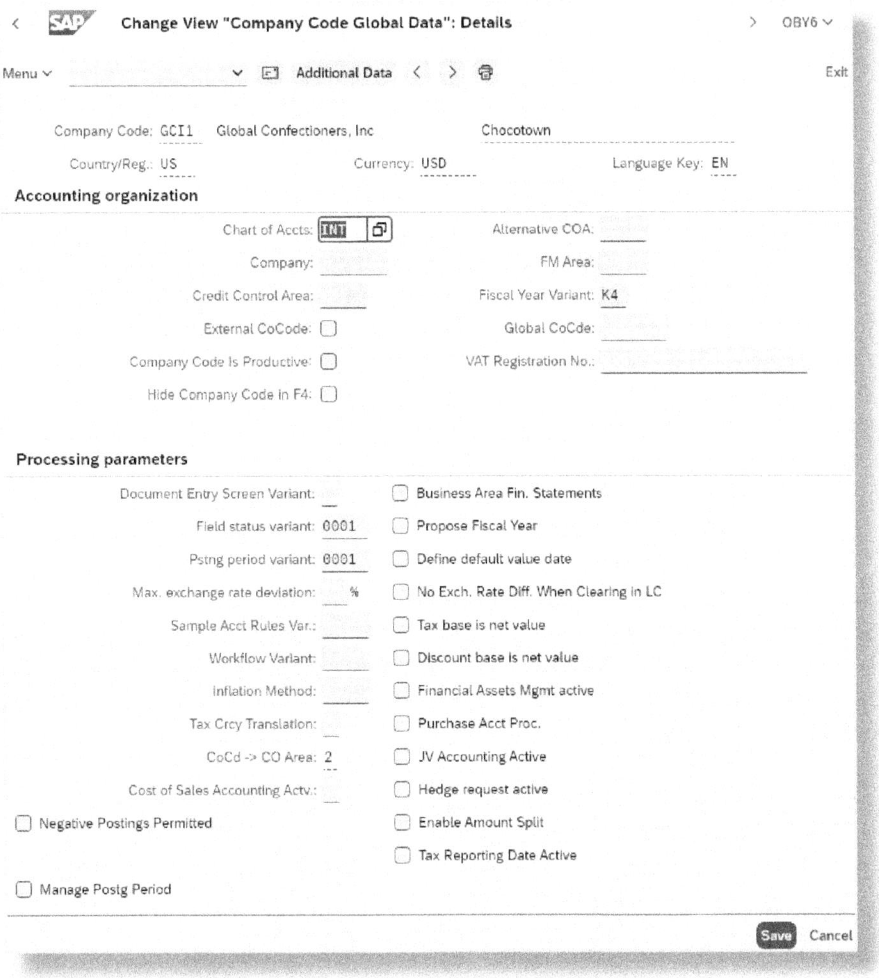


*Figure 3.6: OBY6—Company code*

The menu path for company code setup is: TOOLS • CUSTOMIZING • IMG • SPRO EXECUTE PROJECT • ENTERPRISE STRUCTURE • DEFINITION • FINANCIAL ACCOUNTING • EDIT, COPY, DELETE, CHECK COMPANY CODE.

The menu path for company code global parameters is: TOOLS • CUSTOMIZING • IMG • SPRO EXECUTE PROJECT • FINANCIAL ACCOUNTING • FINANCIAL ACCOUNTING GLOBAL SETTINGS • GLOBAL PARAMETERS FOR COMPANY CODE • ENTER GLOBAL PARAMETERS.

It is possible to post cross-company transactions within FI, provided affiliates are set up as customers and vendors are defined as trading partners. Intercompany eliminations can be performed based on trading partner information.

### 3.5.1 Currencies

Alex researched how GCI uses currencies in the system to assign value to financial postings. He saw that a currency is assigned to each company code. For example, company code GCI1 uses USD (US dollars) and company code GCI2 uses CAD (Canadian dollars). He reasoned that managers responsible for each company code would want to see results in the local currency for that company code.

But what about reporting at the corporate level? If reports showed each of the company codes' currencies, then combining results from GCI1 (Global Confectioners, Inc) and GCI2 (Global Confectioners, CA) would be terribly confusing. Therefore, a group currency (in this case, USD) is also supported when posting financial transactions. Group reporting uses this group currency, which is assigned to the controlling area. To determine how these currencies are defined and used in the system, Alex looked at configuration transaction FINSC_LEDGER, which is used to define how currencies are assigned at the company code level and how different currency types interact with one another in financial postings.

Alex examined the company code settings for currencies after finding FINSC_LEDGER via menu path: TOOLS • CUSTOMIZING • IMG • SPRO EXECUTE PROJECT • FINANCIAL ACCOUNTING • FINANCIAL ACCOUNTING GLOBAL SETTINGS • LEDGERS • LEDGER • DEFINE SETTINGS FOR LEDGERS AND CURRENCY TYPES.

He highlighted the definitions for the two company codes and discovered that the currencies were not directly defined (see Figure 3.7).

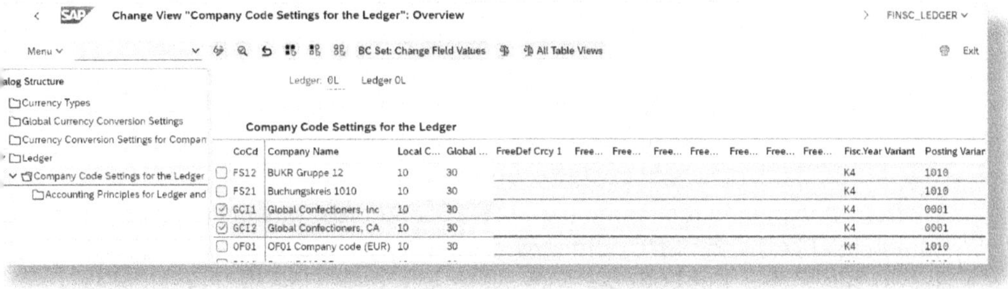


*Figure 3.7: FINSC_LEDGER—Company code currency type settings*

Instead, he saw something called *currency type* in the LOCAL CURRENCY and GLOBAL CURRENCY columns. Currency type 10 refers to the currency assigned to the company code. Currency type 30 is the *group currency* and is defined in transaction SCC4 as the default system currency for the implementation. The currency defined for the controlling area should match this currency, and because of this, group currency is also sometimes referred to as *controlling area currency*.

Alex also noticed that eight "freely defined currencies" could also be set up for the company code. These settings also were defined by currency types. When he asked why these were not used, Bob told Alex that GCI only needed information for these two company codes in local (type 10) and global (type 30) currency.

**Currency types**

Currency types are used to inform the system where to find the actual currency being used:

- Currency type 10 (local currency) uses the currency defined for the company code.
- Currency type 30 (group currency) uses the client-wide currency defined in transaction SCC4.

Other currency types that can be selected include:

- 40 (hard currency)—defined for the country assigned to the company code,
- 50 (index-based currency)—defined for the country, and

- 60 (global company currency)—defined at company level and not at company code level.

In addition, custom currency types can be defined in FINSC_LEDGER. Due to system limitations, avoid the use of currency type 20 (controlling area currency), as this is not supported for financial postings.

In effect, this means that company code GCI2 records transactions in both currencies (CAD and USD). Company code GCI1 also records transactions in two currencies, but both currency types reference USD because that is the group currency.

**Currencies in controlling area and company code**

If, for example, GCI acquired other companies in Mexico, Brazil, and Switzerland, each of the new company codes would have their own currency for local legal reporting (MXN—Mexican pesos, BRL—Brazilian real, CHF—Swiss francs). Internal reporting would be in USD because each of these company codes would be assigned to controlling area GCI1.

If GCI had its headquarters in Europe, then it is likely that controlling area GCI1 would have CHF (Swiss francs) or EUR (Euro) as the controlling area currency. Similarly, if its headquarters were in Asia, we would expect the controlling area currency to be JPY (Japanese yen) or CNY (Chinese yuan).

However, GCI is not limited to recording only company code currency (CAD/USD) and group currency (USD).

Financial accounting also captures transaction currency at the financial accounting document level, also known as *document currency* (e.g., SGD—Singapore dollars). The currency type assigned to this is 00, but it does not need to be defined at the company code level. A transaction in SGD is converted at the prevailing exchange rate into company code currency (also known as *first local currency*). Additionally, group currency is also recorded as *second local currency*. Therefore, for these two company codes, GCI's FI records three currencies:

- transaction/document currency.
- company code/local currency.
- controlling area/group currency.

### Currencies in FI and CO

Financial accounting records transactions in:

- transaction/document currency,
- company code/local currency,
- controlling area/group currency, and
- any of the freely defined currencies assigned to the company code from transaction FINSC_LEDGER.

Controlling transactions are confined to using a maximum of three currency types plus a document currency. These three currencies are the "local" currencies which show up in financial documents. A normal practice is to set up at least two currencies—company code and group.

Alex noted that the names of these fields were a bit different between FI and CO, but that they essentially stored the same values in both modules. Figure 3.8 shows the setup for company code GCI2.

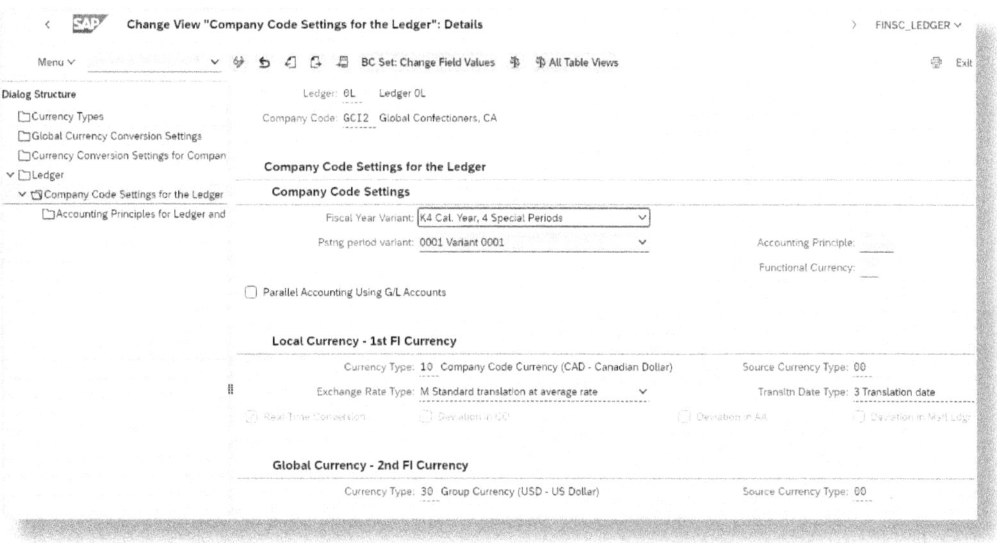


*Figure 3.8: FINSC_LEDGER–FI currencies for company code GCI2*

## 3.6 Profit center

A *profit center* is a business unit in the organization that acts as an independent unit operating in the marketplace. Both income and expenses can be monitored at profit center level and therefore create a complete P&L (and even a partial balance sheet at working capital level) at profit center level. This information can then be summarized using the profit center hierarchy that reflects the management structure. Alternative hierarchy structures can also be defined for summarized analysis; for example, by sector or business/location, to report on and manage operating results.

Objects such as cost centers, projects, materials, sales orders, etc., are assigned to a profit center. This enables costs and revenues to flow to profit center level for reporting. For internal management reporting, a profit center can be assigned to one or many company codes for a cross-company code view. A profit center hierarchy is set up using the MANAGE PROFIT CENTER GROUPS Fiori app (see Figure 3.9).

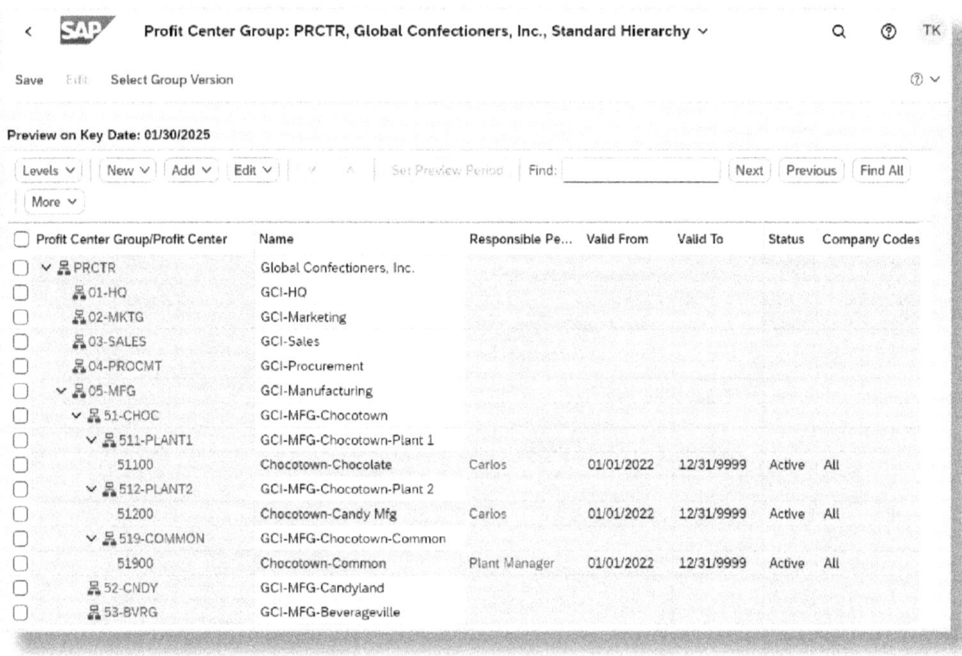


*Figure 3.9: "Manage Profit Center Groups" app—profit center hierarchy*

## 3.7 Controlling versions

*Versions* in SAP Controlling maintain independent sets of planning data and actual data.

Versions are used in planning to set up alternative scenarios based on different assumptions. Different versions can represent best-case, worst-case, or most-likely scenarios. Other examples could be different markets, promotional campaigns, and sales strategies.

The most likely scenario is usually set up in plan version 000. This data is used to calculate planned prices for activity types. Actual data is posted in version 000 to compare *plan versus actual*, as well as *plan versus target*.

Use transaction OKEQ to configure controlling versions, as shown in Figure 3.10.

The menu path is: TOOLS • CUSTOMIZING • IMG • SPRO EXECUTE PROJECT • ENTERPRISE STRUCTURE • CONTROLLING • GENERAL CONTROLLING • ORGANIZATION • MAINTAIN VERSIONS.

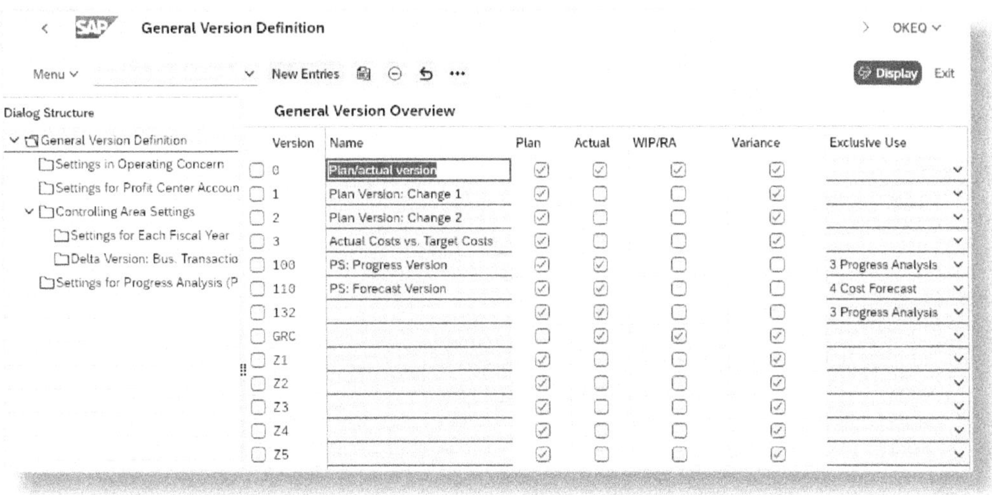


*Figure 3.10: OKEQ—Controlling versions*

## 3.8 Summary

Alex prepared a list of transactions to set up GCI's controlling organization structure (see Table 3.1). The designation *F* indicates a Fiori app and not a transaction code.

| Transaction Code | Description |
|---|---|
| OB13 | Chart of accounts |
| OB29 | Fiscal year variant |
| KEA0 | Operating concern |
| OKKP | Controlling area |
| OBY6 | Company code |
| FINSC_LEDGER | Additional local currencies |
| Manage Profit Center Groups (F) | Profit center hierarchy / group |
| OKEQ | Controlling versions |

*Table 3.1: Transactions to set up controlling organization structure*

Alex understood that master data and transactional data in the SAP application is heavily dependent on the design of the SAP software organization structure. After he reviewed the controlling organization structure at GCI, Alex understood the company's overall technical setup. A good understanding of this structure was going to help him navigate through the data flow relatively quickly.

# 4 Controlling master data—so simple, yet so complex

*"Whenever you are asked if you can do a job, tell 'em, 'Certainly I can!' Then get busy and find out how to do it."*

— Theodore Roosevelt

**Master data plays a critical role in ensuring a system's effectiveness. It sounds simple but meeting the competing requirements of various functions—or at times various business processes within the same function—can be challenging. Consistency and accuracy in maintaining master data contribute significantly to realizing the business benefits of a system. In this chapter, we examine the elements of controlling master data.**

"As you know," Bob said to Alex one morning, "we are setting up a new production line in our plant. We need to create cost centers and all of the related system setup to get this line up and running. Can you go through the system manual and find all of the steps required to complete this task? You may want to reach out to Erin. She is very knowledgeable and can help you if you have any questions."

"Sure, I'll work on it, Bob," replied Alex. Alex turned his attention to the training guide. He had finished the sections regarding the SAP controlling organization structure at GCI1, and he now needed to continue and read about SAP Controlling master data.

From his prior experience at Fork-o-Lift Works (FLW), Alex was aware that master data plays an important role in any system, regardless of whether it is an integrated ERP application such as SAP, or a home-grown system that may or may not be well integrated.

If we visualize organization structure, master data, and transaction data in a pyramid form, organization structure sits at the top of the pyramid, master data is at the center, and transaction processing is at the bottom. Master data inherits a great deal of organization structure information and passes it on to the transaction processing layer. It is therefore important to define organization structure, as well as master data attributes, during the design phase and then build on the design on an ongoing basis.

Once defined, it is not necessary to make frequent changes to the organization structure. However, the master data needs to be maintained on an ongoing basis.

In addition, master data maintenance is handled by the business, usually directly in the production environment. Accurate maintenance of master data is therefore very important to ensure consistent capture of data at the transaction processing layer.

## 4.1 Cost centers—where did we spend all the money?

A *cost center* is one of the most widely used master data elements in controlling. Cost centers enable the departmental breakdown of costs. They are often the lowest level of an organization where costs and departmental performance can be collected and analyzed. Cost centers are therefore useful for departmental budgets and planning versus actual comparison of expenses. Cost centers can also be used for the purpose of interdepartmental cost allocations through sender-receiver relationships. The relationships can be defined in cost center allocations—some of the widely used methods are distribution and assessments.

Cost centers are structured into organizational and/or functional hierarchical groups. Each cost center is assigned to a cost center hierarchy and a profit center.

**Cost center definition—examples**

A cost center is an organizational unit in a controlling area that represents a defined location where costs are incurred. Cost centers can be created based on:

- functional requirements (a department or section),
- allocation criteria (maintenance costs that are allocated to a pool of manufacturing cost centers),
- physical location (headquarters, manufacturing facility 1, manufacturing facility 2, distribution center 1, and distribution center 2), and
- responsibility for costs (finance, accounting, legal, and marketing).

Cost centers are usually set up according to function, machine, responsibility center, or permanent (or long-term) physical location. For example, to set up the new production line in Carl's area, that Bob just referred to, a cost center is the correct controlling object. However, to track costs for a short-term productivity improvement project or a targeted marketing campaign that is temporary in nature, an *internal order* is a better option than a cost center.

### 4.1.1 Cost center hierarchy

*A cost center hierarchy* consists of groups of cost centers in a tree structure, within a controlling area.

Cost centers can be grouped together to provide summary cost information. A cost center hierarchy consists of nodes and sub-nodes that cost centers are attached to.

A cost center hierarchy comprises all cost centers for a given period and therefore represents the entire enterprise. This hierarchy is known as the *standard hierarchy*.

Cost center hierarchies are defined before cost centers are created. Maintenance is handled via the MANAGE COST CENTER GROUPS Fiori app (see Figure 4.1).

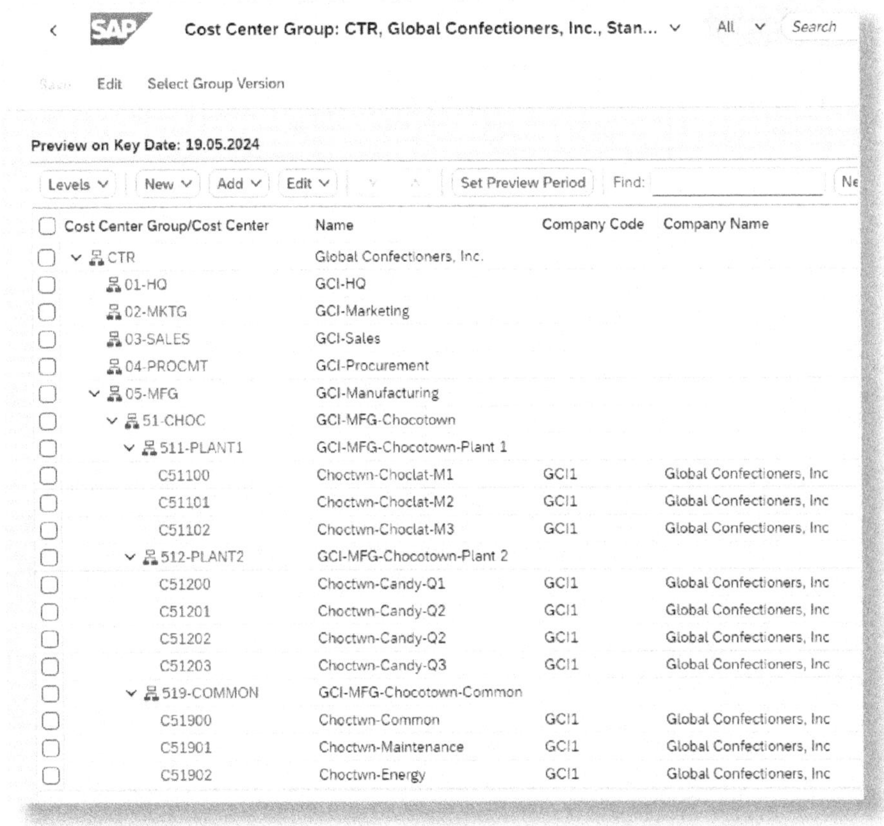


*Figure 4.1: "Manage Cost Center Groups" app—cost center standard hierarchy*

### 4.1.2 Cost center maintenance

*Cost centers* are organizational units in a controlling area that represent a defined location of a cost incurrence. The definition can be based on functional requirements, allocation criteria, physical location, or responsibility for costs.

The cost center defines the smallest area of responsibility within the company that causes and influences costs, meaning the lowest level to which you can meaningfully assign *direct costs* and *indirect costs*.

Cost centers are assigned to a single company code (legal entity), a single profit center (performance entity), a single functional area (type of function), and a single cost center category (what kind of costs can be planned or booked to).

Cost centers are used to plan, capture, track, and report departmental expenses and services consumed or provided by a department using cost center accounting.

Cost centers are maintained using the MANAGE COST CENTERS app (see Figure 4.2).

### 4.1.3 Cost center groups

With *cost center groups*, cost centers are organized into groups according to various criteria in order to reflect the structure of the organization in the system. One cost center group is the standard hierarchy. Other cost center groups are also referred to as *alternative hierarchies*.

Cost center groups utilize cost centers and other groups to build hierarchies, which summarize the decision-making, responsibility and control areas according to the organization's specific requirements. The individual cost centers form the lowest hierarchical level.

Cost center groups are maintained using the MANAGE COST CENTER GROUPS app (see Figure 4.1).

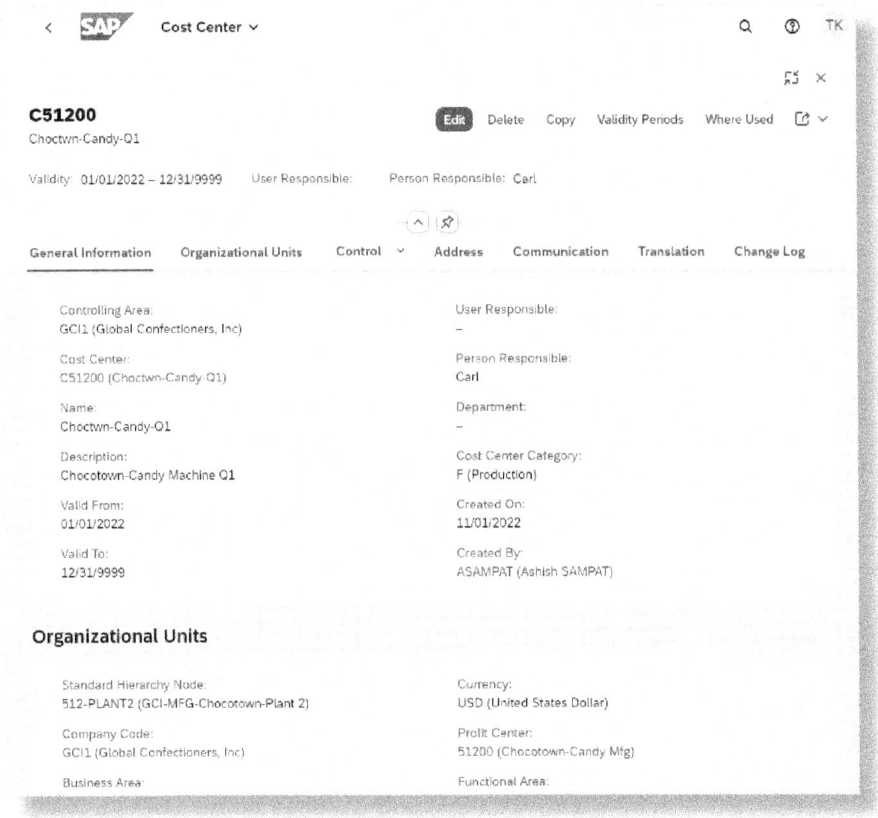


*Figure 4.2: "Manage Cost Centers" app—cost center change*

## 4.2 Cost elements—what kind of money is being spent?

A *cost element* can be defined as a vehicle for carrying costs in CO. It is a special GL account that provides management with a view of where and how money is being spent. It enables management to identify any specific areas where the organization might need to focus on controlling costs.

Cost elements are profit and loss accounts and can be assigned as either primary or secondary. They are maintained using the MANAGE G/L ACCOUNT MASTER DATA app.

### 4.2.1 Primary cost elements

*Primary cost elements* create the link between FI and CO. In general, every P&L type GL account in FI can be defined to be used as a cost element in CO. These elements are called primary cost elements. There may be some exceptions where not all GL accounts are created as cost elements. An example is interest expenses—when management does not want to track a cost center's interest expenses.

The following cost element categories are used to create PRIMARY COSTS OR REVENUE elements (see Figure 4.3):

- 1 (Primary cost element)—can be debited with all primary postings, for example, in FI or MM.
- 11 (Revenue element)—used to post revenues.
- 12 (Sales deduction)—used to post sales deductions, adjustments, or revenue deduction postings, such as discounts and rebates.

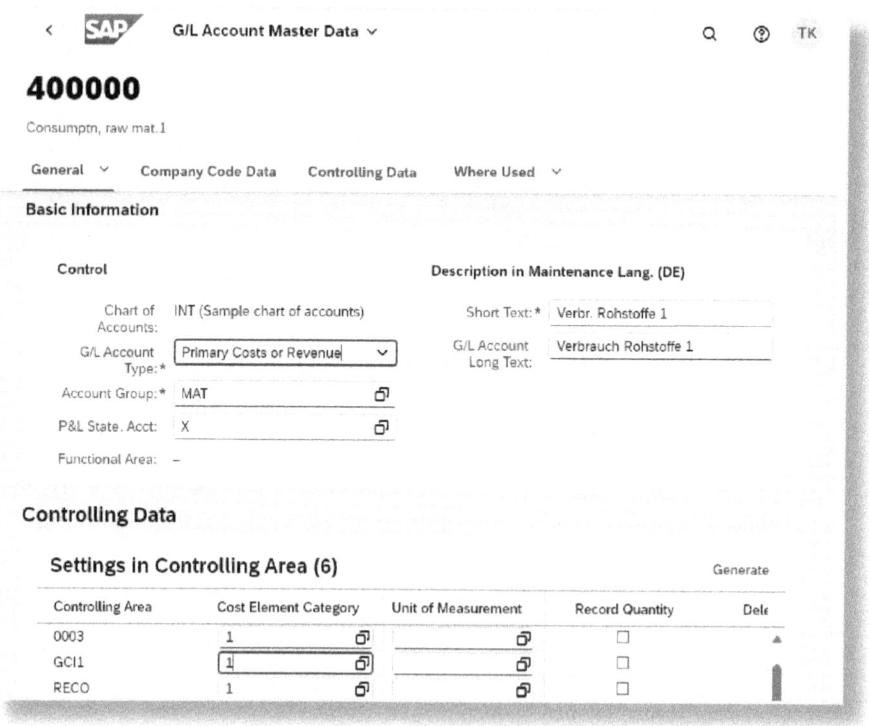


Figure 4.3: "Manage G/L Account Master Data" app—primary cost element

The example shows a G/L account that is defined with COST ELEMENT CATEGORY 1 (primary).

### 4.2.2 Secondary cost elements

*Secondary cost elements* (see Figure 4.4) can be created to record controlling-specific transactions such as settlement, overhead rates, assessment, and activity allocation. They describe cost flows that occur within SAP Controlling.

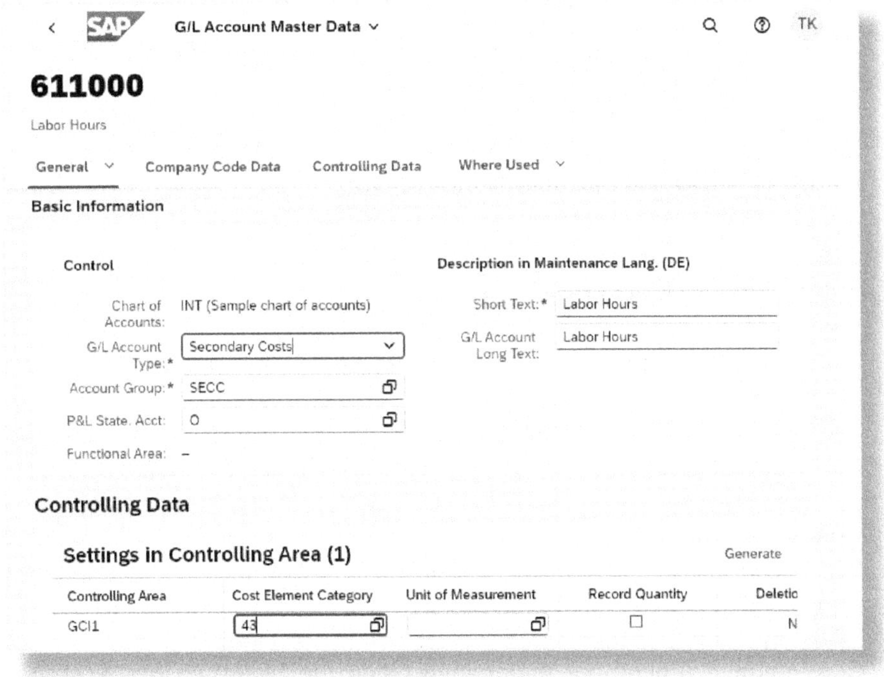


*Figure 4.4: "Manage G/L Account Master Data" app—Secondary cost element*

Because accounts defined as secondary cost elements are used for moving costs from one cost object to another, the overall balance in the account will be 0. However, there will be a balance when looking at postings for a given cost object.

The following cost element categories can be used for SECONDARY COSTS elements:

- 21 (Internal settlement)—used to settle (further allocate) order or project costs to CO-internal objects. CO-internal objects include orders, profitability segments, cost centers, and projects.
- 31 (Order/project results analysis)—system-required accounts for posting WIP.
- 41 (Overhead rates)—used to load overheads using costing sheets.
- 42 (Assessment)—used to allocate costs using the assessment method.
- 43 (Allocation of activities/processes)—used during internal activity allocation.

Figure 4.4 shows the SECONDARY COSTS element defined as COST ELEMENT CATEGORY 43, for internal activity allocation.

### 4.2.3 Cost element groups

*Cost element groups* collect cost elements with similar characteristics.

Cost element groups can be utilized for reporting, for example, using the cost element group structure to define the row structure of the reports.

Cost element groups can also be used when several cost elements need to be used in one transaction; for example, in cost center planning, distribution, or assessment.

Cost element groups are maintained using the MANAGE COST ELEMENT GROUPS app (see Figure 4.5).

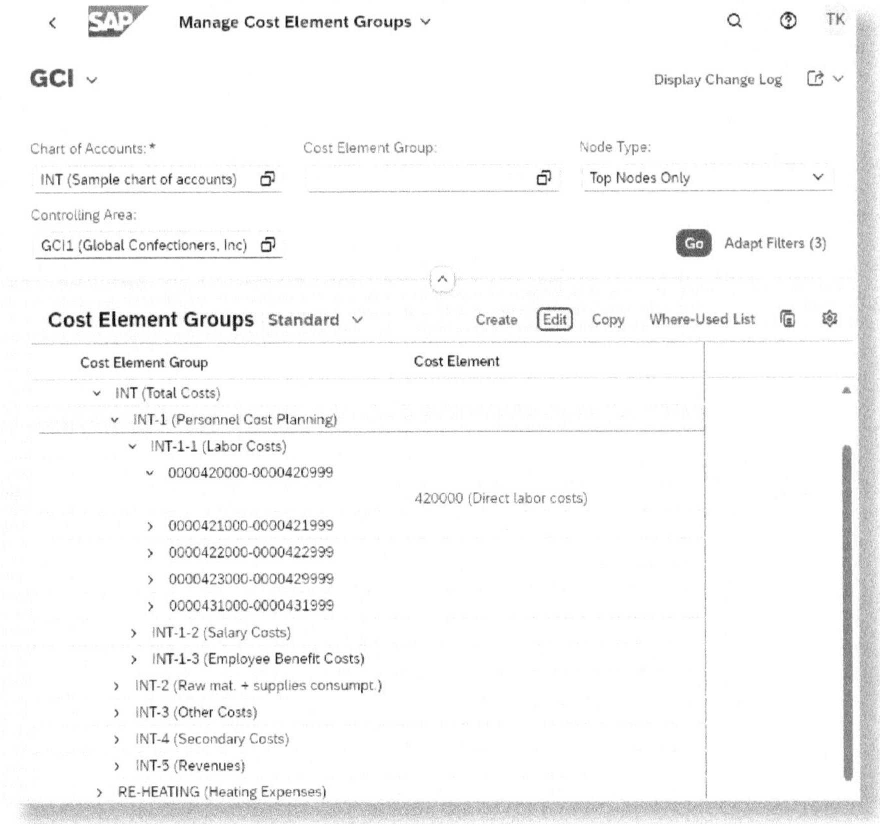


*Figure 4.5: "Manage Cost Element Groups" app*

## 4.3 Activity types—are these the cost drivers we keep talking about?

*Activity types* refer to activities performed in cost centers within a controlling area; for example, labor hours or maintenance hours for a maintenance cost center.

Activity types describe the specific activity output provided by a cost center to other cost objects such as work orders, internal orders, etc. They are measured in units of time and quantity, and are valued using a rate per hour, or per unit, of activity:

- Total planned cost / Planned activity hours = Planned activity rate per hour
- Total actual cost / Actual activity hours = Actual activity rate per hour

Activity types are maintained with the MANAGE ACTIVITY TYPES app (see Figure 4.6).

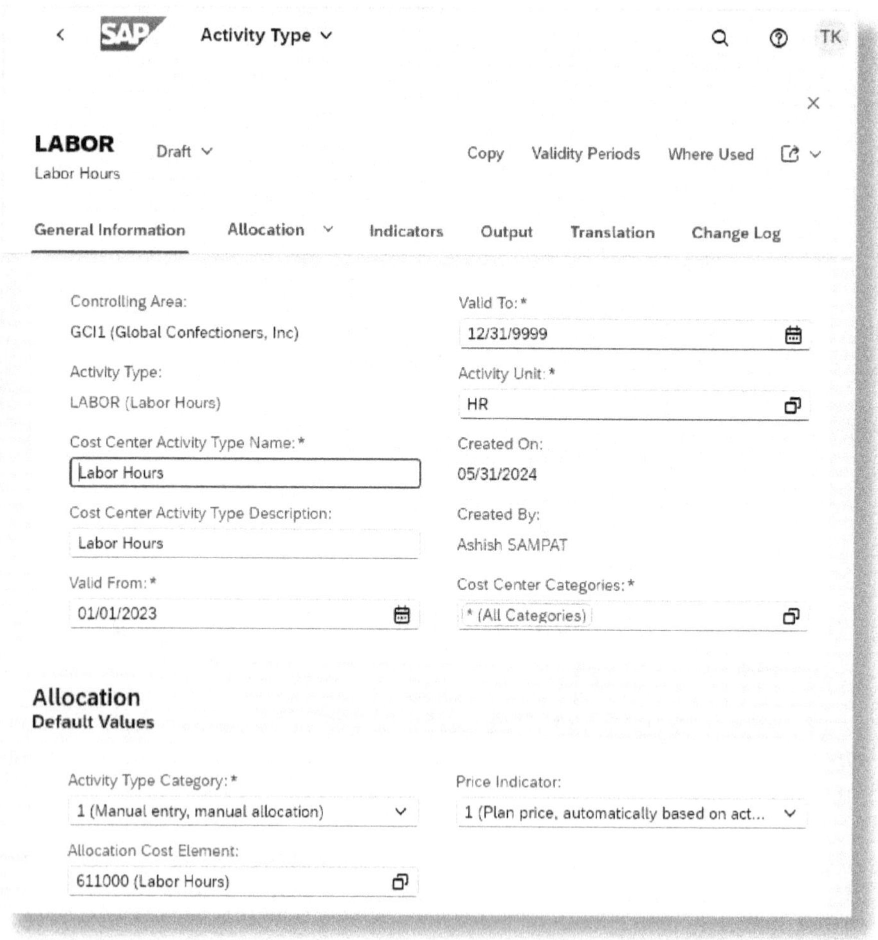


*Figure 4.6: "Manage Activity Types" app*

## 4.4 SKFs—it's all statistical data after all

A *statistical key figure (SKF)* is used to track quantities and values for various operating activities. SKFs are designed for use in reporting and analysis and can also be used to assist in the allocation of costs.

An SKF can be defined as either a fixed value or a total value. Key figures defined as fixed values are valid as of the posting period and in all subsequent posting periods of the fiscal year. In contrast, key figures defined as total values are only valid for the posting period in which they are entered.

SKFs are maintained using the MANAGE STATISTICAL KEY FIGURES app (see Figure 4.7).

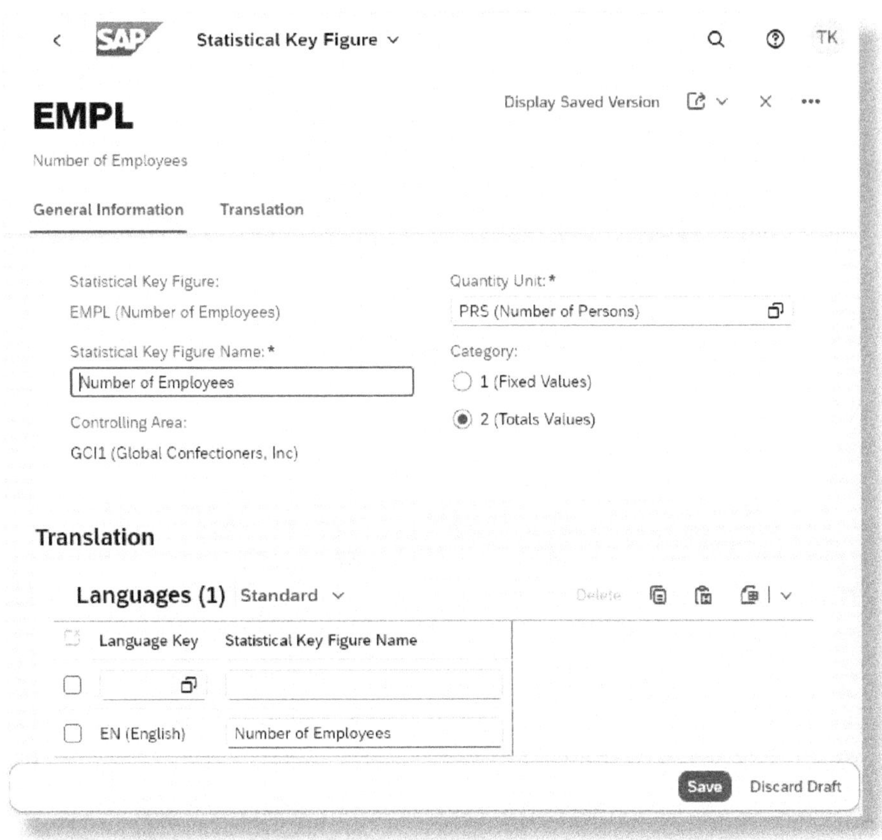


*Figure 4.7: "Manage Statistical Key Figures" app—display*

## 4.5 Allocations—who is sending, who is receiving? an internal Web?

A typical manufacturing facility incurs costs in multiple departments. For example, the maintenance department can provide a service to the production department to keep the machines running. Similarly, the information systems department helps keep the systems running. Usually, the goal is to transfer costs from these service departments to production departments, so that the costs are added to the cost of the product. This internal transfer of costs is achieved within CO using *allocations*. Most allocations are processed using the MANAGE ALLOCATIONS app. Figure 4.8 shows part of the definition of a cost allocation cycle.

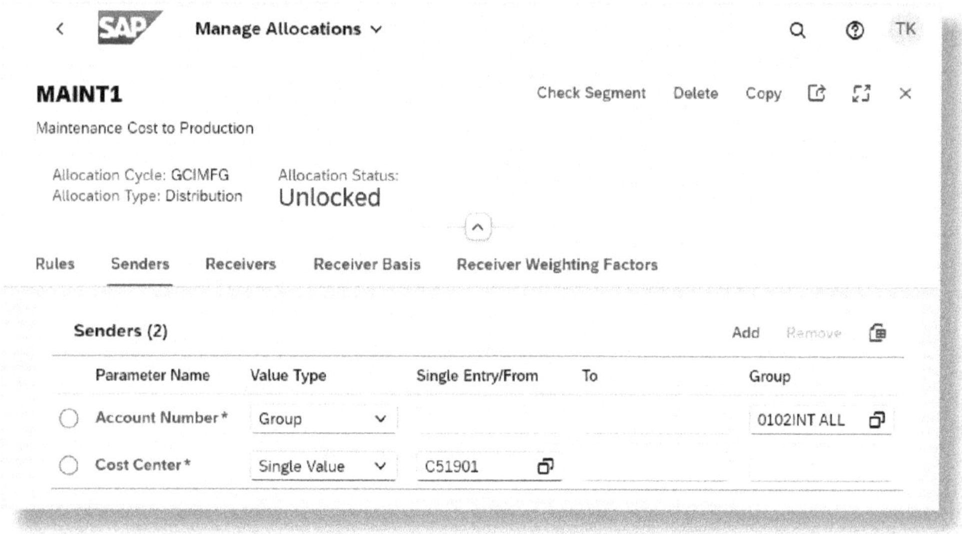


*Figure 4.8: "Manage Allocations" app—defining the sender*

There are two main types of allocations in controlling—distribution and assessments.

Using *distribution*, the original primary cost element is retained and passed on to the receiver. The sender and receiver information are documented with line items in the CO document.

Using *assessments*, original cost elements are grouped together into assessment cost elements (secondary cost elements), which are passed on to the receivers; original cost elements are not displayed for the receivers.

The sender and receiver information is displayed in the CO document.

**Distribution versus assessment—example**

Let's look at an example of a facilities department—with one *sending* cost center—which is responsible for a building. This cost center incurs three primary costs:

- rent for the building,
- telephone expenses, and
- beverage expenses (such as tea and coffee) for staff working in that building.

This building houses four departments:

- marketing,
- finance and accounting,
- purchasing, and
- human resources (four *receiving* cost centers).

Costs should be allocated in predefined percentages for each department.

If the *distribution* method of allocation is used, then the same primary cost element is used to allocate costs. The sender cost center receives a credit using three original primary cost elements. Four receiving cost centers will each see three original primary cost elements as debits to their cost centers. This means each department is able to identify how much money was allocated on each of the three expense categories of rent, telephone, and beverages.

If the *assessment* method of allocation is used, then a secondary cost element for assessment, say *facilities expense*, is used to allocate costs. The sender cost center receives a credit via the assessment cost element. Four receiving cost centers will each see one secondary cost element as a debit to their cost center. This means each department only knows how much money was allocated to them under *facilities expenses*. The receivers do not know the breakdown of the facilities expenses with respect to rent, telephone, and beverage. They need to look up the sending cost center's report to identify the cost split.

**! Allocations based on activity type postings**

As of S/4HANA on-premise version 2023, the MANAGE ALLOCATIONS app cannot process allocations based on posted activity type quantities. For distribution, transaction KSVB is used for planned allocations and KSV5 is used for actual allocations. For assessment, transaction KSUB is used for planned allocations and KSU5 is used for actual allocations.

To maintain distributions using activity quantities as a tracing factor, use the following transactions for planned distributions:

- KSV7 (create)
- KSV8 (change)
- KSV8 (display)
- KSV9 (delete).

For actual distributions, use:

- KSV1 (create)
- KSV2 (change)
- KSV3 (display)
- KSV4 (delete).

The corresponding assessment transactions are KSU7 through KSUA for planned assessments, and KSU1 through KSU4 for actual assessments. All distributions and assessments that do not involve activity type quantities should use the MANAGE ALLOCATIONS app.

## 4.6 Internal orders—another tool for cost tracking?

*Internal orders* are used to collect, monitor, and settle direct and indirect costs incurred by a specific project. They are cost collectors that have a more dynamic nature than cost or profit centers. Orders can be used as a primary cost object which is then settled to a cost center or as a statistical posting object where the primary posting goes to the cost center. Plan data can be entered for orders and can be tracked against actual spend.

**Internal orders**

Internal orders can be used for a variety of purposes in CO.

An internal order is created for a customer event to track budget and actual amounts for that event. Once the event is complete, costs are settled (or moved) to the appropriate cost center.

For example, vehicle repair and maintenance costs are booked to one cost center, but the costs for each vehicle are also tracked "statistically" using a statistical internal order created for each vehicle.

As a further example, each of a company's research and development (R&D) projects requires actual spending to be tracked. R&D internal orders help capture an individual project's costs.

## 4.7 Summary

Alex now turned to Bob's request to list all of the steps that were necessary to reflect the new production line in the system. Since the chart of accounts was common, Alex did not think that there was a need to set up additional cost elements. Additionally, the design required that a common set of activity types and statistical key figures (SKFs) be used. Therefore, there was no need to set up new activity types or SKFs.

The CO master data changes that are necessary for a new production line include:

- Create a new cost center under the same hierarchy node as that of existing lines ("512-PLANT2").
- Add the new cost center in an alternate (separate) cost center group for Chocotown.
- Create a new *segment* in plan distribution for the new cost center.
- Create a new segment in actual distribution for the new cost center.

Alex learned that consistent ongoing maintenance of master data is fundamental for the accuracy of transaction data and reporting. Due to the sensitive nature of the data, access to create and change data has been restricted to a handful of individuals in GCI. Access to view data is more open, because several business users may need to review this data from time to time.

The training manual referred to numerous master data objects and apps, so Alex created a table as a quick reference tool (see Figure 4.9).

**Controlling Master Data Objects and their Fiori Apps**

| Controlling Master Data Object | Fiori App |
|---|---|
| | |
| Cost Center | Manage Cost Centers |
| Cost Center Group | Manage Cost Center Groups |
| Cost Element / G/L Account | Manage G/L Account Master Data |
| Cost Element Group | Create Cost Element Groups |
| Activity Type | Manage Activity Types |
| Activity Type Group | Manage Activity Type Groups |
| Statistical Key Figure | Manage Statistical Key Figures |
| Statistical Key Figure Group | Manage Statistical Key Figure Groups |
| Internal Order | Manage Internal Orders |
| Internal Order Group | Manage Internal Order Groups |

| Allocation Object ** | Fiori App "Manage Allocations" |
|---|---|
| | Allocation Context "Cost Centers" |
| Plan Distribution | Allocation Type "Distribution" |
| Plan Assessment | Allocation Type "Overhead Allocation" |
| | |
| Actual Distribution | Allocation Type "Distribution" |
| Actual Assessment | Allocation Type "Overhead Allocation" |

** Distribution / Assessment will be covered with further details in subsequent chapters

*Figure 4.9: Controlling master data objects and Fiori apps*

# 5 Cost center planning—an annual marathon

*"Let our advance worrying become advance thinking and planning."*
—Winston Churchill

**Most organizations undergo an annual budgeting (planning) process that helps them prepare for the following year. Planning methods might involve one approach or a combination of methods. An organization could take the previous year's plan as the base, the previous twelve months' actual as the base, or they could even plan from scratch (popularly referred to as "zero-based" budgeting). The planning process typically starts with sales and operations (S&OP) planning, which is then broken down into a production plan, a procurement plan, a labor cost plan, and an overhead cost plan. This chapter provides an overview of cost center planning, which typically covers overhead planning and labor cost planning.**

The ultimate goal of a manufacturing unit is to consistently deliver throughput at a consistent quality, while maintaining optimum inventory levels. In doing so, it must accurately determine and control the cost at which it has produced this material.

Product costs include direct costs and indirect costs. *Direct costs* consist of the cost of raw materials, packaging materials, and all the direct conversion costs of producing the finished material. This typically includes the cost of personnel who have 'touched' the product (those directly involved in manufacturing the product). *Indirect costs* include the cost of personnel who might not have directly "touched" the product, but have indirectly contributed to producing the material. For example, maintenance staff, housekeeping staff, warehouse staff, security, finance, human resources, facilities, systems, etc.

Another way to look at conversion costs is that a product must *carry* (or absorb) the cost of the departments it passes through. A predetermined absorption rate is used to load the product with the cost of the department.

For example, if the total planned budget for a department is $10,000.00 for the month, with 200 hours of planned operation, then the predetermined absorption rate is $10,000.00 / 200 hours = $ 50.00/hr.

This cost can be further broken down into labor hours, machine hours, and any other additional cost drivers based on the business requirement. These drivers are often defined as *activity types* in the SAP system.

At GCI, labor hours and machine hours are defined as the two main activity types. These drivers have a rate called an *activity rate*, or *planned activity rate*.

Alex remembered that FLW used similar cost drivers in their legacy system—direct labor hours, indirect labor hours, and machine hours. However, at FLW they were called *burden rates*.

GCI carried out their planning cycle between August and November. The sales team created the sales forecast at SKU (stock keeping unit) level for the upcoming year. The production planning team compared demand to capacity and arrived at the planned production volume. The planning team could then arrive at the planned procurement of raw materials. Alex recalled the methodology at FLW—planning was not as detailed and was often done at the product group level. However, he could relate to the objective of the exercise, because manufacturing always needs to be operationally ready for the following year!

Planned exchange rates for various currency combinations need to be maintained for the planning period before feeding plan data into the system for the next year. This ensures that all plan costs are converted at a consistent exchange rate.

Alex decided to familiarize himself with the system by using a hands-on example. He logged into a test system and started entering plan data, step by step, following the instructions in the user manual.

## 5.1 Activity quantity planning

Let's look at the steps Alex followed.

#### Step 1: Setting the planner profile

The first step in cost center planning is to set the *planner profile* using transaction KP04. The planner profile is used to pick and choose the right combination of fields suitable for your planning needs. GCI decided to use the SAP-delivered standard planner profile SAPALL (see Figure 5.1), which includes all possible combinations for planning.

The menu path is: ACCOUNTING • CONTROLLING • COST CENTER ACCOUNTING • PLANNING • SET PLANNER PROFILE.

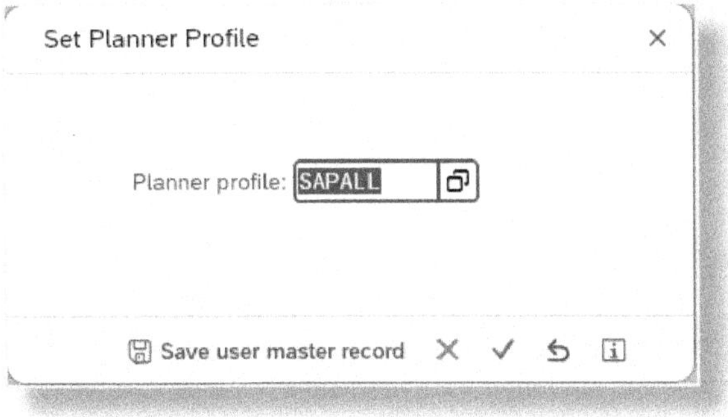


*Figure 5.1: KP04—Set Planner Profile*

**Step 2: Activity quantity planning—cost centers**

Alex's next cost center planning step was to carry out *activity quantity planning* to determine the base for absorption. Typically, the activity quantity is determined by the production volume for the planning period, which can be further constrained by production capacity and potential downtime for maintenance, if any. Activity quantity is planned using the EDIT PRICES FOR ACTIVITY TYPES app (see Figure 5.2). This app executes GUI transaction KP26 to enter the activity plan information.

*Figure 5.2: Fiori app for planning activity quantities*

As shown in Figure 5.3, the initial planning screen requires the user to enter the VERSION, FROM PERIOD/TO PERIOD, and FISCAL YEAR that the planning relates to.

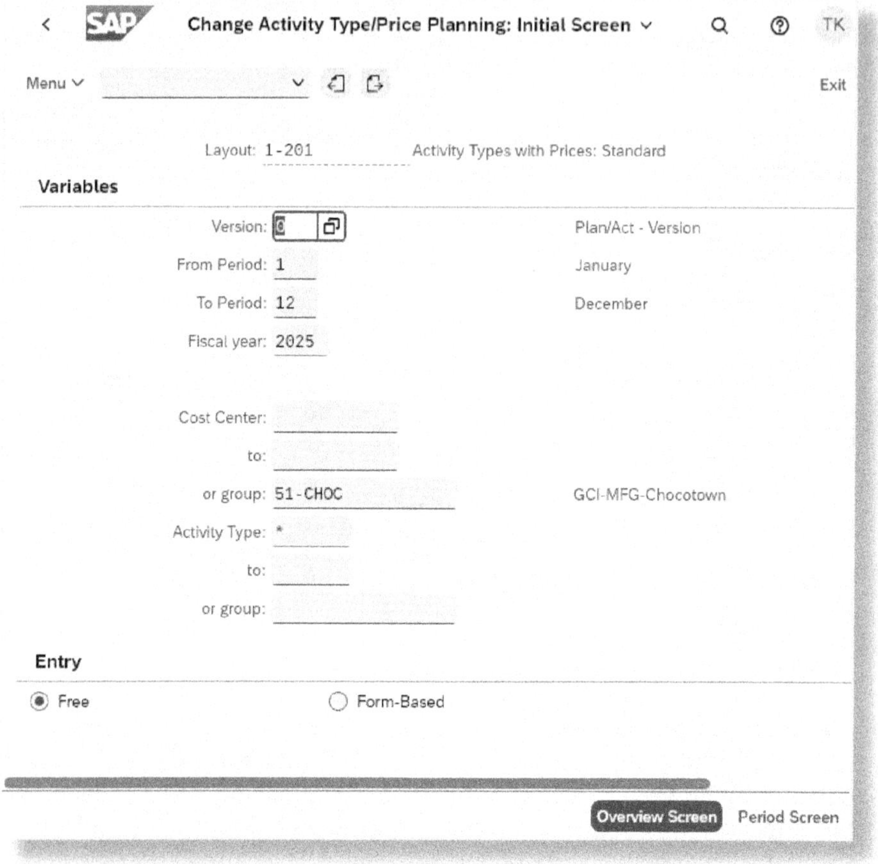


*Figure 5.3: "Edit Prices for Activity Types" app—Initial Screen*

The COST CENTER (or cost center group) and ACTIVITY TYPE (or activity type group) are also entered. Finally, the user can add FREE entries (user enters the values), or they can use FORM-BASED entries (the system pre-populates possible combinations of master data, and the user enters the quantities). GCI decided to use the free-form option for entering plan data.

In his example, Alex wanted to see what planning for cost center group 51-CHOC looked like for 2025.

Alex clicked on the Overview Screen button on the initial screen and the overview screen appeared (see Figure 5.4).

He saw that two activities were planned for the year—6,000 hours for LABOR and 1,800 machine hours (MCHRS). When Alex clicked on PERIOD SCREEN, a new window opened, where he saw that the 6,000 hours planned for labor were distributed evenly across 12 months (see Figure 5.5).

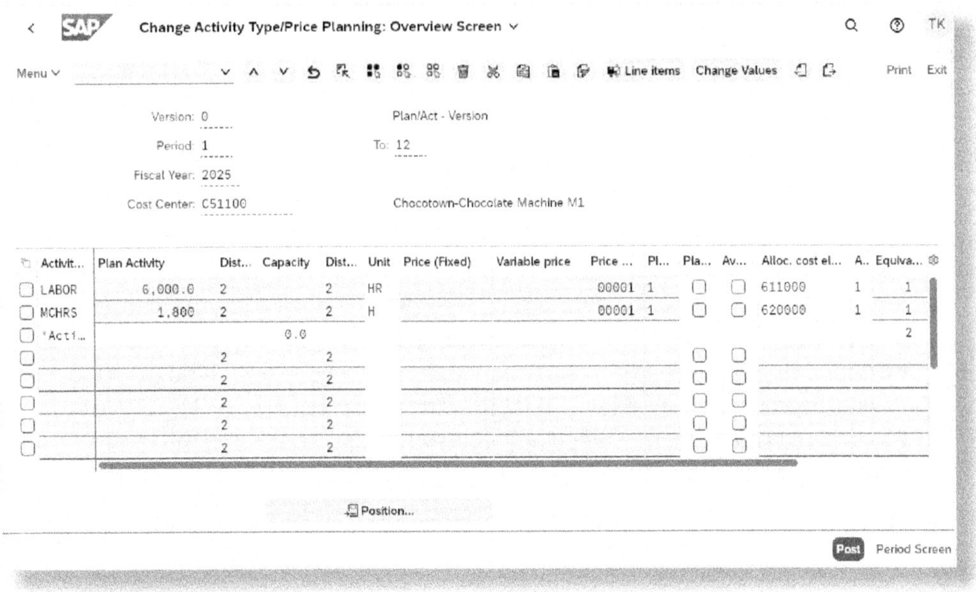


*Figure 5.4: "Edit Prices for Activity Types" app—Overview Screen*

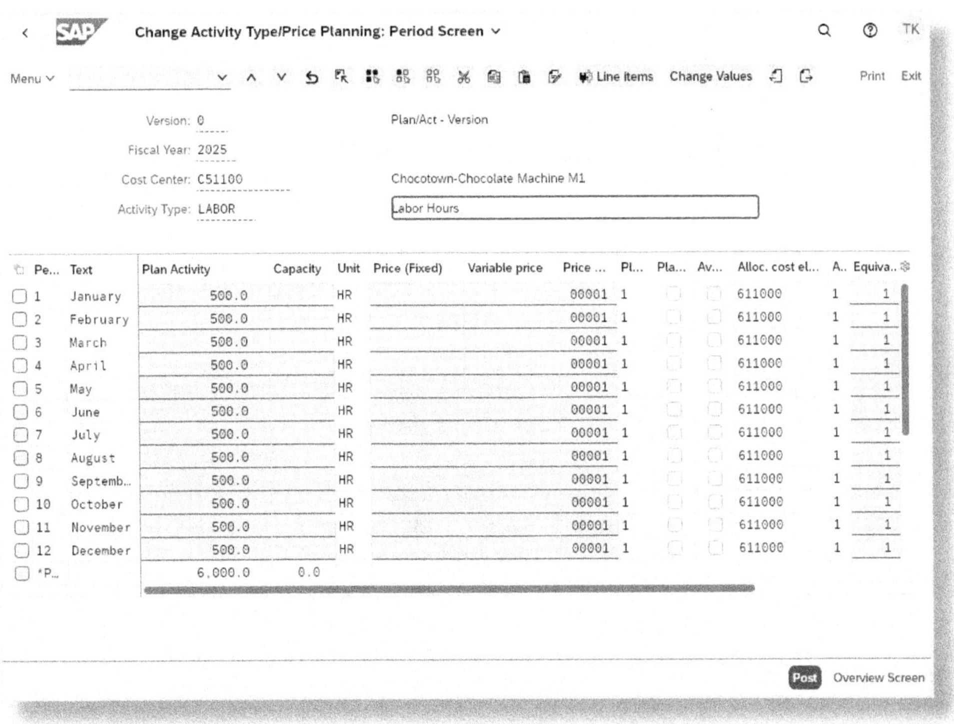


*Figure 5.5: "Edit Prices for Activity Types" app—activity quantity planning, Period Screen*

Alex had the possibility to edit this data and plan for different activity quantities for each month (which is usually the case in manufacturing); however, for the purpose of this example, he decided to use the evenly distributed activity quantities.

**Uploading cost center plans from Excel**

Instead of manually entering the cost center plans, SAP provides a method of uploading the data from Excel spreadsheets. As part of system configuration, file formats are created and assigned to cost center planning layouts in order to process activity quantity planning and activity-dependent and activity-independent cost planning. The upload is processed from any one of the planning transaction codes (KP06, KP26/ EDIT PRICES FOR ACTIVITY TYPES app, or KP46) by navigating to the menu option EXTRAS • EXCEL PLANNING • UPLOAD from the transaction.

## 5.2 Direct costs (activity-dependent)

**Step 3: Activity-dependent cost planning**

Now that the quantities were planned, it was time for Alex to plan the dollars (or amounts). GCI uses GUI transaction KP06 to do this because there is no SAP-delivered Fiori tile to call up the transaction.

Alex noticed that the KP06 screen (see Figure 5.6) looked very similar to the initial EDIT PRICES FOR ACTIVITY TYPES app screen, except that there were additional fields for entering cost element information.

The menu path is: ACCOUNTING • CONTROLLING • COST CENTER ACCOUNTING • PLANNING • COST AND ACTIVITY INPUTS • CHANGE.

The same screen is used for both *activity-dependent* cost planning and *activity-independent* cost planning. Leaving the ACTIVITY TYPE field blank results in *activity-independent* cost planning. However, if the activity type field is populated with a * or a specific activity, this results in *activity-dependent* cost planning. Fixed-cost planning is usually activity-independent, because these costs occur regardless of whether any tasks have been performed.

*Figure 5.6: Activity-dependent cost planning—Initial Screen*

> **Planning for activity-dependent/independent costs**
>
> Activity-independent cost planning is carried out by leaving the ACTIVITY TYPE field blank on the KP06 initial screen.
>
> Activity-dependent cost planning is carried out by entering a * or a specific ACTIVITY TYPE on the initial screen.

Alex went ahead and planned for activity type LABOR with COST ELEMENT 420000 for direct labor costs and 449000 for other personnel costs, as shown in Figure 5.7.

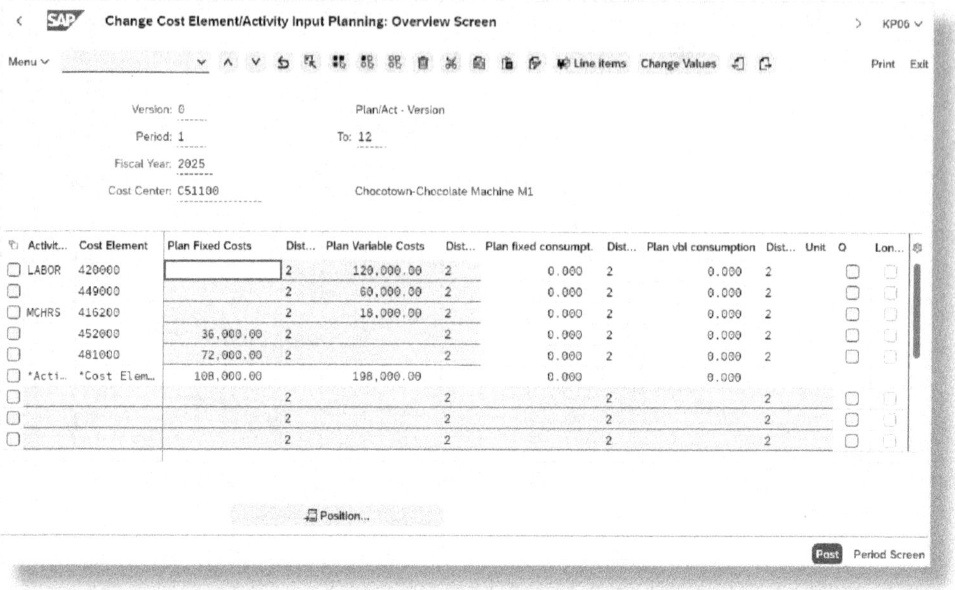

*Figure 5.7: Activity-dependent cost planning—Overview Screen*

He ensured that the dollars planned for this combination were entered into the PLAN VARIABLE COSTS column due to the nature of these costs—variable costs directly proportional to activity quantity.

Next, Alex planned for activity type MCHRS using COST ELEMENT 452000 for machine maintenance, 481000 for cost accounting depreciation—both fixed costs—and 416200 for electricity use, which is variable in nature.

After entering plan data for the activity-dependent costs, Alex wanted to see what the report would look like. He navigated to transaction code S_ALR_87013611 (see Figure 5.8), which provided the actual/plan/variance data for the cost centers. There was no actual data in the test system, so all Alex could see was the planning data he entered.

The menu path for this is: ACCOUNTING • CONTROLLING • COST CENTER ACCOUNTING • INFORMATION SYSTEM • REPORTS FOR COST CENTER ACCOUNTING • PLAN/ACTUAL COMPARISONS • COST CENTERS: ACTUAL/PLAN/VARIANCE.

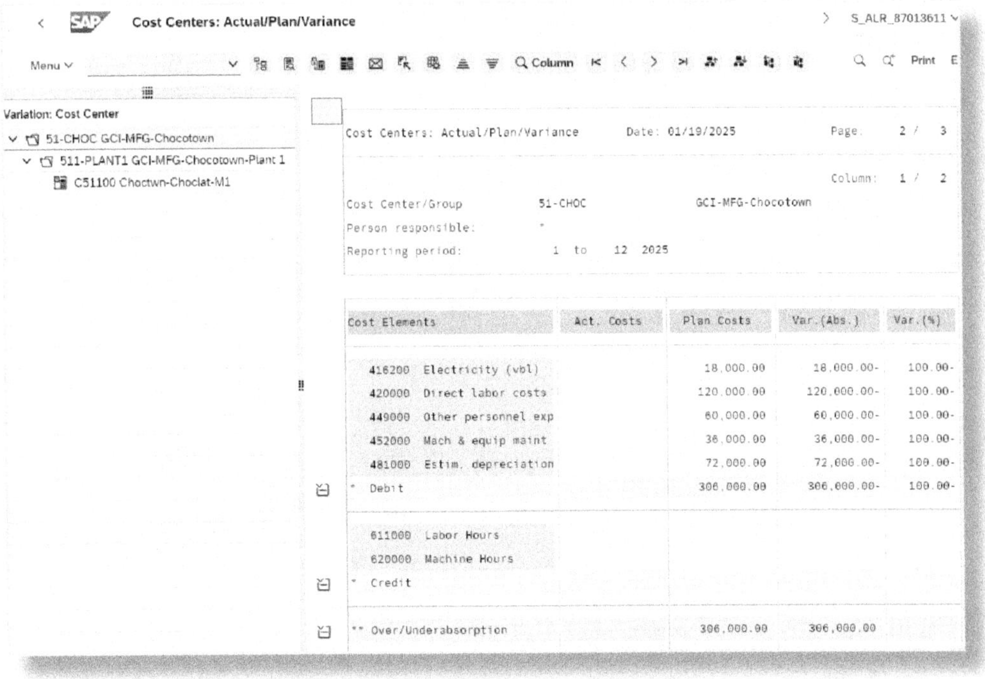


*Figure 5.8:* S_ALR_87013611—*Cost center report (after activity-dependent planning)*

Alex noticed that there was data on the debit side, but the credit side was blank. He learned that information on the credit side is populated once the plan price calculation has been carried out (see Section 5.5).

## 5.3 Overhead costs (activity-independent)

### Step 4: Activity-independent cost planning (KP06)

Alex moved on to enter fixed-cost information in transaction KP06 (see Figure 5.9), which is independent of the activity being performed by the department. For this, he needed to leave the ACTIVITY TYPE field blank.

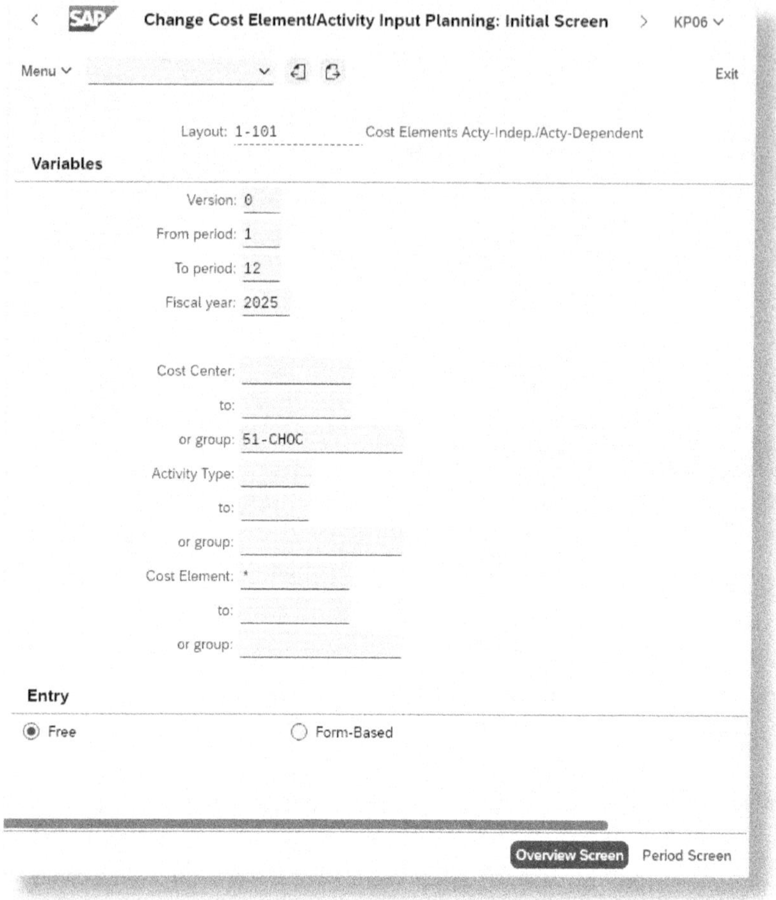


*Figure 5.9: KP06—Activity-independent cost planning, Initial Screen*

Alex used the following cost elements for the fixed-cost plan (see Figure 5.10):

- 405200 (Office supplies use)
- 430000 (Salaries)
- 435000 (Annual bonus)
- 470101 (Meals)
- 473000 (Postage)

Once the fixed cost was entered, he went back to the S_ALR_87013611 report to review the impact. He was then able to see all the costs planned for the cost center, including the fixed costs, as shown in Figure 5.11.

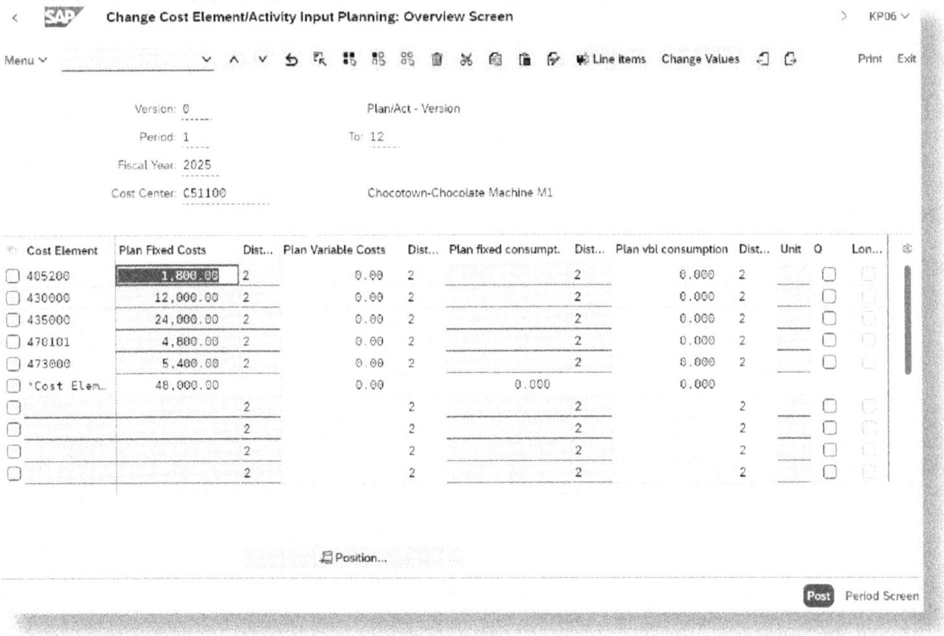


*Figure 5.10: KP06—Activity-independent cost planning, Overview Screen*

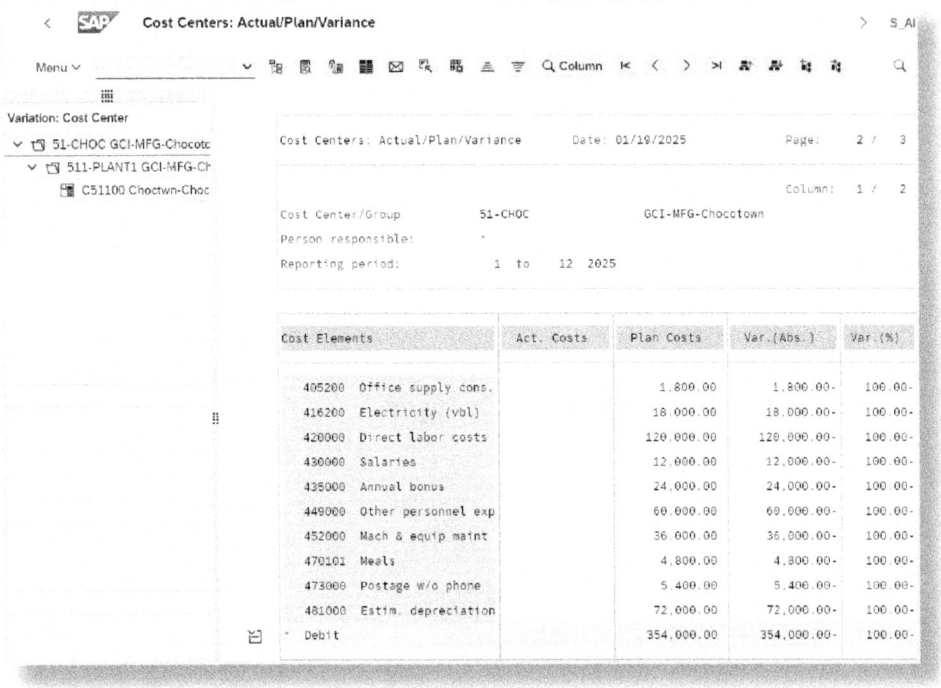


*Figure 5.11: S_ALR_87013611—Cost center report (after activity-independent planning)*

Alex used transaction KSBL (Cost Centers: Planning Report) to review the activity-dependent and activity-independent costs for each cost center, as shown in Figure 5.12. He could also see the planned activity quantities for the cost center.

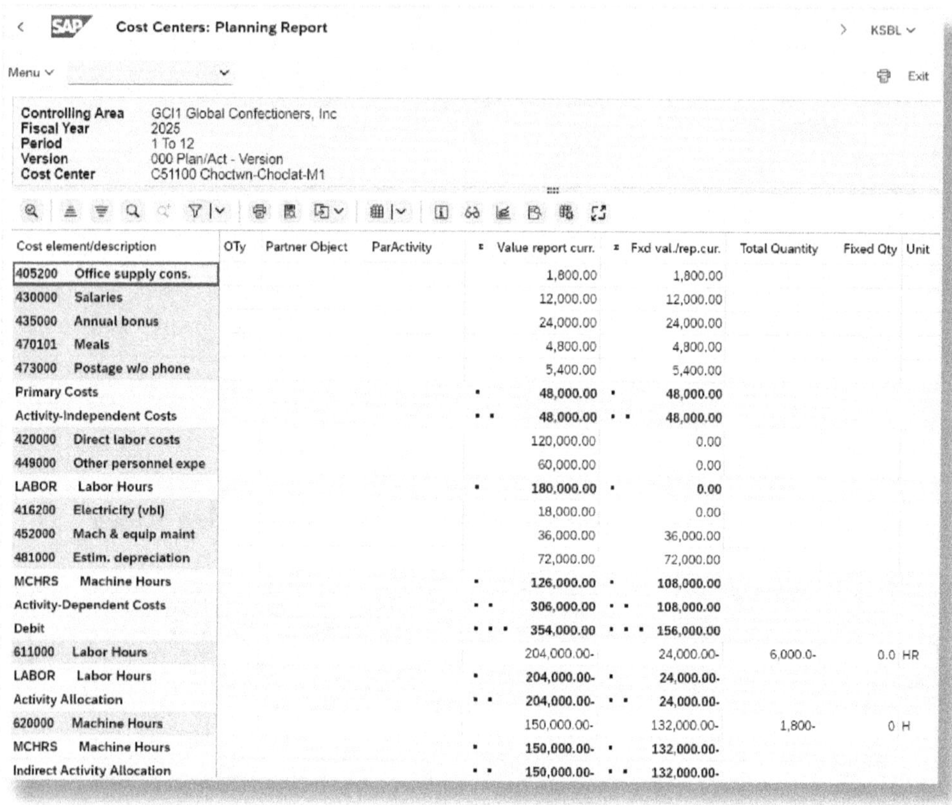

Cost Centers: Planning Report

| | |
|---|---|
| Controlling Area | GCI1 Global Confectioners, Inc |
| Fiscal Year | 2025 |
| Period | 1 To 12 |
| Version | 000 Plan/Act - Version |
| Cost Center | C51100 Choctwn-Choclat-M1 |

| Cost element/description | OTy | Partner Object | ParActivity | Value report curr. | Fxd val./rep.cur. | Total Quantity | Fixed Qty | Unit |
|---|---|---|---|---|---|---|---|---|
| 405200 Office supply cons. | | | | 1,800.00 | 1,800.00 | | | |
| 430000 Salaries | | | | 12,000.00 | 12,000.00 | | | |
| 435000 Annual bonus | | | | 24,000.00 | 24,000.00 | | | |
| 470101 Meals | | | | 4,800.00 | 4,800.00 | | | |
| 473000 Postage w/o phone | | | | 5,400.00 | 5,400.00 | | | |
| Primary Costs | | | | • 48,000.00 | • 48,000.00 | | | |
| Activity-Independent Costs | | | | •• 48,000.00 | •• 48,000.00 | | | |
| 420000 Direct labor costs | | | | 120,000.00 | 0.00 | | | |
| 449000 Other personnel expe | | | | 60,000.00 | 0.00 | | | |
| LABOR Labor Hours | | | | • 180,000.00 | • 0.00 | | | |
| 416200 Electricity (vbl) | | | | 18,000.00 | 0.00 | | | |
| 452000 Mach & equip maint | | | | 36,000.00 | 36,000.00 | | | |
| 481000 Estim. depreciation | | | | 72,000.00 | 72,000.00 | | | |
| MCHRS Machine Hours | | | | • 126,000.00 | • 108,000.00 | | | |
| Activity-Dependent Costs | | | | •• 306,000.00 | •• 108,000.00 | | | |
| Debit | | | | ••• 354,000.00 | ••• 156,000.00 | | | |
| 611000 Labor Hours | | | | 204,000.00- | 24,000.00- | 6,000.0- | 0.0 | HR |
| LABOR Labor Hours | | | | • 204,000.00- | • 24,000.00- | | | |
| Activity Allocation | | | | •• 204,000.00- | •• 24,000.00- | | | |
| 620000 Machine Hours | | | | 150,000.00- | 132,000.00- | 1,800- | 0 | H |
| MCHRS Machine Hours | | | | • 150,000.00- | • 132,000.00- | | | |
| Indirect Activity Allocation | | | | •• 150,000.00- | •• 132,000.00- | | | |

*Figure 5.12: KSBL—Cost center planning report*

The menu path is: ACCOUNTING • CONTROLLING • COST CENTER ACCOUNTING • INFORMATION SYSTEM • REPORTS FOR COST CENTER ACCOUNTING • PLANNING REPORTS • COST CENTERS: PLANNING OVERVIEW.

## 5.4 Plan cost center splitting

### Step 5: Splitting activity-dependent costs

The next task for Alex was *plan cost splitting* (transaction KSS4), where activity-independent costs are attached to specific activity types. This is necessary because the ultimate goal is to load costs for the department to the product, which is done via cost drivers (activity types).

Alex recalled that he had planned $48,000.00 as activity-independent costs. He wanted to see how the system divided (or split) this cost between the two activity types LABOR and MCHRS.

Transaction KSS4 requires a cost center, a cost center group, a selection variant (a predefined list of cost centers), or all cost centers to be entered (see Figure 5.13).

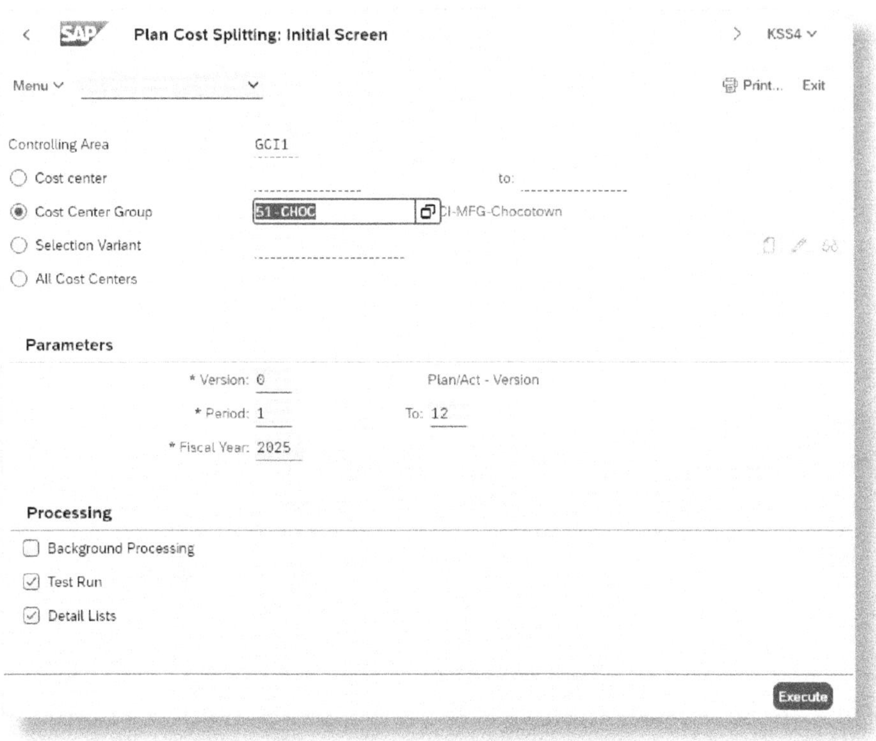


*Figure 5.13: KSS4—Plan Cost Splitting, Initial Screen*

VERSION, FISCAL YEAR, and PERIOD also need to be provided. In addition, the system provides checkboxes to select BACKGROUND PROCESSING (for performance reasons, especially if the data set is large), TEST RUN (to review data before posting it for good), and DETAIL LISTS.

The menu path is: ACCOUNTING • CONTROLLING • COST CENTER ACCOUNTING • PLANNING • ALLOCATIONS • SPLITTING.

Alex hit the EXECUTE button at the bottom right corner of the initial KSS4 screen and was taken to the detail LIST screen where he noticed that the activity-independent plan amount of $48,000.00 was split evenly between the activity types LABOR and MCHRS (see Figure 5.14). Because no splitting rules were maintained, the system divided the costs equally. However, it is possible to split this cost into a ratio of quantities between the two activity types if required.

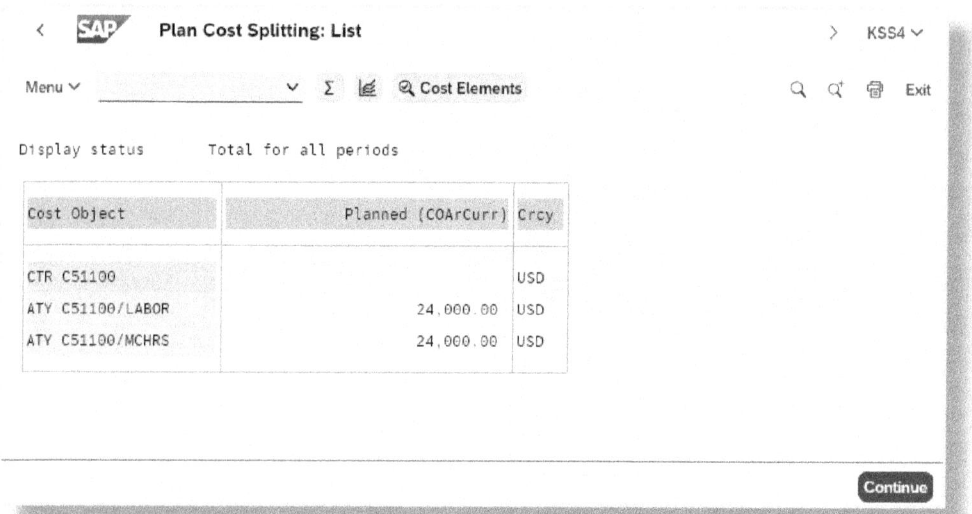


*Figure 5.14: KSS4—Plan Cost Splitting, result screen*

## 5.5 Plan activity price calculation

### Step 6: Activity price calculation

Alex's next step in cost center planning was the *plan activity price calculation,* which he carried out by running transaction KSPI. Similar to other planning transactions, Alex noted various fields such COST CENTER GROUP, VERSION, PERIOD, and FISCAL YEAR on the selection screen, as well as options BACKGROUND PROCESSING, TEST RUN, and DETAIL LISTS (see Figure 5.15).

The menu path for this is: ACCOUNTING • CONTROLLING • COST CENTER ACCOUNTING • PLANNING • ALLOCATIONS • PRICE CALCULATION.

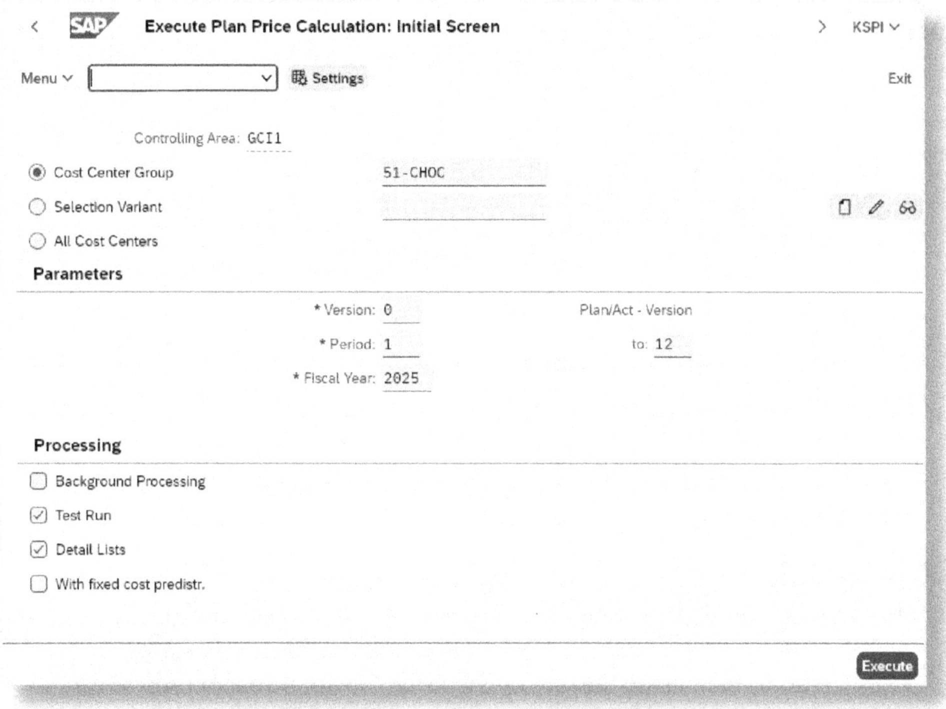


*Figure 5.15: KSPI—Plan price calculation, Initial Screen*

Alex hit the EXECUTE button on the initial KSPI screen and was taken to the detail screen where he saw the activity prices calculated for cost center/ activity type combinations C51100/LABOR and C51100/MCHRS (see Figure 5.16).

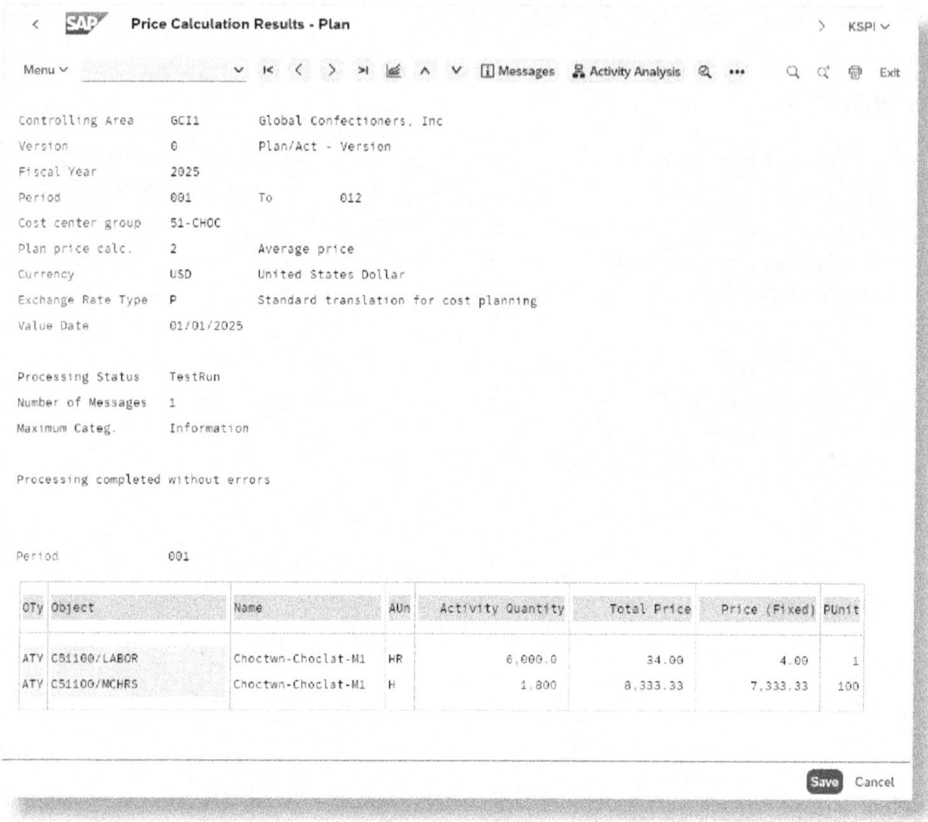


*Figure 5.16: KSPI—Plan price calculation, result screen*

Alex went through the calculations and validated his understanding of the numbers in KSPI.

Activity type LABOR had a total activity-dependent cost of $180,000.00 (from KP06) for 6,000 planned hours (from KP26), bringing the activity rate to $30.00/hr. In addition, the activity-independent cost was $24,000.00 (in KSS4), thereby increasing the rate by $4.00/hr. The total cost of LABOR was $34.00/hr, of which the fixed component was $4.00.

Activity type MCHRS had a total activity-dependent cost of $128,000.00 (from KP06) for 1,800 planned hours (from KP26), bringing the activity rate to $70.00/hr. Additionally, there was an activity-independent cost of $24,000.00 (in KSS4 cost splitting), thereby increasing the rate by $13.33/hr. The total cost of LABOR was $83.33/hr, of which the fixed component was $73.33. Alex noticed that the system showed a fixed price for MCHRS as $7,333.33—with a price unit (PUNIT) of 100. This was automatically determined to avoid rounding differences in calculations using the activity price.

Alex now wanted to view the report to see the final impact of the plan price calculation step. He jumped back into the S_ALR_87013611 report and noted that the credit side of the plan costs were now populated with the respective amounts attributable to the two activity types (see Figure 5.17). The net amount of debits minus credits was zero. This means the cost center plan was fully absorbed.

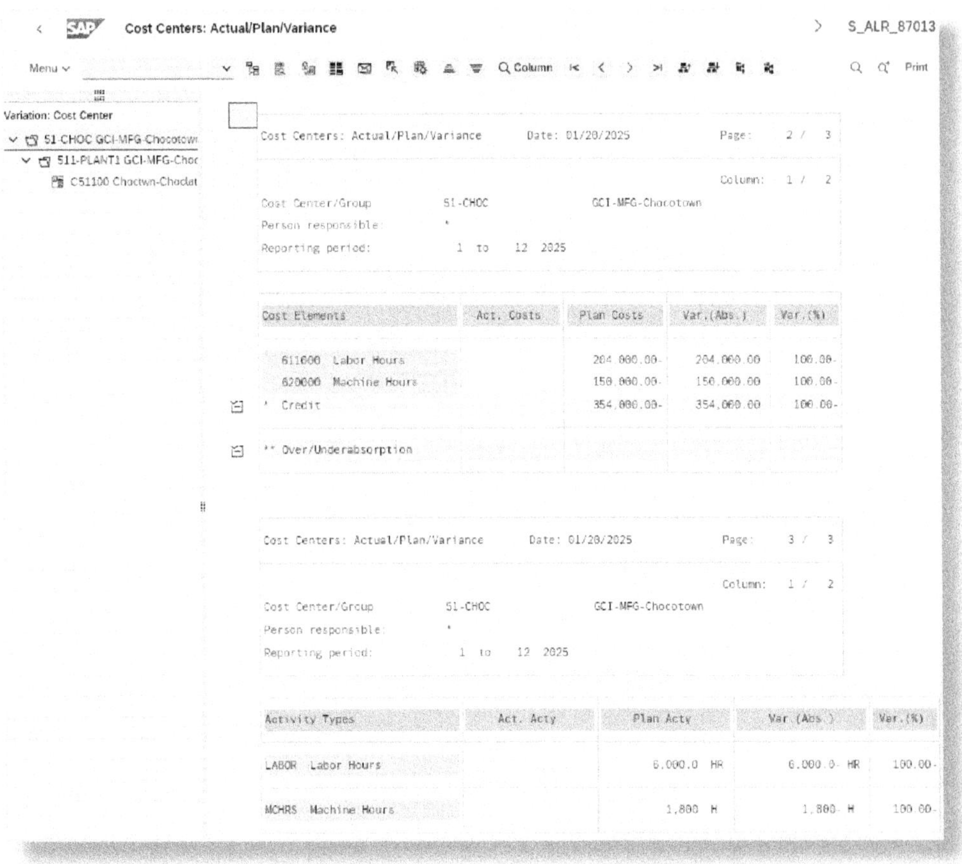


*Figure 5.17: S_ALR_87013611—Cost center report (after activity price calculation)*

Alex took a final look at his example in the spreadsheet and was impressed by the way this played out in the system (see Figure 5.18).

| | | | Quantity | Amount ($) | | | Rate ($ / Hr) | | |
|---|---|---|---|---|---|---|---|---|---|
| Cost Element | Description | Activity | (Hours) | Variable | Fixed | Total | Variable | Fixed | Total |
| 420000 | Direct labor costs | LABOR | | 120,000.00 | | 120,000.00 | | | |
| 449000 | Other pers. costs | LABOR | | 60,000.00 | | 60,000.00 | | | |
| | | KP26 | 6,000 | 180,000.00 | 0.00 | 180,000.00 | 30.00 | 0.00 | 30.00 |
| | | | | | | KP06 | | | |
| | | | | | | | | | |
| 452000 | Machine maintenance | MCHRS | | | 36,000.00 | 36,000.00 | | | |
| 481000 | Cost-acctg deprec. | MCHRS | | | 72,000.00 | 72,000.00 | | | |
| 416200 | Electricity Usage | MCHRS | | 18,000.00 | | 18,000.00 | | | |
| | | KP26 | 1,800 | 18,000.00 | 108,000.00 | 126,000.00 | 10.00 | 60.00 | 70.00 |
| | | | | | | KP06 | | | |
| | | | | | | | | | |
| 405200 | Usage OfficeSupplies | | | | 1,800.00 | 1,800.00 | | | |
| 430000 | Salaries | | | | 12,000.00 | 12,000.00 | | | |
| 435000 | Annual Bonus | | | | 24,000.00 | 24,000.00 | | | |
| 470101 | Meals | | | | 4,800.00 | 4,800.00 | | | |
| 473000 | Postage | | | | 5,400.00 | 5,400.00 | | | |
| | | * | | 0.00 | 48,000.00 | 48,000.00 | | | |
| | | | | | | KP06 | | | |
| | | | | | | | | | |
| | Cost Splitting | LABOR | | | 24,000.00 | 24,000.00 | 0.00 | 4.00 | 4.00 |
| | | MCHRS | | | 24,000.00 | 24,000.00 | 0.00 | 13.33 | 13.33 |
| | | | | | | KSS4 | | | |
| | | | | | | | | | |
| | Price Calculation | LABOR | | 180,000.00 | 24,000.00 | 204,000.00 | 30.00 | 4.00 | 34.00 |
| | | MCHRS | | 18,000.00 | 132,000.00 | 150,000.00 | 10.00 | 73.33 | 83.33 |
| | | | | 198,000.00 | 156,000.00 | 354,000.00 | | | |
| | | | | | | | | | KSPI |

* These costs were planned on the Production Line Cost Center to simplify this example. These costs can also be planned on Support Cost Centers and then flow via Plan Assessment (KSUB) or / and Plan Distribution (KSVB).

*Figure 5.18: Cost center planning—snapshot from the spreadsheet*

For simplicity purposes, this example only involved one cost center and a handful of cost elements, but Alex wanted to prove the concept and ensure that he understood the dependencies from one step to another. No doubt, when there are multiple cost centers involving the entire plant, as well as multiple cost elements for each of the cost centers, the planning process is much more complex. This is where the system's functionalities can be relied on.

## 5.6 Transferring planned costs to the HANA database

### Step 7: Transferring planned costs for Fiori reports

Alex also learned from his studies of SAP that manufacturing, product costing, and cost center planning data is stored in special CO controlling tables. Most financial reporting applications now use special planning tables that have been introduced to support newer system functionality as part of the Universal Journal—the ACDOCP table for planning data and the ACCOSTRATE table for calculated rates. All actual postings are processed in the Universal Journal ACDOCA table regardless of whether the special controlling tables or the newer planning tables are used in the planning process. Special Fiori reports access the newer planning tables but not the special CO tables. The planning data should be made available to support these Fiori reports, and SAP has provided a means of updating the planning tables from the CO tables. Two programs are provided:

- R_FINS_PLAN_TRANS_CO_ERP_2_S4H —for copying the cost center plan data.
- R_FINS_PLAN_TRANS_ACTY_ERP_S4H —for copying the calculated activity rates.

These programs are accessed by using transaction SA38 to run the updates. First, copy the cost center plans by executing program R_FINS_PLAN_TRANS_CO_ERP_2_S4H from SA38, as shown in Figure 5.19.

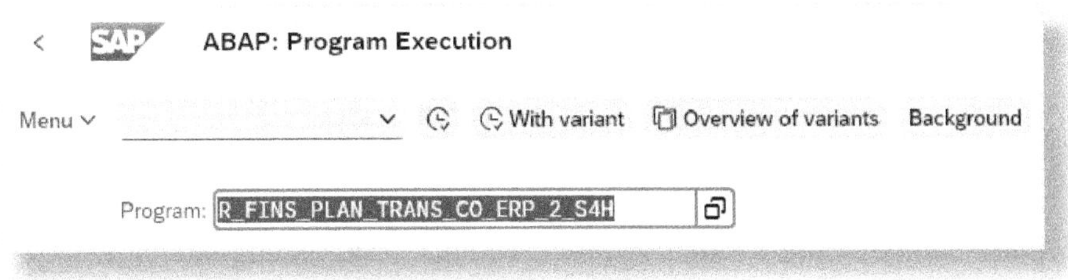


*Figure 5.19: SA38 program to copy cost center plans*

After pressing the EXECUTE button, enter the required parameters for the transfer. Planning category PLN is usually used for this, but other planning categories can also be used if required. Figure 5.20 shows the typical selections.

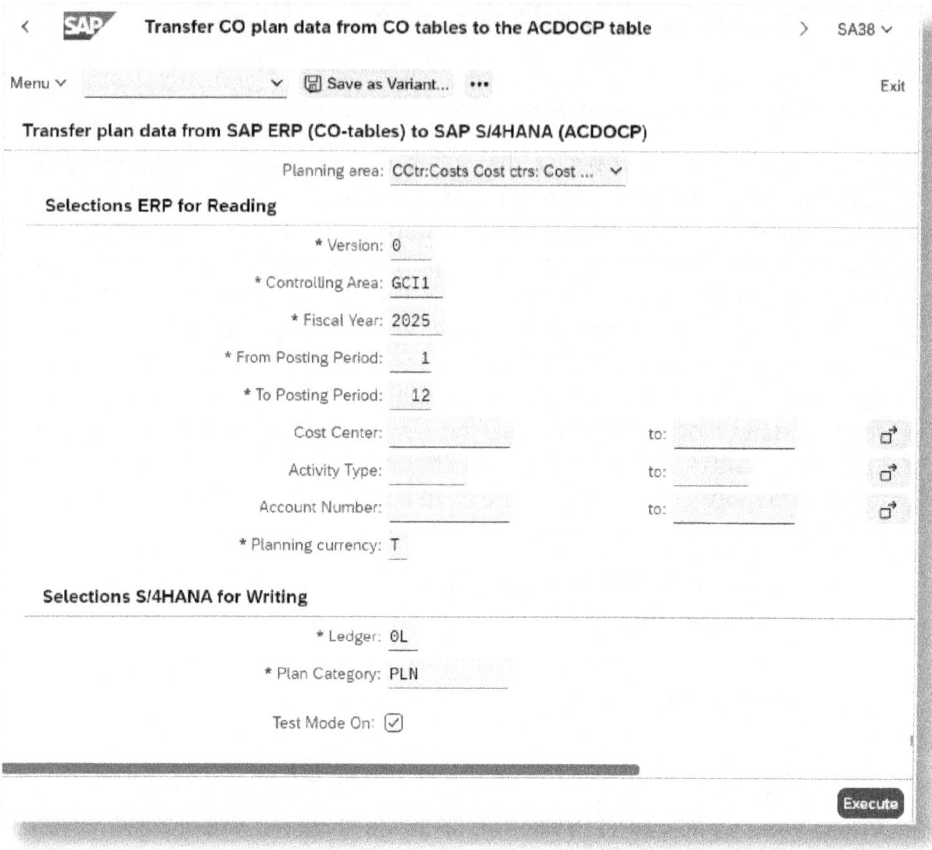


*Figure 5.20: Required information to copy the cost center plan*

> **! Using transaction SA38 to run programs**
>
> GUI transaction SA38 enables you to run any available program, not only programs specific to cost center planning. This transaction is normally heavily restricted for use by ordinary users. The recommended way to handle these transfers is to have your ABAP development team create special Fiori tiles that execute these particular programs. Fiori tiles can also be created to execute standard GUI transactions. Using this method enables you to execute the necessary GUI transactions from the Fiori launchpad without having to establish a separate GUI user session. A few transactions already have Fiori tiles predefined by SAP. For example, GUI transaction KP26 is also delivered as the EDIT PRICES FOR ACTIVITY TYPES Fiori app. However, most transactions do not have a Fiori equivalent.

Reviewing the log is important to make sure that all the data has been copied (see Figure 5.21).

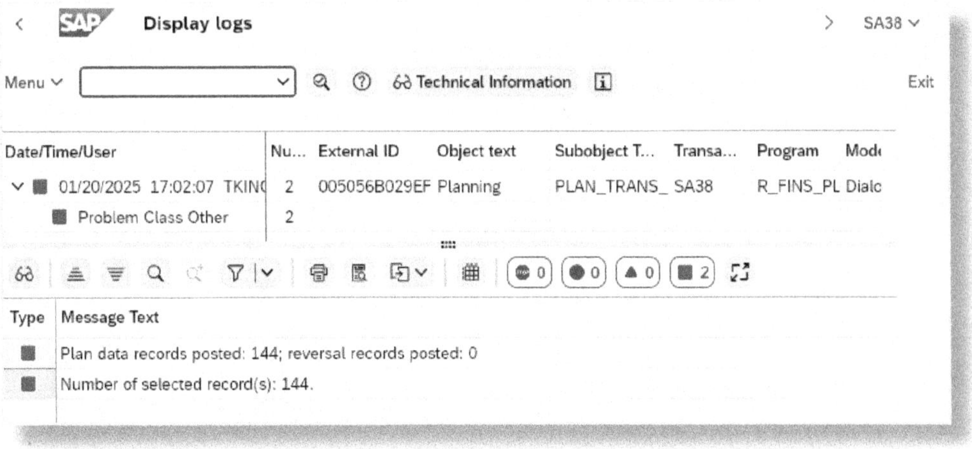


*Figure 5.21: Log for transferring planning data from CO tables*

**Step 8: Transferring activity prices for Fiori reports**

A separate program, R_FINS_PLAN_TRANS_ACTY_ERP_S4H, is used to update the calculated activity rates. This is also processed using transaction SA38, as shown in Figure 5.22.

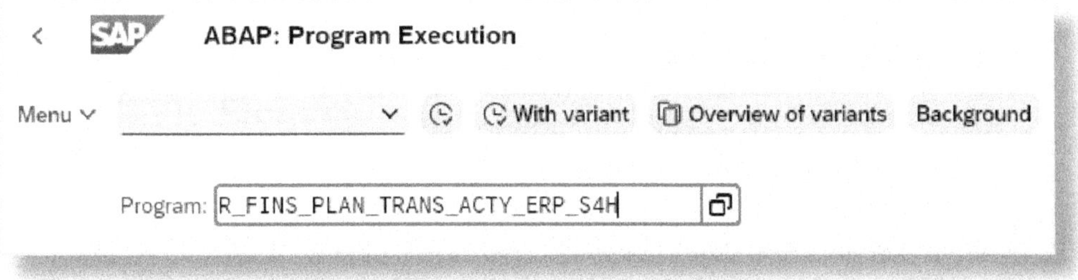


*Figure 5.22: Program to transfer activity rates*

Enter the required information to identify the rates to be transferred (see Figure 5.23).

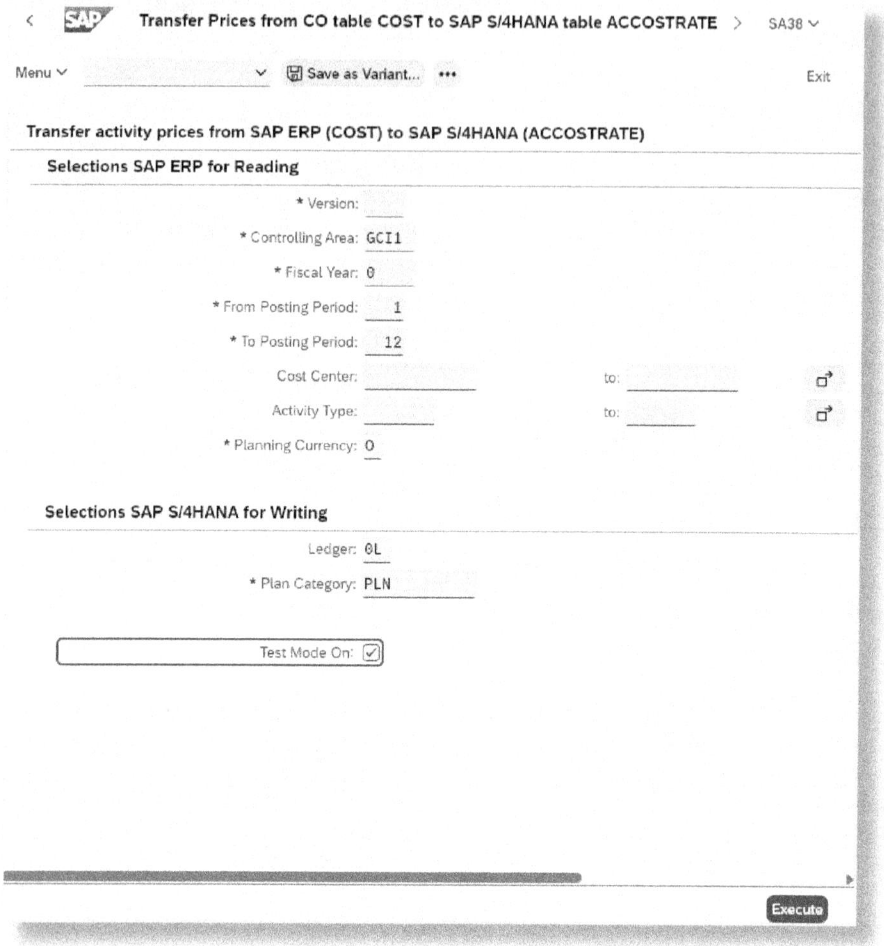


*Figure 5.23: Transfer activity rate parameters*

After the transfer, Alex could check the results by running the COST CENTERS PLAN/ACTUAL Fiori application by selecting the tile shown in Figure 5.24.

*Figure 5.24: Cost Centers Plan/Actual report—Fiori tile*

Figure 5.25 shows that the planned costs match what was entered in the original planning process, meaning that the plan was successfully transferred to the Universal Journal planning tables.

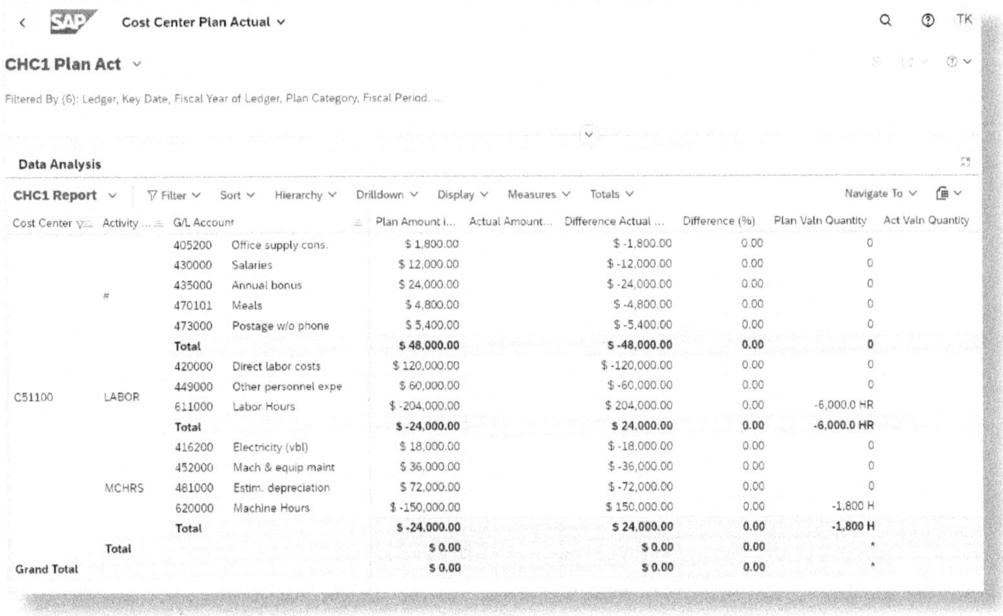


| Cost Center | Activity ... | G/L Account | | Plan Amount i... | Actual Amount... | Difference Actual ... | Difference (%) | Plan Valn Quantity | Act Valn Quantity |
|---|---|---|---|---|---|---|---|---|---|
| C51100 | # | 405200 | Office supply cons. | $ 1,800.00 | | $ -1,800.00 | 0.00 | 0 | |
| | | 430000 | Salaries | $ 12,000.00 | | $ -12,000.00 | 0.00 | 0 | |
| | | 435000 | Annual bonus | $ 24,000.00 | | $ -24,000.00 | 0.00 | 0 | |
| | | 470101 | Meals | $ 4,800.00 | | $ -4,800.00 | 0.00 | 0 | |
| | | 473000 | Postage w/o phone | $ 5,400.00 | | $ -5,400.00 | 0.00 | 0 | |
| | | **Total** | | **$ 48,000.00** | | **$ -48,000.00** | **0.00** | **0** | |
| | LABOR | 420000 | Direct labor costs | $ 120,000.00 | | $ -120,000.00 | 0.00 | 0 | |
| | | 449000 | Other personnel expe | $ 60,000.00 | | $ -60,000.00 | 0.00 | 0 | |
| | | 611000 | Labor Hours | $ -204,000.00 | | $ 204,000.00 | 0.00 | -6,000.0 HR | |
| | | **Total** | | **$ -24,000.00** | | **$ 24,000.00** | **0.00** | **-6,000.0 HR** | |
| | MCHRS | 416200 | Electricity (vbl) | $ 18,000.00 | | $ -18,000.00 | 0.00 | 0 | |
| | | 452000 | Mach & equip maint | $ 36,000.00 | | $ -36,000.00 | 0.00 | 0 | |
| | | 481000 | Estim. depreciation | $ 72,000.00 | | $ -72,000.00 | 0.00 | 0 | |
| | | 620000 | Machine Hours | $ -150,000.00 | | $ 150,000.00 | 0.00 | -1,800 H | |
| | | **Total** | | **$ -24,000.00** | | **$ 24,000.00** | **0.00** | **-1,800 H** | |
| | **Total** | | | **$ 0.00** | | **$ 0.00** | **0.00** | * | |
| **Grand Total** | | | | **$ 0.00** | | **$ 0.00** | **0.00** | * | |

*Figure 5.25: Cost center plan versus actual report*

## 5.7 Plan allocations

During his orientation, Alex learned about GCI's Chocotown manufacturing facility, which was divided into two plants. Plant-specific costs were captured in their respective cost centers. However, there were certain costs that were captured in common cost center C51900.

Costs captured in the common cost center were allocated to plant-specific cost centers using distributions and assessments.

*Distribution* is an allocation process in which the original primary cost element is carried over from the sender to the receiver. However, in the case of *assessments*, the cost allocation takes place using a secondary cost element. In other words, using an assessment means that the identity of the cost element is lost.

GCI uses a combination of both distribution and assessment in its planning and actual processes. Both functions can be handled using the MANAGE ALLOCATIONS Fiori app (see Figure 5.26) as long as activity type posting quantities are not used in the calculation of the allocation amounts.

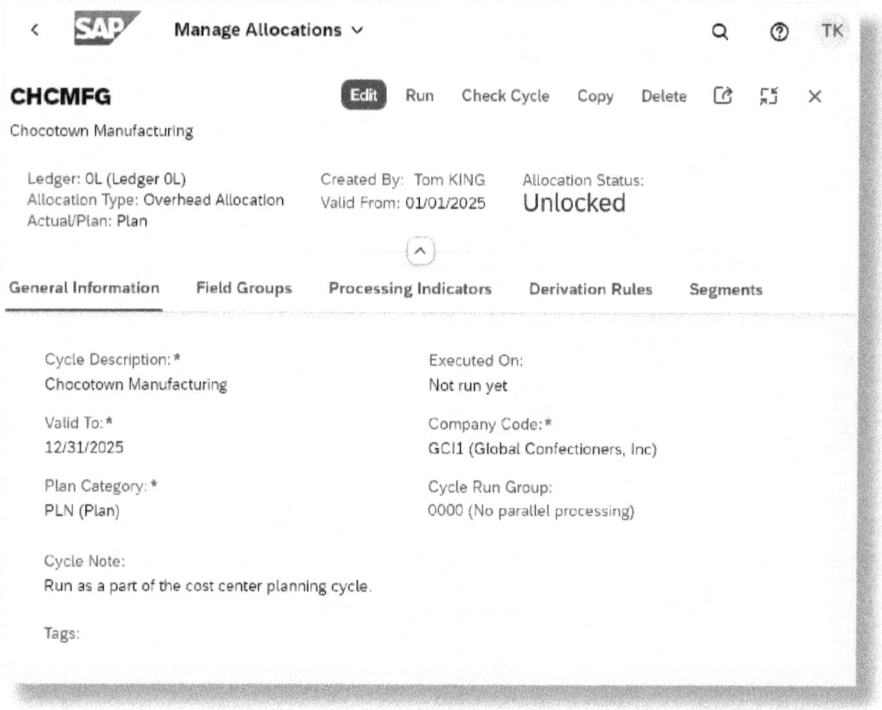


*Figure 5.26: "Manage Allocations" Fiori app— for processing cost allocations*

When planned activity quantities are used in the calculation, transaction KSUB is used for distributions and KSVB is used for assessments.

For KSUB (plan distribution), the menu path is: ACCOUNTING • CONTROLLING • COST CENTER ACCOUNTING • PLANNING • ALLOCATIONS • DISTRIBUTION.

For KSVB (plan assessment), the menu path is ACCOUNTING • CONTROLLING • COST CENTER ACCOUNTING • PLANNING • ALLOCATIONS • ASSESSMENT.

Alex also came across various tools for cost center planning. He summarized them in a table for reference (see Figure 5.27).

**Steps for Planning for Cost Centers at GCI**

| Description of transaction | Create / Change | Purpose | Display |
|---|---|---|---|
| Set Planner Profile | KP04 (transaction) | Provides combination of fields suitable for your planning needs | |
| Activity Quantity Planning | Edit Prices for Activity Types | Planning of activity quantity for the planning period | KP27 |
| Activity Dependent Cost Planning | KP06 (transaction) | Planning of activity dependent (direct) costs | KP07 |
| Activity Independent Cost Planning | KP06 (transaction) | Planning of activity independent (indirect / overhead) costs | KP07 |
| Plan Cost Center Splitting | KSS4 (transaction) | Attach activity independent costs to specific Activity Types | |
| Plan Activity Price Calculation | KSPI (transaction) | Calculate predetermined absorption rate (burden rate) | |
| Transfer Plan to Universal Journal | SA38 (transaction) | Update plan in table ACDOCP (R_FINS_PLAN_TRANS_CO_ERP_2_S4H) | |
| Transfer Prices to Universal Journal | SA38 (transaction) | Update activity rates in ACCOSTRATE (R_FINS_PLAN_TRANS_ACTY_ERP_S4H) | |

**Tools for Cost Center Planning**

| Description of transaction | Transaction / Fiori app | Purpose |
|---|---|---|
| Direct input of activity prices | Edit Prices for Activity Types | Activity type rates are fed manually instead of being calculated via KSPI |
| Mass upload of activity quantities | Edit Prices for Activity Types | Upload activity quantities using a comma separated (csv) file |
| Quantity data from long term planning | KSPP (transaction) | Transfers Long Term Planning (LTP) data to cost centers (activity quantity input via KP26 can be avoided or reduced) |
| Mass upload of planned costs | KP06 (transaction) | Upload costs using a comma separated (csv) text file |
| Copy from previous year's plan | KP97 (transaction) | Previous year's plan is the base for upcoming year's plans |
| Copy from previous year's actuals | KP98 (transaction) | Previous year's actual is the base for upcoming year's plans |
| Plan cost distribution | Manage Allocations | Allocation of costs (sender cost element retained) |
| Cost center planning report | KSBL (transaction) | Displays activity-dependent and -independent costs for a cost center |
| Plan cost assessment | Manage Allocations | Allocation of costs (sender cost element not available) |
| Activity price report | Analyze Prices for Activity Types | Report of activity prices for cost center / cost center group |

*Figure 5.27: Planning steps and tools for cost center planning*

# 6 Absorption—aren't cost centers like sponges?

*"I kind of like to be a sponge, in a way. So everywhere that I am, I like to keep an open mind and just get ideas from everything."*
—Bethany Mota

**Once the plan for the upcoming year was complete, it was time for Alex to look at how actual costs are booked and absorbed at cost center level. Cost centers collect costs every month and then pass along some of the costs during, and at the end of, each month. The process of collecting and passing along costs is called "absorption".**

## 6.1 Actual cost booking

Not all costs end up in cost centers. There are certain costs that are recorded as other cost objects; for example, production orders, process orders, internal orders, work breakdown structure (WBS) elements, and product cost collectors. Costs that are directly attributable to a cost object and that are booked on the cost object, such as a raw material consumed during manufacturing, will be consumed at process order level. A raw material that is consumed for a specific trial purpose will be consumed at internal order level. Labor hours spent assembling a new set of machinery that will be used for production can be charged to a WBS element. A cost center, however, is usually the most common sender/receiver of costs in a manufacturing setup.

Examples of cost center postings in a manufacturing facility are:

- *production line cost center*—typically receives the wage costs of shopfloor staff dedicated to that particular production line, as well depreciation of machinery that makes up the production line.
- *maintenance cost center*—receives costs related to spare parts consumed for regular maintenance.
- *energy cost center*—receives costs related to power, steam, and other utilities consumed for the plant.

- *common cost center* (for the plant)—receives costs for a plant manager's salary and all other common costs that a plant incurs.

Let's look at an example that illustrates the flow of costs in cost center report S_ALR_87013611.

Figure 6.1 shows that several cost elements had actual postings to COST CENTER/GROUP C51100, including cost element 404000 (spare parts) in the amount of $200.00.

The menu path is: ACCOUNTING • CONTROLLING • COST CENTER ACCOUNTING • INFORMATION SYSTEM • REPORTS FOR COST CENTER ACCOUNTING • PLAN/ACTUAL COMPARISONS • COST CENTERS: ACTUAL/PLAN/VARIANCE.

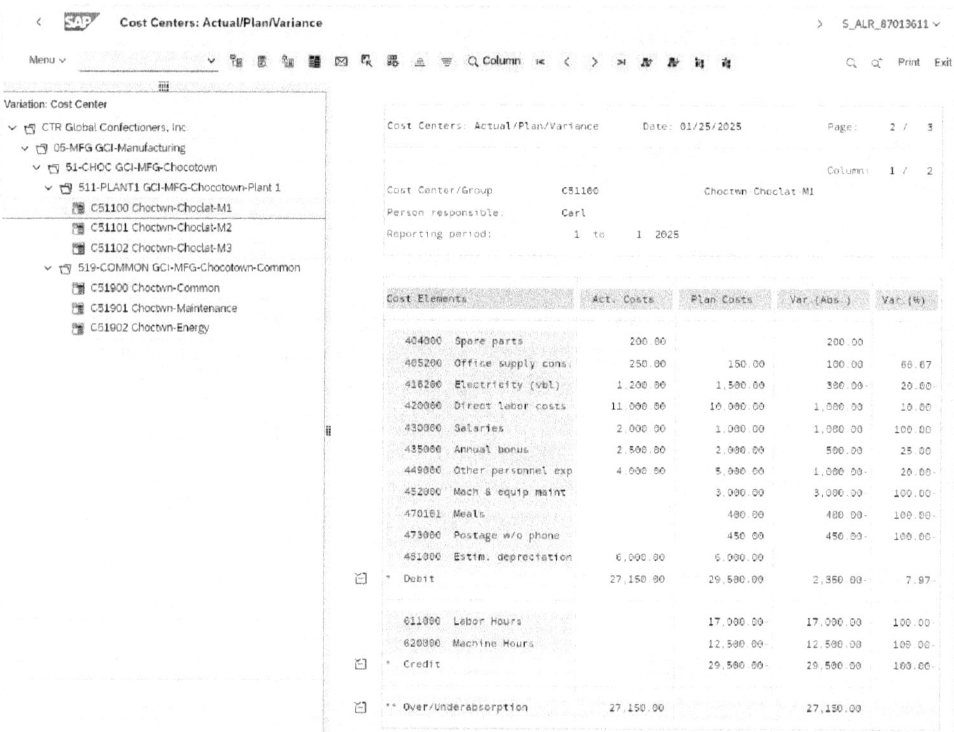


*Figure 6.1: S_ALR_87013611—Actual cost booking on production line cost center*

Figure 6.2 shows that COST CENTER/GROUP C51901 had a posting of $2,000.00 for cost element 404000 (spare parts) and $6,000.00 for cost element 452000 (machine maintenance).

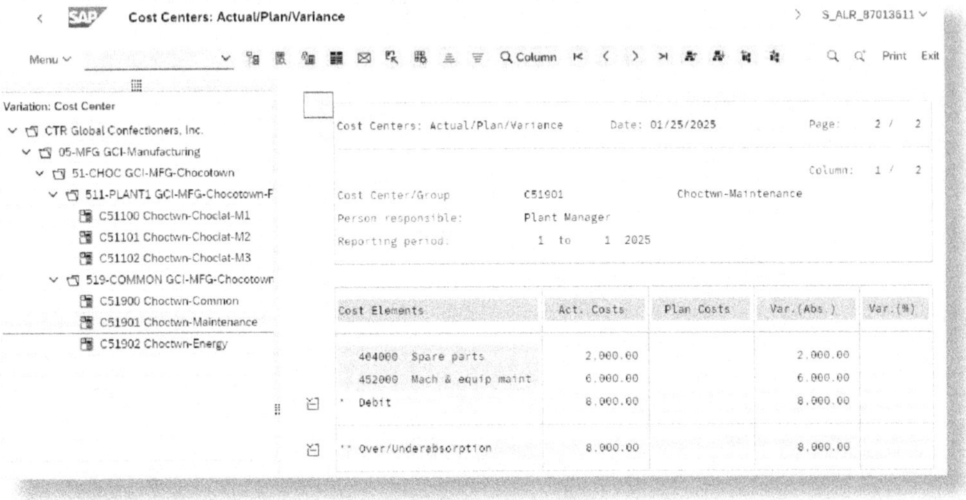


*Figure 6.2: S_ALR_87013611—Actual cost booking on maintenance cost center*

## 6.2 Activity absorption

A product carries the costs of materials, labor, and overhead that are involved in its manufacture. The material cost can be more or less tangible and identifiable with the inputs. However, labor and overhead calculations are usually based on the number of hours spent on manufacturing the product. In effect, this is the *conversion cost* for making the product—the cost of converting a raw material into a semi-finished material, or a semi-finished material into a finished material.

Plan activity costs are calculated during the planning phase. These prices are nothing more than predetermined absorption rates that will be used for each activity type unit.

## Plan activity costs—example

If the activity price for direct labor is $30.00/hour and the machine hour is $120.00/hour, then a product that consumes two hours of direct labor and three hours of machine hours will carry $60.00 absorption of direct labor and $360.00 absorption of machine hours. At that time, the process order is debited for the cost of $420.00 and the cost center is credited. This credit provides absorption, whereas the debits provide the actual cost.

It is highly likely that the actual cost debit on the cost center will not be equal to what was absorbed in the cost center. The difference is called *over absorption/under absorption* (see Figure 6.3). Perfect absorption (no under/over absorption), purely by activity posting, is very rare.

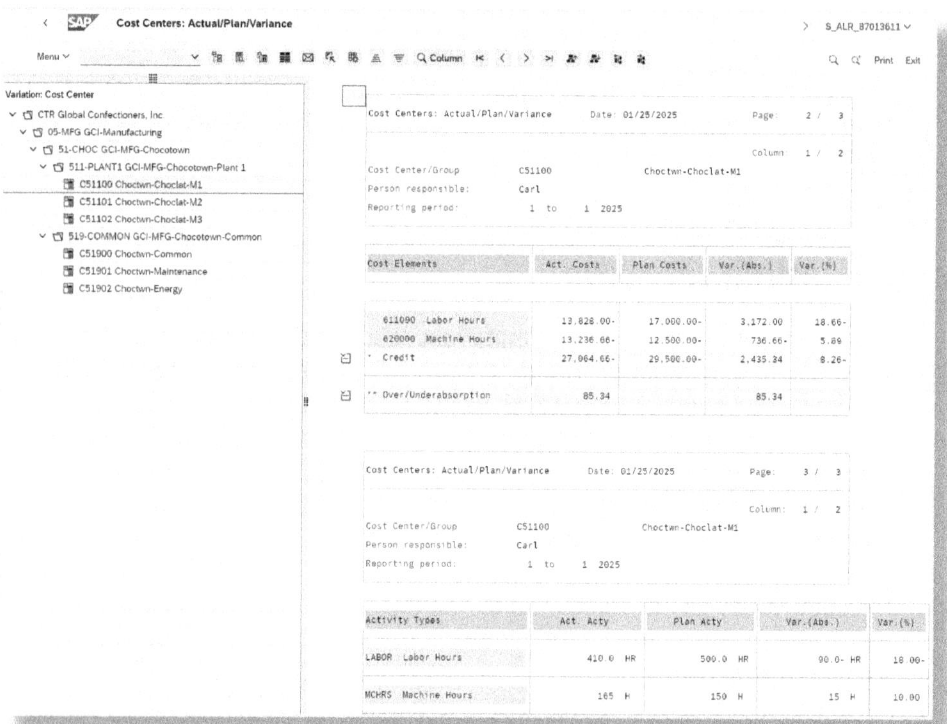


*Figure 6.3: S_ALR_87013611—Activity absorption on production line cost center*

There could be several reasons for over/under absorption, including:

- *spending variances* (e.g., spent more than planned),
- *volume variances* (e.g., produced less than planned or activity quantity was less than planned),
- *mix variances* (e.g., mix or types of products produced were different than planned), or
- *efficiency variances* (e.g., labor was too fast and consumed fewer labor hours, or machines were too slow and consumed more machine hours).

This over/under absorption must be passed over to:

- the product—via either KSII actual activity price calculation with CON2 revaluation of orders or as a part of the Actual Costing run, or
- another cost center—by way of cost-center to cost-center allocation (MANAGE ALLOCATIONS Fiori app or GUI transactions KSU5/KSV5), or
- profitability segment (MANAGE ALLOCATIONS app), or
- a combination of all the above.

## 6.3 Actual allocations

In addition to the costs booked directly at cost-center level, such as wages and depreciation, a production line cost center receives costs from various other cost centers in the plant. Some examples of cost center allocations are:

- Maintenance costs from a maintenance cost center—the most commonly used drivers are machine hours across various production line cost centers.
- Energy costs from an energy cost center—production volume across various production line cost centers can be used as the basis of allocation. If there are meters installed in each department that enable actual energy consumption to be tracked, then an accurate allocation can be made using statistical key figures, or in the allocation cycle.

- Support staff costs such as the plant manager's salary, finance costs, IT costs, warehouse costs, R&D costs, and quality costs—here too, production volume across various production line cost centers can be used as the basis of allocation.

**! "Manage Allocations" Fiori app**

Alex asked Erin from IT why GCI does not use the MANAGE ALLOCATIONS Fiori app to run its allocations and distributions. Erin pointed him to SAP Note 2936255—"FAQs on Fiori apps for Controlling Overhead Management...". The first question in the note relates to the app's limitations. Point 4 of the answer states the following:

*"Allocation Context: Cost Center --> If the receiver rule 'variable portion type' is selected, there is no option to use activity types as reference. Only statistical key figures are provided.*

*Regarding the requirement as Activity Type as Receiver Tracing Factors are planned to be delivered in future OP releases and it is in the scope of development. However, there is no roadmap about the timeline/OP version being fixed."*

Due to the requirement that GCI perform its allocations based on activity type postings, the GUI transactions are used instead.

Costs can be allocated using distribution (transaction KSV5, where original cost element is used to allocate costs), or assessments (transaction KSU5—a secondary cost element, known as *assessment cost element*—is used to allocate costs). Other methods include template allocation (transaction KPAS) and actual cost reposting (KB11N). These functions are performed as part of the month-end closing function to ensure that all postings for the period have been completed.

Figure 6.4 shows transaction KSV3—SEGMENT HEADER tab for CYCLE MAINT. We can see that 100% of actual values are to be allocated in the ACTUAL ACTIVITY proportion.

The menu path is: ACCOUNTING • CONTROLLING • COST CENTER ACCOUNTING • PLANNING • ALLOCATIONS • DISTRIBUTION • EXTRAS • CYCLE • DISPLAY.

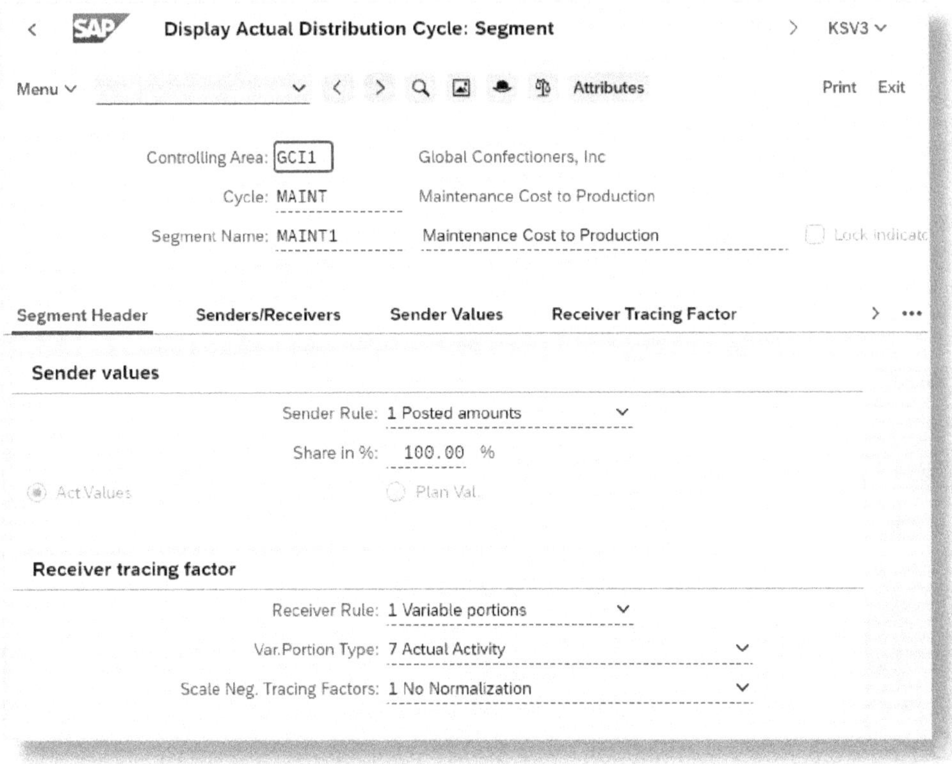


*Figure 6.4: KSV3—Distribution Cycle MAINT—Segment Header tab*

Figure 6.5 shows the SENDERS/RECEIVERS tab, where the SENDER: COST CENTER *C51901* sends costs incurred in COST ELEMENT: GROUP *ALL* to the RECEIVER: COST CENTER GROUP 511-PLANT1.

This means that cost center C51901 (Chocotown-Maintenance) will transfer all costs to cost center group 511-PLANT1, which includes the following cost centers:

- C51100 Chocotown-Chocolate Machine M1
- C51101 Chocotown-Chocolate Machine M2
- C51102 Chocotown-Chocolate Machine M3

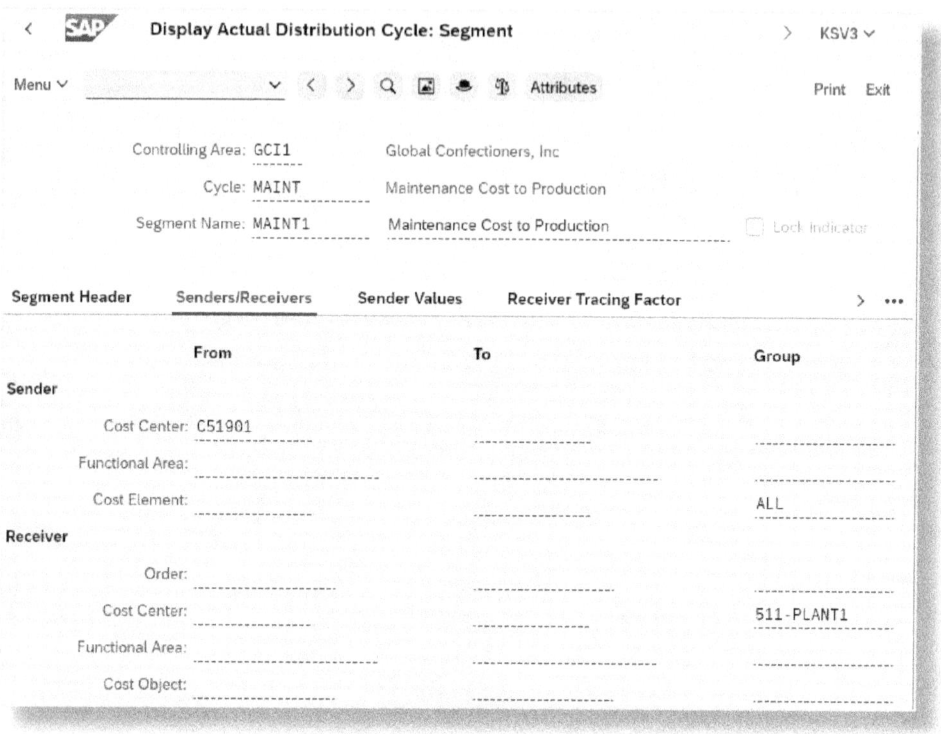


*Figure 6.5: KSV3—Distribution Cycle MAINT—Senders/Receivers tab*

Figure 6.6 shows the RECEIVER TRACING FACTOR tab, where ACTIVITY TYPE MCHRS (machine hours) is used to proportionately allocate the costs to receiver cost centers.

Figure 6.7 shows the EXECUTE ACTUAL DISTRIBUTION initial screen (transaction KSV5), where three cycles have been executed, including cycle MAINT.

The menu path is: ACCOUNTING • CONTROLLING • COST CENTER ACCOUNTING • PLANNING • ALLOCATIONS • DISTRIBUTION.

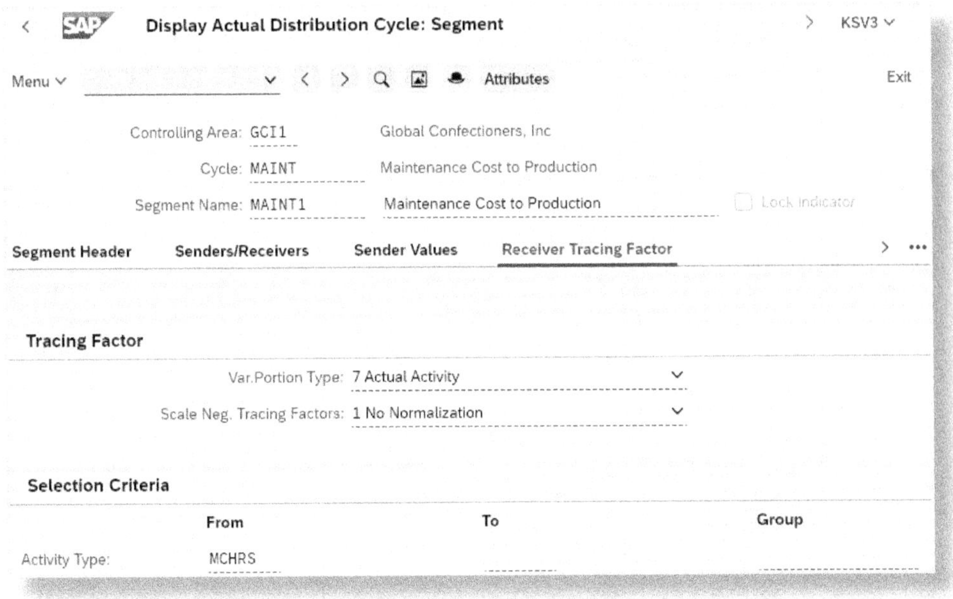


*Figure 6.6: KSV3—Distribution Cycle MAINT—Receiver Tracing Factor tab*

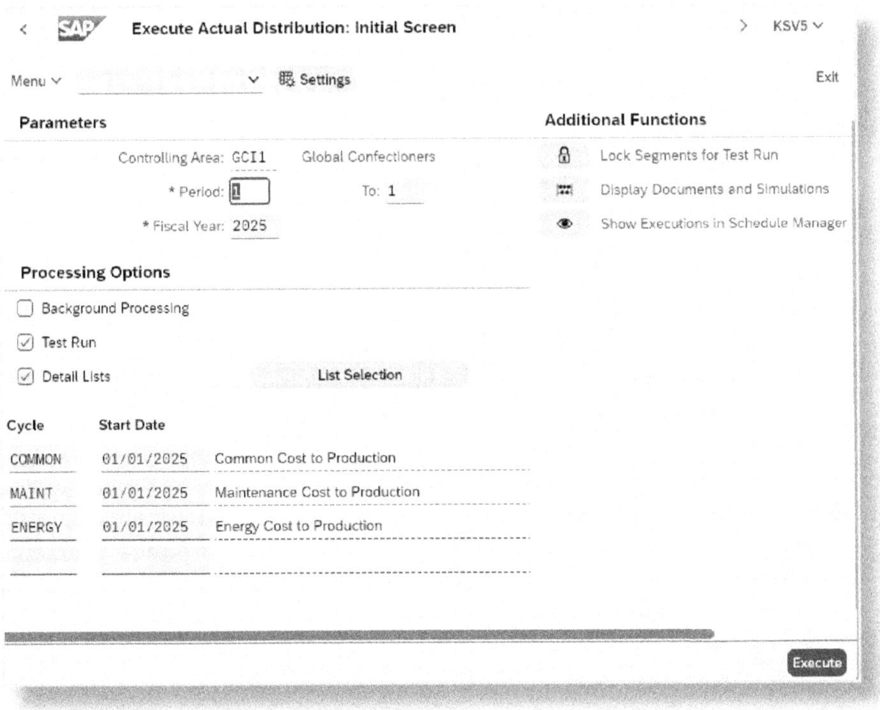


*Figure 6.7: KSV5—Distribution execution*

Figure 6.8 shows the results of the actual distribution in report S_ALR_87013611. Cost center C51901 distributed its cost of $2,000.00 for cost element 404000 and $6,000.00 for cost element 452000 to receiver cost centers C51100, C51101, and C51102.

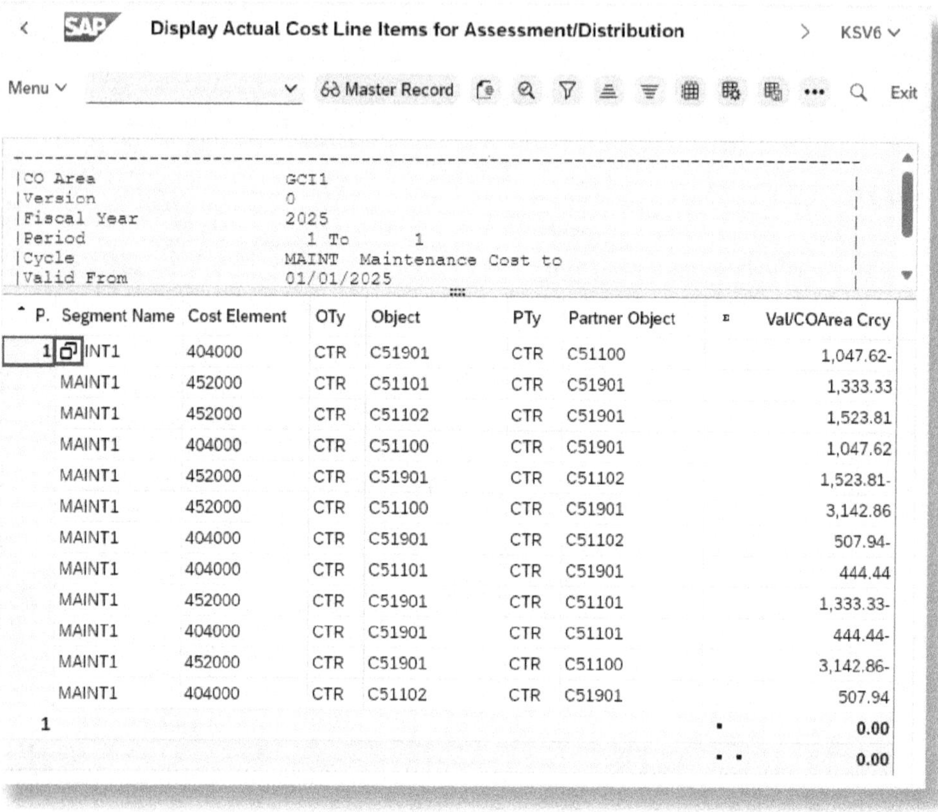

Display Actual Cost Line Items for Assessment/Distribution

| CO Area | GCI1 |
|---|---|
| Version | 0 |
| Fiscal Year | 2025 |
| Period | 1 To 1 |
| Cycle | MAINT Maintenance Cost to |
| Valid From | 01/01/2025 |

| P. | Segment Name | Cost Element | OTy | Object | PTy | Partner Object | Σ | Val/COArea Crcy |
|---|---|---|---|---|---|---|---|---|
| 1 | MAINT1 | 404000 | CTR | C51901 | CTR | C51100 | | 1,047.62- |
| | MAINT1 | 452000 | CTR | C51101 | CTR | C51901 | | 1,333.33 |
| | MAINT1 | 452000 | CTR | C51102 | CTR | C51901 | | 1,523.81 |
| | MAINT1 | 404000 | CTR | C51100 | CTR | C51901 | | 1,047.62 |
| | MAINT1 | 452000 | CTR | C51901 | CTR | C51102 | | 1,523.81- |
| | MAINT1 | 452000 | CTR | C51100 | CTR | C51901 | | 3,142.86 |
| | MAINT1 | 404000 | CTR | C51901 | CTR | C51102 | | 507.94- |
| | MAINT1 | 404000 | CTR | C51101 | CTR | C51901 | | 444.44 |
| | MAINT1 | 452000 | CTR | C51901 | CTR | C51101 | | 1,333.33- |
| | MAINT1 | 404000 | CTR | C51901 | CTR | C51101 | | 444.44- |
| | MAINT1 | 452000 | CTR | C51901 | CTR | C51100 | | 3,142.86- |
| | MAINT1 | 404000 | CTR | C51102 | CTR | C51901 | | 507.94 |
| 1 | | | | | | | • | 0.00 |
| | | | | | | | •• | 0.00 |

*Figure 6.8: KSV5—Distribution results*

Figure 6.9 shows that the C51901 costs are now fully absorbed (there is no over/under absorption).

Cost center C51100 originally had a cost of $200.00 for cost element 404000 (spare parts), as we saw in Figure 6.1. After the distribution of $1,047.62 for cost element 404000 from cost center C51901 (see Figure 6.8), the remaining cost for cost element 404000 in C51100 is now $1,247.62 (see Figure 6.10).

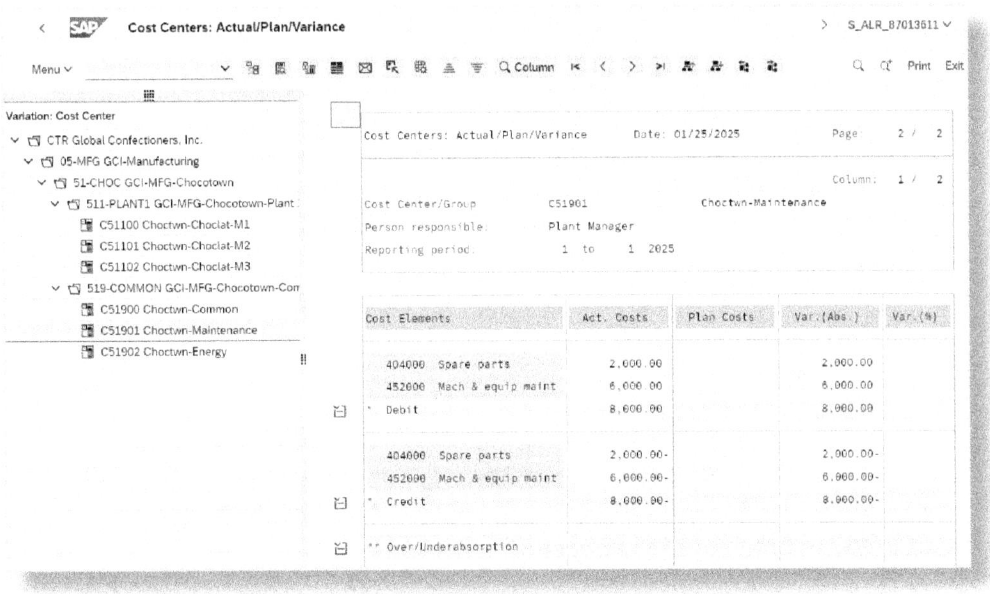


*Figure 6.9: S_ALR_87013611—Maintenance cost center after actual allocations*

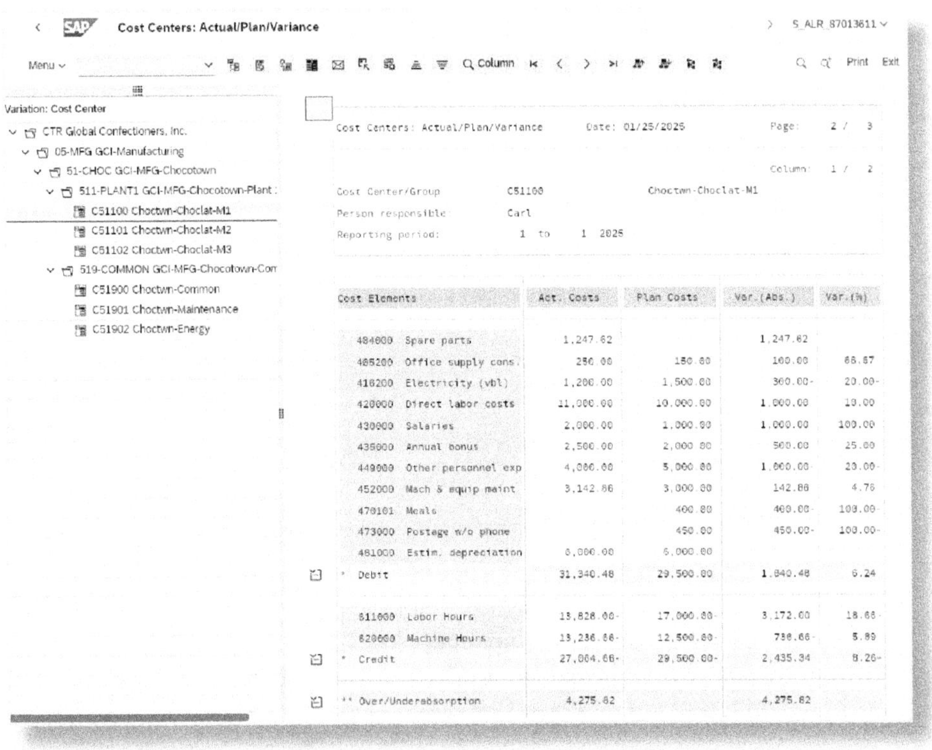


*Figure 6.10: S_ALR_87013611 Production line cost center after allocation*

## 6.4 Actual cost center splitting

Similar to plan cost center splitting, *actual cost center splitting* associates activity-independent costs to a specific activity. Costs associated with a specific cost element (or a cost element group) can be attached to an activity using splitting rules maintained in the splitting structure (transaction OKES) and assignment of cost centers to splitting structure (transaction OKEW).

### 6.4.1 Splitting structure

The menu path is: TOOLS • CUSTOMIZING • IMG • SPRO EXECUTE PROJECT • CONTROLLING • COST CENTER ACCOUNTING • ACTUAL POSTINGS • PERIOD-END CLOSING • ACTIVITY ALLOCATION • SPLITTING • DEFINE SPLITTING STRUCTURE.

Figure 6.11 shows splitting structure GC for ASSIGNMENT line LAB (LABOR), where all costs in Cost Element Group SPLIT_LAB are attached to ACTIVITY TYPE: LABOR.

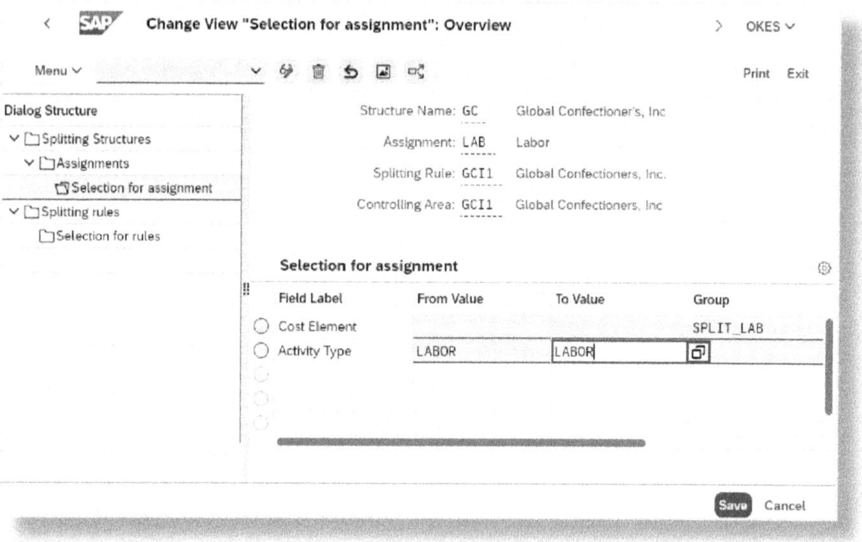


*Figure 6.11: OKES—Splitting structure setup for labor*

Similarly, Figure 6.12 shows the splitting structure GC for ASSIGNMENT line MCH (machine hours), where all costs in cost element group SPLIT_MCH are attached to ACTIVITY TYPE: MCHRS.

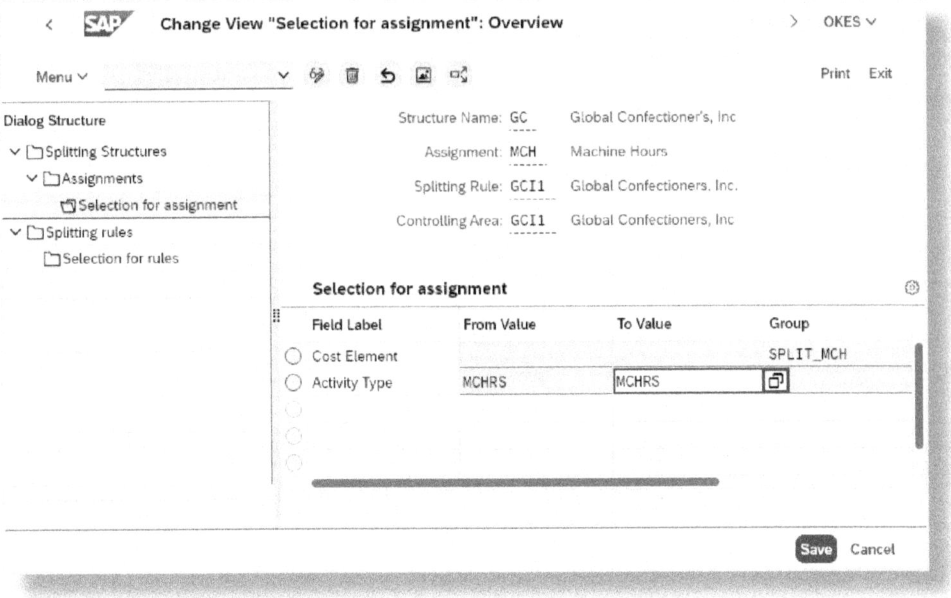


*Figure 6.12: OKES—Splitting structure setup for machine hours*

The definition of cost element group SPLIT_LAB is shown in Figure 6.13 (MANAGE COST ELEMENT GROUPS Fiori app).

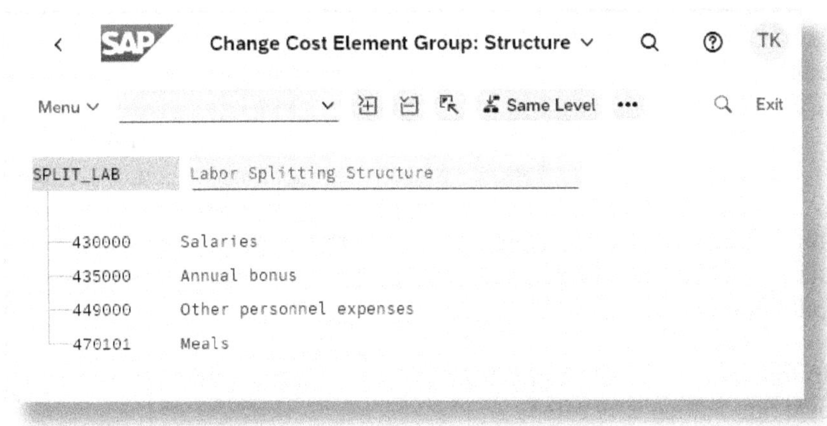


*Figure 6.13: Cost element group for splitting labor*

The definition of cost element group SPLIT_MCH is shown in Figure 6.14 (MANAGE COST ELEMENT GROUPS Fiori app).

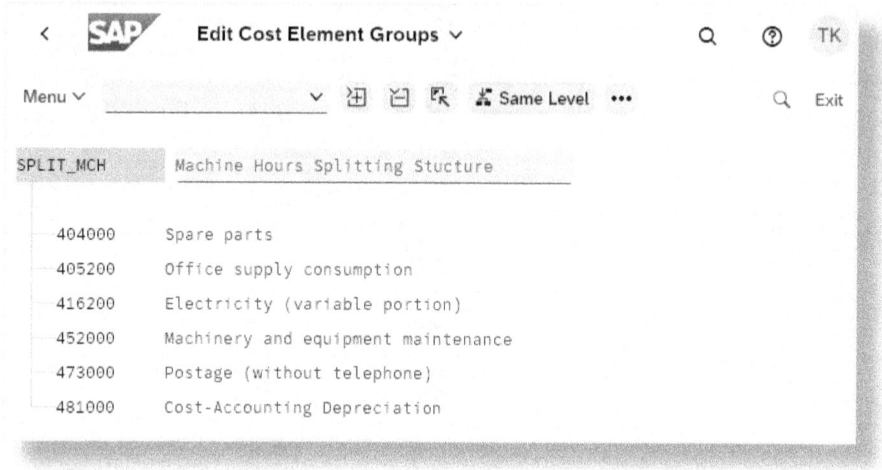


*Figure 6.14: Cost element group for splitting machine hours*

## 6.4.2 Assignment of cost centers to splitting structure

Cost centers are attached to a specific splitting rule (transaction OKEW) (see Figure 6.15).

The menu path is: TOOLS • CUSTOMIZING • IMG • SPRO EXECUTE PROJECT • CONTROLLING • COST CENTER ACCOUNTING • ACTUAL POSTINGS • PERIOD-END CLOSING • ACTIVITY ALLOCATION • SPLITTING • ASSIGN SPLITTING STRUCTURE TO COST CENTERS.

All production line cost centers are attached to splitting structure GC. Neither common cost centers nor sending cost centers are mapped to the splitting structure. In other words, cost centers that are associated with an activity type and have a calculated plan/actual price need to be assigned to a spitting structure.

Both transactions OKES and OKEW are part of a configuration setup that should not change very often.

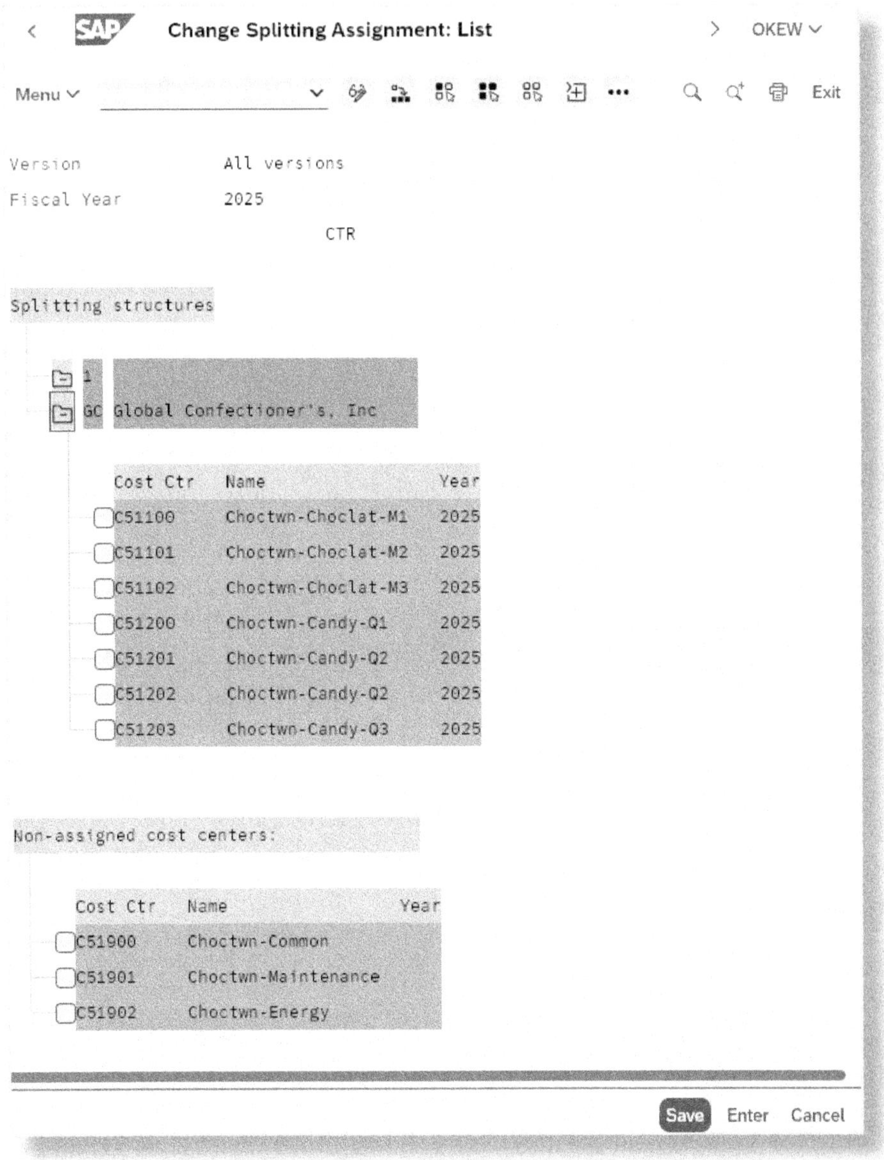


*Figure 6.15: OKEW—Assigning cost centers to splitting structure*

### 6.4.3 Actual cost splitting

Actual cost splitting is performed during month-end closing by running transaction KSS2.

The menu path is: ACCOUNTING • CONTROLLING • COST CENTER ACCOUNTING • PERIOD-END CLOSING • SINGLE FUNCTIONS • SPLITTING.

Figure 6.16 shows the ACTUAL COST SPLITTING: INITIAL SCREEN (KSS2). Splitting can be performed at cost center or cost center group level.

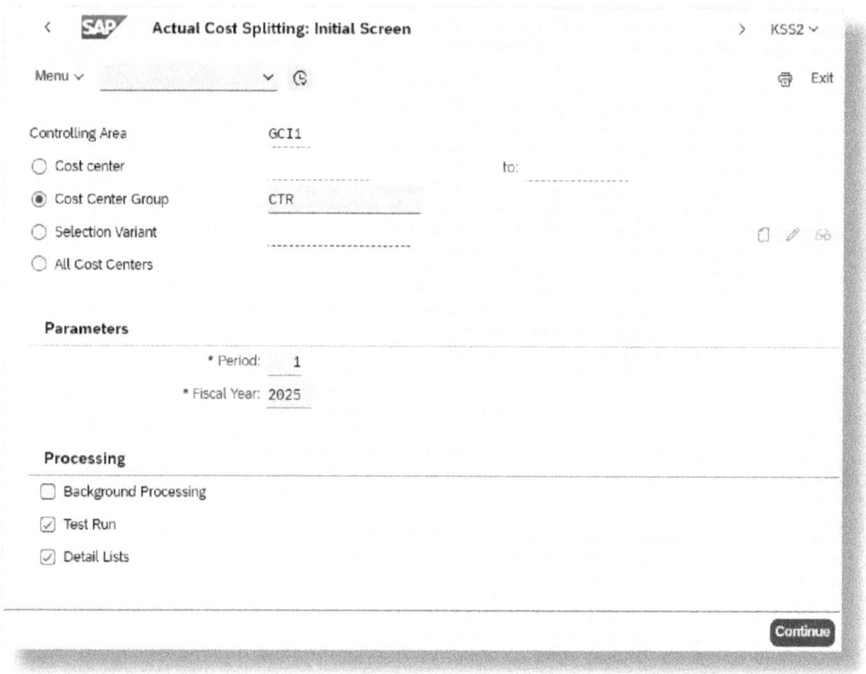


*Figure 6.16: KSS2—Actual cost splitting*

Figure 6.17 shows the actual cost splitting (KSS2) results screen. Cost element group and activity price combinations are maintained in splitting rules (transaction OKES), and cost element groups (MANAGE COST ELEMENT GROUPS app) are used during splitting.

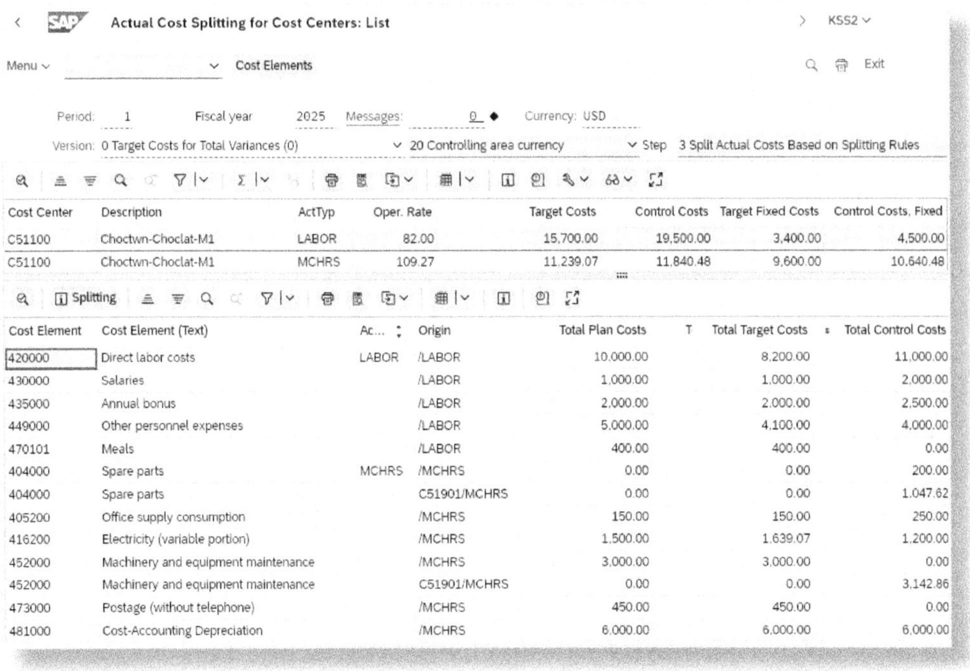


*Figure 6.17: KSS2—Actual cost splitting results*

## 6.5 Actual activity price calculation

Once you have established a link between an activity-independent cost and an activity type via cost center splitting, you are ready to perform the *actual activity price calculation* using transaction KSII. Price calculation can be performed only at cost center group level—it cannot be performed at individual cost center level (see Figure 6.18). It should also only be processed during month-end closing activities.

The menu path is: ACCOUNTING • CONTROLLING • COST CENTER ACCOUNTING • PERIOD-END CLOSING • SINGLE FUNCTIONS • PRICE CALCULATION.

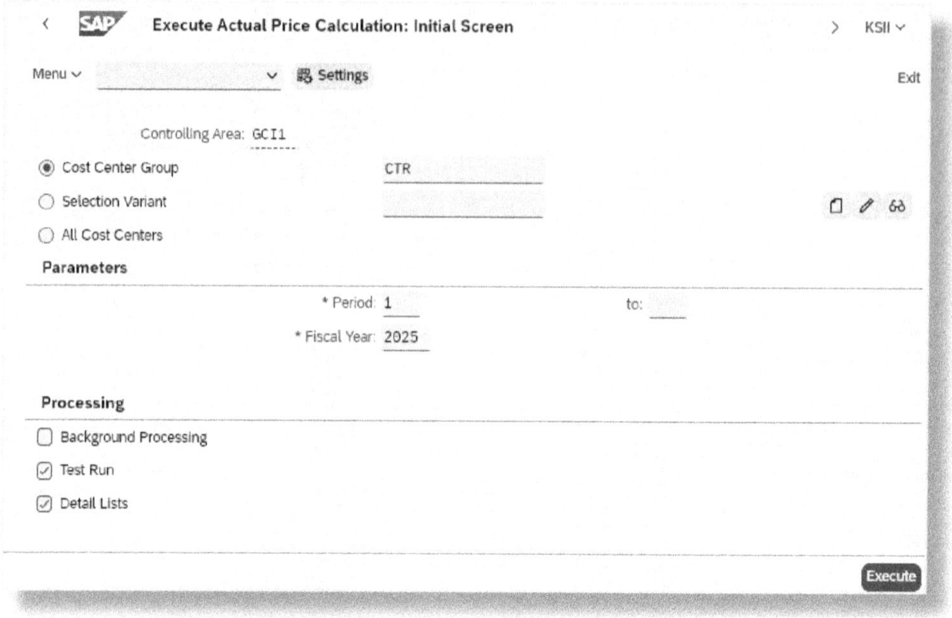


*Figure 6.18: KSII—Initial actual activity price calculation screen*

The actual price is calculated for each activity type that was attached to the cost center within the cost center group. As shown in Figure 6.19, the actual activity price was calculated for activity types LABOR and MCHRS for three production line cost centers—C51100, C51101, and C51102. Price units of 10, 100, 1,000, or 10,000 are used to reduce rounding errors.

## 6.6 Revaluation of activities on orders

Using transaction CON2, the system posts the difference between the plan rate and the actual rate and revalues the orders with the actual rate at month end. This transaction provides additional postings to the cost center on the credit side and effectively fully absorbs the cost center.

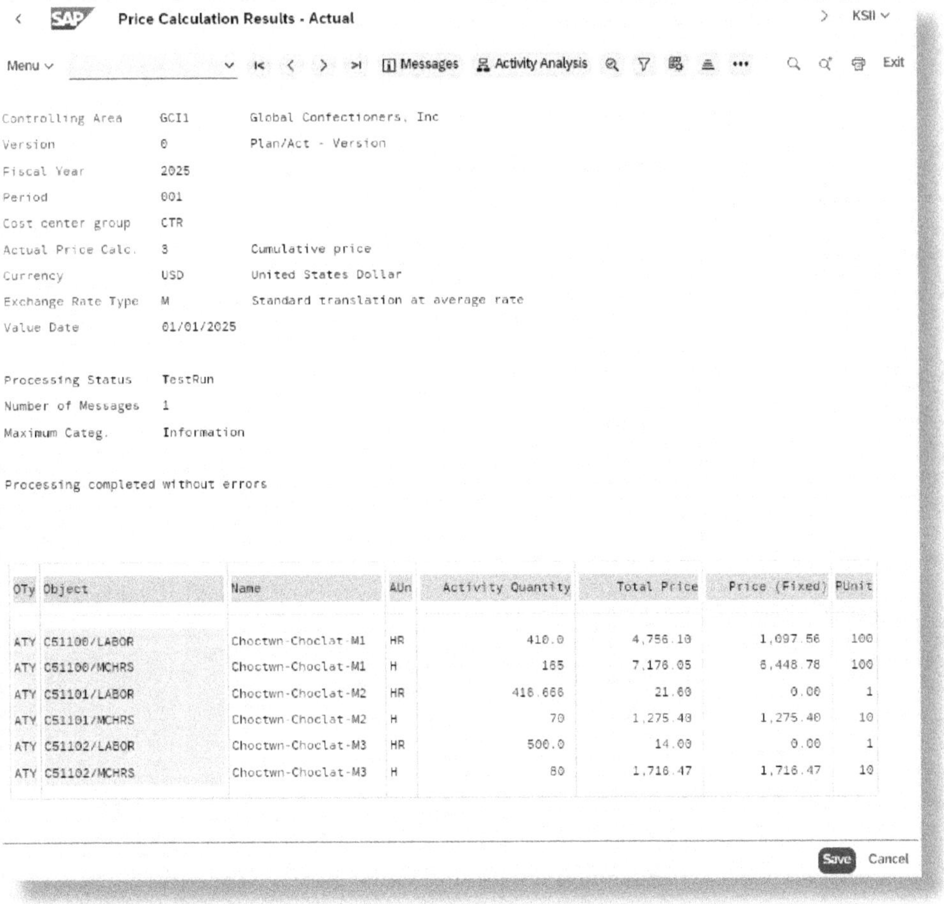
Price Calculation Results - Actual

| | | |
|---|---|---|
| Controlling Area | GCI1 | Global Confectioners, Inc |
| Version | 0 | Plan/Act - Version |
| Fiscal Year | 2025 | |
| Period | 001 | |
| Cost center group | CTR | |
| Actual Price Calc. | 3 | Cumulative price |
| Currency | USD | United States Dollar |
| Exchange Rate Type | M | Standard translation at average rate |
| Value Date | 01/01/2025 | |
| Processing Status | TestRun | |
| Number of Messages | 1 | |
| Maximum Categ. | Information | |

Processing completed without errors

| OTy | Object | Name | AUn | Activity Quantity | Total Price | Price (Fixed) | PUnit |
|---|---|---|---|---|---|---|---|
| ATY | C51100/LABOR | Choctwn-Choclat-M1 | HR | 410.0 | 4,756.10 | 1,097.56 | 100 |
| ATY | C51100/MCHRS | Choctwn-Choclat-M1 | H | 165 | 7,176.05 | 6,448.78 | 100 |
| ATY | C51101/LABOR | Choctwn-Choclat-M2 | HR | 416.666 | 21.60 | 0.00 | 1 |
| ATY | C51101/MCHRS | Choctwn-Choclat-M2 | H | 70 | 1,275.40 | 1,275.40 | 10 |
| ATY | C51102/LABOR | Choctwn-Choclat-M3 | HR | 500.0 | 14.00 | 0.00 | 1 |
| ATY | C51102/MCHRS | Choctwn-Choclat-M3 | H | 80 | 1,716.47 | 1,716.47 | 10 |

*Figure 6.19: KSII—Actual activity price calculation results*

The menu path is: ACCOUNTING • CONTROLLING • PRODUCT COST CONTROLLING • COST OBJECT CONTROLLING • PRODUCT COST BY ORDER • PERIOD-END CLOSING • SINGLE FUNCTIONS • REVALUATION AT ACTUAL PRICES • COLLECTIVE PROCESSING.

Figure 6.20 shows the initial screen for revaluation of orders at actual activity prices. This transaction is executed at plant level.

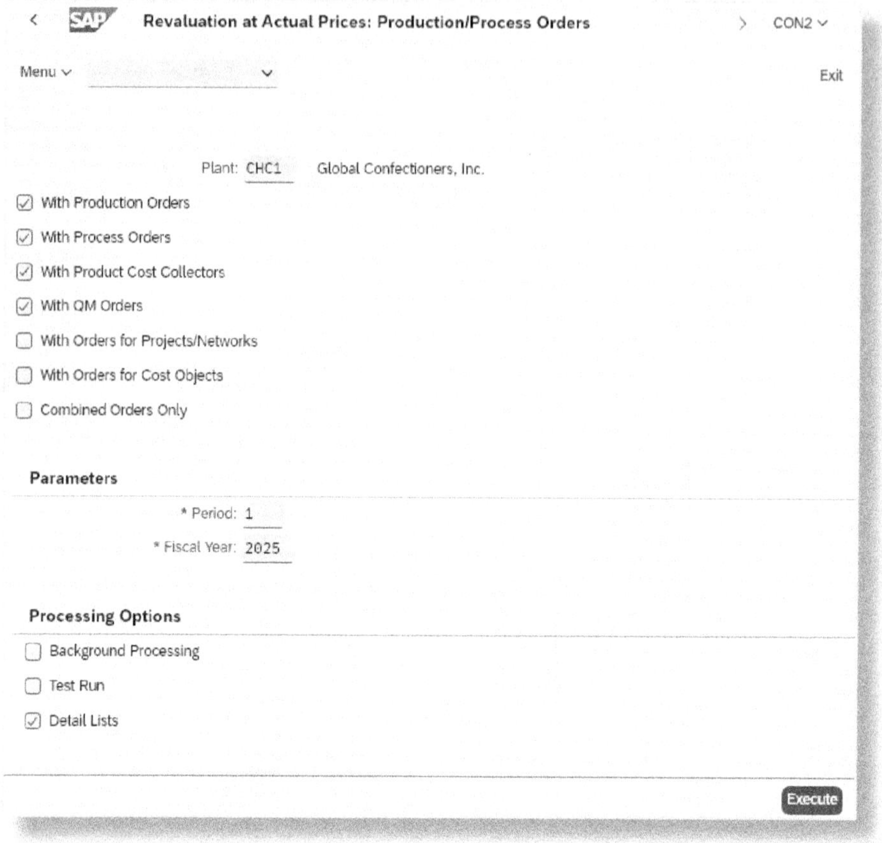


*Figure 6.20: CON2—Revaluating orders with actual price—initial screen*

Figure 6.21 shows the results of the revaluation. The output provides SENDERS (cost center and activity type combination), RECEIVER (order number), COST ELEM. (cost element), and VAL/CO AREA CRCY (value in controlling area currency—amount of revaluation).

Orders 1000840, 1000841, 1000860, and 1000861 were revalued with activity LABOR in the amount of $5,672.00 and MCHRS in the amount of $(1,396.17). The total revaluation for the cost center was $4,275.83.

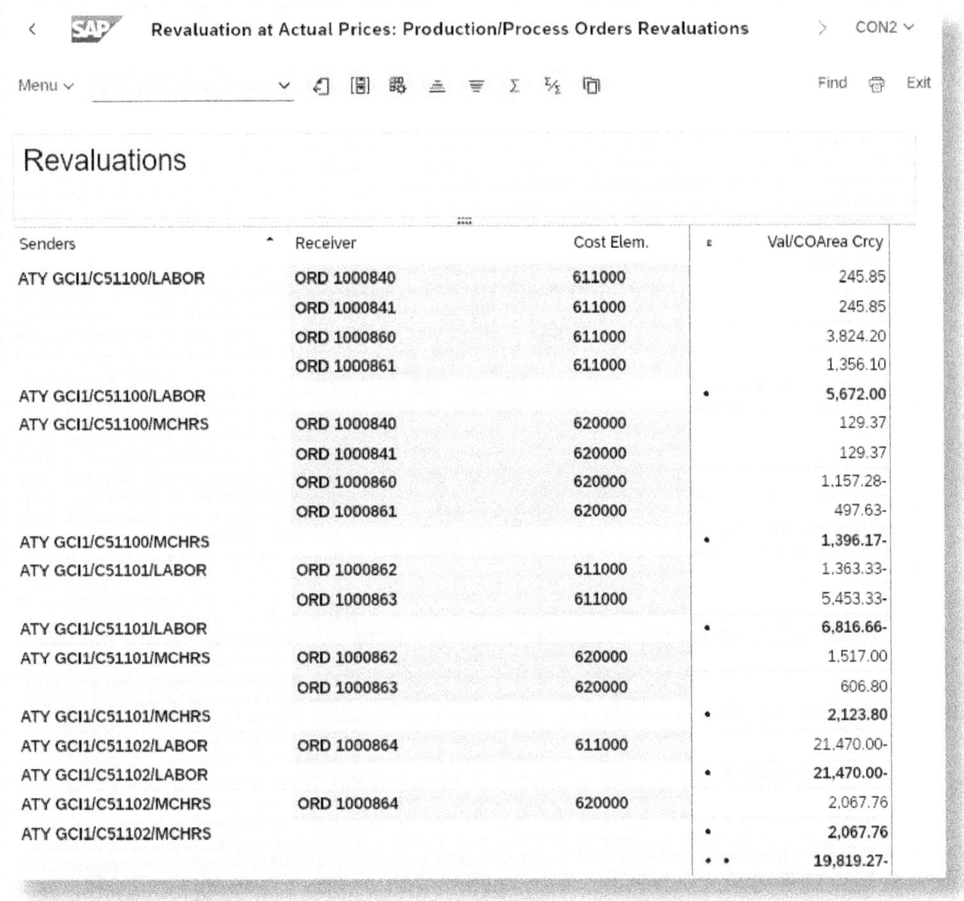

Revaluation at Actual Prices: Production/Process Orders Revaluations

Revaluations

| Senders | Receiver | Cost Elem. | Σ | Val/COArea Crcy |
|---|---|---|---|---|
| ATY GCI1/C51100/LABOR | ORD 1000840 | 611000 | | 245.85 |
| | ORD 1000841 | 611000 | | 245.85 |
| | ORD 1000860 | 611000 | | 3,824.20 |
| | ORD 1000861 | 611000 | | 1,356.10 |
| ATY GCI1/C51100/LABOR | | | • | **5,672.00** |
| ATY GCI1/C51100/MCHRS | ORD 1000840 | 620000 | | 129.37 |
| | ORD 1000841 | 620000 | | 129.37 |
| | ORD 1000860 | 620000 | | 1,157.28- |
| | ORD 1000861 | 620000 | | 497.63- |
| ATY GCI1/C51100/MCHRS | | | • | **1,396.17-** |
| ATY GCI1/C51101/LABOR | ORD 1000862 | 611000 | | 1,363.33- |
| | ORD 1000863 | 611000 | | 5,453.33- |
| ATY GCI1/C51101/LABOR | | | • | **6,816.66-** |
| ATY GCI1/C51101/MCHRS | ORD 1000862 | 620000 | | 1,517.00 |
| | ORD 1000863 | 620000 | | 606.80 |
| ATY GCI1/C51101/MCHRS | | | • | **2,123.80** |
| ATY GCI1/C51102/LABOR | ORD 1000864 | 611000 | | 21,470.00- |
| ATY GCI1/C51102/LABOR | | | • | **21,470.00-** |
| ATY GCI1/C51102/MCHRS | ORD 1000864 | 620000 | | 2,067.76 |
| ATY GCI1/C51102/MCHRS | | | • | **2,067.76** |
| | | | • • | **19,819.27-** |

*Figure 6.21: Revaluate orders with actual price—results*

This revaluation amount is almost identical to the unabsorbed amount of $4,275.82 for cost center C51100 as shown in Figure 6.10. Note that there is a minor balance of $0.01 due to rounding. If necessary, this can be allocated to Margin Analysis or transferred to an internal order.

Figure 6.22 shows the results of revaluation in report S_ALR_87013611. Cost center C51100 is now considered to be fully absorbed.

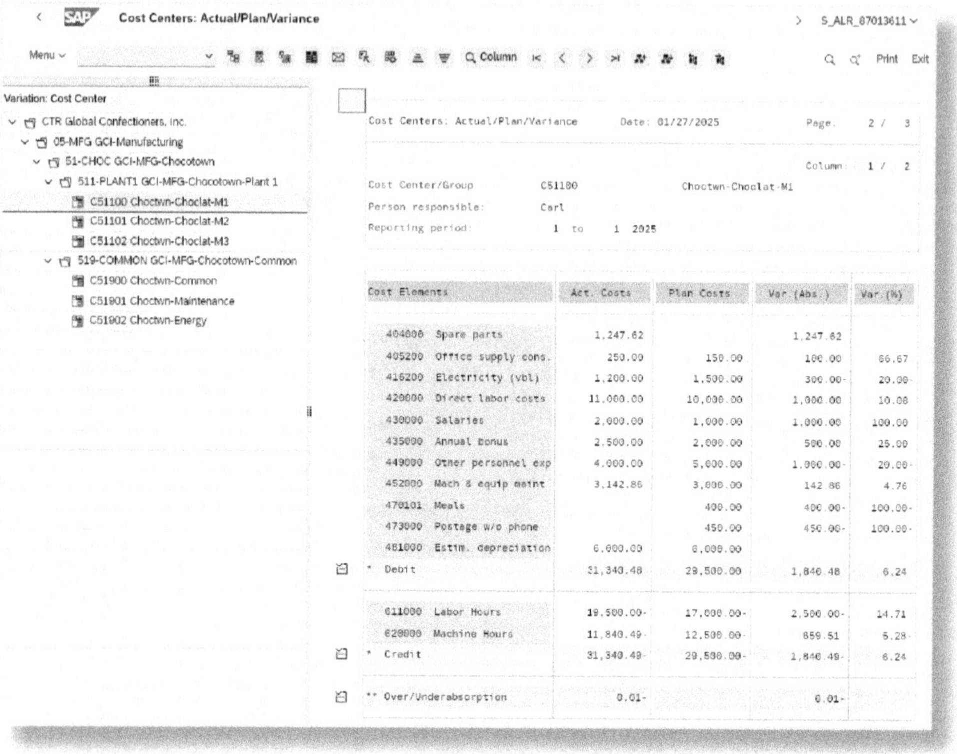


Cost Centers: Actual/Plan/Variance Date: 01/27/2025 Page: 2 / 3

Column: 1 / 2

Cost Center/Group C51100 Choctwn-Choclat-M1

Person responsible: Carl

Reporting period: 1 to 1 2025

| Cost Elements | Act. Costs | Plan Costs | Var.(Abs.) | Var.(%) |
|---|---|---|---|---|
| 404000 Spare parts | 1,247.62 | | 1,247.62 | |
| 405200 Office supply cons. | 250.00 | 150.00 | 100.00 | 66.67 |
| 416200 Electricity (vbl) | 1,200.00 | 1,500.00 | 300.00- | 20.00- |
| 420000 Direct labor costs | 11,000.00 | 10,000.00 | 1,000.00 | 10.00 |
| 430000 Salaries | 2,000.00 | 1,000.00 | 1,000.00 | 100.00 |
| 435000 Annual bonus | 2,500.00 | 2,000.00 | 500.00 | 25.00 |
| 449000 Other personnel exp | 4,000.00 | 5,000.00 | 1,000.00- | 20.00- |
| 452000 Mach & equip maint | 3,142.86 | 3,000.00 | 142.86 | 4.76 |
| 470101 Meals | | 400.00 | 400.00- | 100.00- |
| 473000 Postage w/o phone | | 450.00 | 450.00- | 100.00- |
| 481000 Estim. depreciation | 6,000.00 | 6,000.00 | | |
| * Debit | 31,340.48 | 29,500.00 | 1,840.48 | 6.24 |
| 611000 Labor Hours | 19,500.00- | 17,000.00- | 2,500.00- | 14.71 |
| 620000 Machine Hours | 11,840.49- | 12,500.00- | 659.51 | 5.28- |
| * Credit | 31,340.49- | 29,500.00- | 1,840.49- | 6.24 |
| ** Over/Underabsorption | 0.01- | | 0.01- | |

*Figure 6.22: S_ALR_87013611—Production line cost center after revaluation at actual price*

Figure 6.23 shows the results of the revaluation in report S_ALR_87013611. All cost centers are now fully absorbed.

The system design might sometimes require that not all cost elements be included in the cost center split. In such cases, those cost elements are not passed along to the production/process/internal orders using revaluation. These costs need to be cleared manually using a journal entry or an assessment to a profitability segment using the MANAGE ALLOCATIONS app.

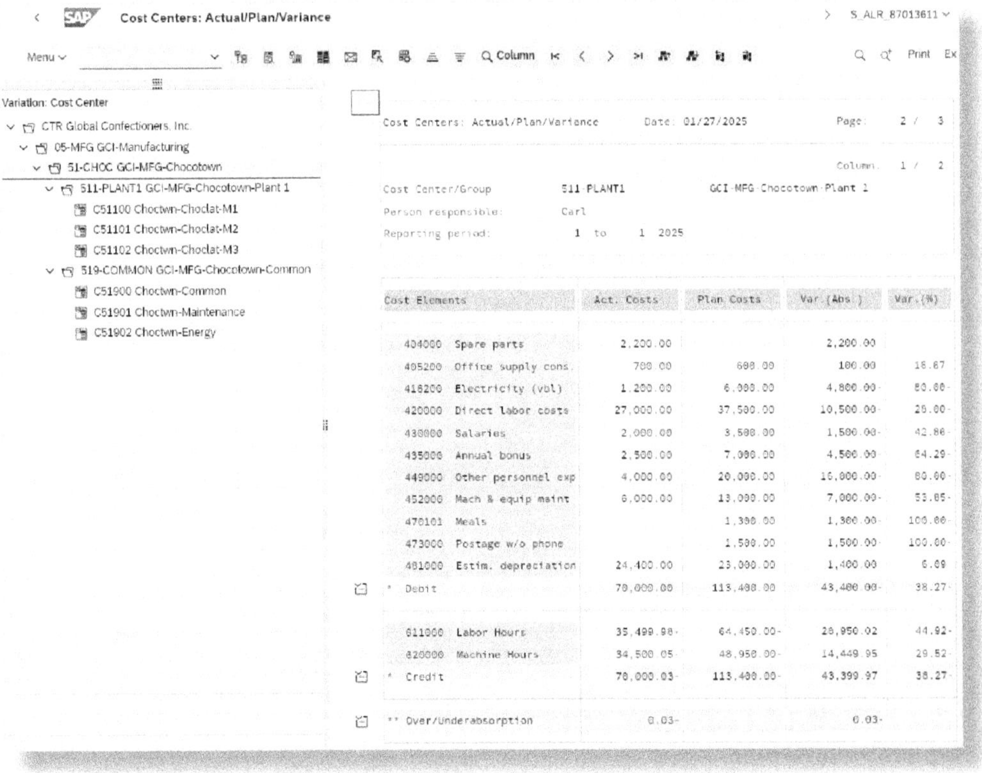

Cost Centers: Actual/Plan/Variance

S_ALR_87013611

Variation: Cost Center

- CTR Global Confectioners, Inc.
  - 05-MFG GCI-Manufacturing
    - 51-CHOC GCI-MFG-Chocotown
      - 511-PLANT1 GCI-MFG-Chocotown-Plant 1
        - C51100 Choctwn-Choclat-M1
        - C51101 Choctwn-Choclat-M2
        - C51102 Choctwn-Choclat-M3
      - 519-COMMON GCI-MFG-Chocotown-Common
        - C51900 Choctwn-Common
        - C51901 Choctwn-Maintenance
        - C51902 Choctwn-Energy

Cost Centers: Actual/Plan/Variance    Date: 01/27/2025    Page: 2 / 3

Column: 1 / 2

Cost Center/Group    511 PLANT1    GCI-MFG-Chocotown-Plant 1

Person responsible:    Carl

Reporting period:    1 to 1 2025

| Cost Elements | Act. Costs | Plan Costs | Var.(Abs.) | Var.(%) |
|---|---|---|---|---|
| 404000 Spare parts | 2,200.00 | | 2,200.00 | |
| 405200 Office supply cons. | 700.00 | 600.00 | 100.00 | 16.67 |
| 418200 Electricity (vbl) | 1,200.00 | 6,000.00 | 4,800.00- | 80.00- |
| 420000 Direct labor costs | 27,000.00 | 37,500.00 | 10,500.00- | 28.00- |
| 430000 Salaries | 2,000.00 | 3,500.00 | 1,500.00- | 42.86- |
| 435000 Annual bonus | 2,500.00 | 7,000.00 | 4,500.00- | 64.29- |
| 449000 Other personnel exp | 4,000.00 | 20,000.00 | 16,000.00- | 80.00- |
| 452000 Mach & equip maint | 6,000.00 | 13,000.00 | 7,000.00- | 53.85- |
| 470101 Meals | | 1,300.00 | 1,300.00- | 100.00- |
| 473000 Postage w/o phone | | 1,500.00 | 1,500.00- | 100.00- |
| 481000 Estim. depreciation | 24,400.00 | 23,000.00 | 1,400.00 | 6.09 |
| * Debit | 70,000.00 | 113,400.00 | 43,400.00- | 38.27- |
| 611000 Labor Hours | 35,499.98- | 64,450.00- | 28,950.02 | 44.92- |
| 620000 Machine Hours | 34,500.05- | 48,950.00- | 14,449.95 | 29.52- |
| * Credit | 70,000.03- | 113,400.00- | 43,399.97 | 38.27- |
| ** Over/Underabsorption | 0.03- | | 0.03- | |

*Figure 6.23: S_ALR_87013611—All cost centers after revaluation at actual price*

### Methods for allocating actual activity prices to materials

There are two methods for associating the actual activity price to a material when using submodule Material Ledger Actual Costing. The method described in this chapter revalues the activity price and assigns the difference directly to the manufacturing orders, and this becomes part of the variance when manufacturing orders are settled.

Another method is to use the actual calculated activity price and assign that value to the material during the actual costing run at period end. Orders are not updated, and the activity price difference is assigned to a special account and posted to the source cost center. This is controlled in configuration at: TOOLS • CUSTOMIZING • IMG • SPRO EXECUTE PROJECT • CONTROLLING • PRODUCT COST CONTROLLING • ACTUAL COSTING/MATERIAL LEDGER • ACTUAL COSTING • ACTIVATE ACTUAL COSTING.

When enabling the plant for Actual Costing, set the ACTACT field to 1 to assign the actual price to the orders, or set it to 2 to calculate the differences as part of the actual costing run. In either case, KSII must be run to calculate the actual price—CON2 can only be executed when ACTACT is set to 1. GCI wants to look at the actual activity price as a part of order variances, and so it has used 1 as the parameter.

For reference, Alex summarized the important transactions in a table (see Figure 6.24).

**Cost center absorption transactions used at CGI**

| Description of transaction | Transaction / Fiori app | Purpose |
|---|---|---|
| Actual cost distribution | KSV5 (transaction) | Allocation of costs (sender cost element retained) |
| Actual cost assessment | KSU5 (transaction) | Allocation of costs (sender cost element not available) |
| Maintain splitting structure | OKES (transaction) | Configure splitting structure (cost elements, groups, activities) |
| Assign cost centers to splitting structure | OKEW (transaction) | Configure assignment of cost centers to splitting structure |
| Actual cost center splitting | KSS2 (transaction) | Attach activity independent costs to specific activity types |
| Actual activity price calculation | KSII (transaction) | Calculate actual absorption rate (burden rate) |
| Revaluation at actual prices | CON2 (transaction) | Revalue process / production orders with actual activity price |

**Tools for Cost Center Planning**

| Description of transaction | Transaction / Fiori app | Purpose |
|---|---|---|
| Cost Centers: Actual/Plan/Variance Report | S_ALR_87013611 (transaction) | Cost center report (amount, activities, SKFs) – plan vs. actual |
| Activity price report | Analyze Prices for Activity Types | Report of activity prices for cost center / cost center group |
| Cost center display | Manage Cost Centers | Display of cost center used in allocation cycles |
| Cost center group display | Manage Cost Center Groups | Display of cost center group used in allocation cycles |
| Cost element display | Manage G/L Account Master Data | Display of cost element used in allocation cycles |
| Cost element group display | Manage Cost Element Groups | Display of cost element group used in allocation cycles |
| Activity type display | Manage Activity Types | Display of activity type used in allocation cycles |
| Statistical key figure (SKF) display | Manage Statistical Key Figures | Display of SKF used in allocation cycles |

*Figure 6.24: Cost center absorption transactions used at GCI*

# 7 Product costs—where do all the direct costs end up?

*"In the beginning God created man ... and the costs followed afterwards."*

—"Profound Patricia", Management Accountant

***Product costing* is the valuation of material components and activities on a process or production order, utilizing material prices and activity rates. Plan and actual values are recorded and reported with variances, and variances are disposed of according to company policy. Product costing is where all the direct costs for a product end up. The indirect costs in this context are sales, general, and administrative (SG&A) expenses that are usually not absorbed into the product costs.**

From the perspective of inventory valuation, a manufacturing unit should include all of the costs of raw materials and conversion costs, including any overhead that went into manufacturing a finished product.

## 7.1 Product costing drivers

The user manual listed the following drivers for product costing:

- Material quantities are derived (read) from the bill of material (BoM or BOM).
- Components are costed as per costing method (standard or moving/weighted average), by reading the values stored in the material masters, purchasing information records (PIRs), or some other planned price valuation method such as trending (historical average) price.

- Activities are costed by applying activity rates as the product moves through the routing (or recipe in the case of process industry) or operations performed in the work centers (resources in case of process industry) in the manufacturing facility.
- Overhead costs are absorbed into the product cost via activity types and/or costing sheet.

## 7.2 Master data dependencies

BOM and routing (or recipe) are commonly referred to as the *quantity structure*, meaning that quantities for costing are read from these master data elements. As Alex knew, a BOM requires the material master to be set up, whereas a routing (or recipe) requires a work center (or resource) to be set up.

A BOM uses the material master to retrieve component material quantities and uses PIRs or other planned prices to obtain the rates at which materials will be costed.

A routing (or recipe) uses a work center (or resource) to obtain activity quantities. Activity prices are maintained for a specific combination of activity type and cost center using cost center planning.

For raw materials, or procured semi-finished or finished materials, the price from the material master or PIR is used during costing. A *valuation variant* determines the access sequence of prices (which price should be used first—PIR or standard price from the material master, or moving average price from the material master).

If a recipe uses an activity type for setup time, then the costing lot size used during costing will have an impact on the setup cost per unit. A larger costing lot size will result in a smaller setup cost per unit. In contrast, a smaller costing lot size provides a higher setup cost per unit.

The training manual discussed various production master data in detail, specifically material master, BOM, work center (resource), and routing (recipe). Even though these master data elements are not owned, or always maintained, by finance or product costing teams, they are an integral part of SAP ERP. These master data elements provide very powerful integration between the production process and product costing.

## 7.3 Material master

*Material master* (or simply *material*) is an alphanumeric key that identifies a material. Types of materials include raw materials, semi-finished materials, finished materials, and spare parts. Material refers to a physical or logical grouping with the same form, fit, and function. Use of the material master is fundamental to goods movement. Material and its use spans across multiple SAP modules and organizational processes. Once transactions are posted, it is very difficult to change some of these fields without significant rework. Therefore, material definition is very important at an early stage of each SAP implementation.

A material can be displayed using the DISPLAY MATERIAL app. Because there can be multiple uses of a material, a material master is defined with views that are logically grouped together by function or process area. Some of the views in a material master include BASIC DATA, MRP, WORK SCHEDULING, GENERAL PLANT DATA / STORAGE, ACCOUNTING, COSTING, etc.

### 7.3.1 Settings impacting product costs—owned by finance

**Accounting 1 tab**

Figure 7.1 shows the material view ACCOUNTING 1 tab.

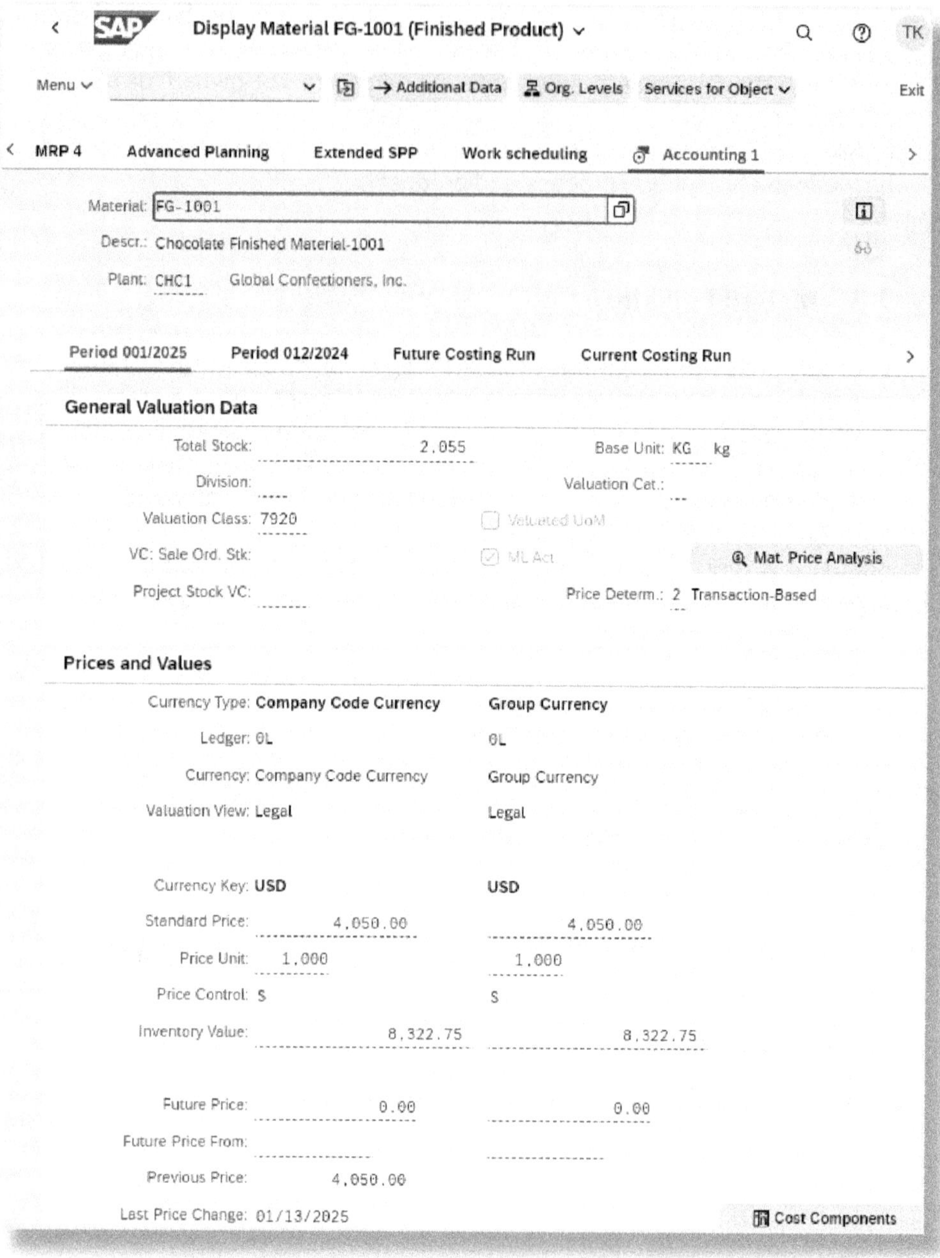


*Figure 7.1: Display Material—Accounting 1 tab*

Let's take a look at some of the fields on this tab.

The VALUATION CLASS provides a link between the material master and FI. It facilitates the posting of stock values of materials of the same material types to the same GL accounts.

PRICE CONTROL refers to the method of *inventory valuation*. SAP CO offers two methods of inventory valuation and product costing: *standard cost* (S) and *moving/weighted average* (V). This is identified at the material master level. Different materials can therefore use different valuation methods within a plant.

**Standard versus moving average price control**

Finished and semi-finished materials that are produced in-house must always use the standard cost indicator S. Procured items can use S or V, depending on corporate policy/project decision.

The STANDARD PRICE (or standard cost) field stores the price for the material. The price should be expressed in price per unit, per base unit of measure, in the given currency (e.g., USD 4,590/1,000 KG or EUR 2,961.29/1,000 KG). If a material is valued by moving average price control, then the value in the standard price field is statistical in nature; i.e., this field is not used when recording goods movement transactions.

The PRICE UNIT prevents rounding issues while carrying out goods movement transactions.

**Using price unit—example**

A material priced at 29.37 cents ($0.2937) per unit should be created with a price unit of at least 100, so that the price is $29.37/100 or, even better, $293.70/1,000. This prevents rounding differences.

The ML ACT. (material ledger active) checkbox indicates if the material ledger is active for this plant. This flag is automatically set when the material ledger is activated for that plant. The material ledger is always activated for the S/4HANA versions of SAP. If this flag is not set, you need to contact your system administrator.

The PRICE DETERM (price determination) setting indicates whether the material has been activated for use in the actual costing run, which is processed during month-end closing activities. A value of *3* indicates that the material is relevant for actual costing. A value of *2* indicates that the material will not be included in an actual costing run. Materials for which the PRICE DETERMINATION is set to *3* must have price control set to *S* (standard cost).

The *periodic unit price* is the price at which the material is valuated after an actual costing run. This field only appears for the material in the previous period after the actual calculation. Chapter 10 covers how this is determined and updated.

The VALUATION CAT (valuation category) is used when *split valuation* is activated. This setting determines whether stocks for the material should be valuated together or separately. If the valuation category is maintained, as with a batch indicator, then the material is valued at *batch* level; i.e., each individual batch will have its own cost. If the valuation category is blank, then all batches are valued with the same cost. This indicator also determines which valuation types are allowed, meaning the criteria by which stocks can be valuated.

The VALUATION TYPE field (not shown here) is the individual value below material level. This field is only used when split valuation is activated—when each batch is a valuation type. If a material is valued by origin, domestic or imported, then each origin is a valuation type.

Material valuation can be seen for the current period by clicking on the appropriate tab. In the example shown in Figure 7.1, refer to the PERIOD 001/2025 tab. There is also a tab for the previous period and one for the last period in the previous fiscal year. In this case, both are the same, so only one previous period is displayed (PERIOD 012/2024). When clicking on a previous period tab, the values displayed reflect the inventory and actual cost situation as at the end of that fiscal period.

## Accounting 2 tab

Figure 7.2 shows the ACCOUNTING 2 tab.

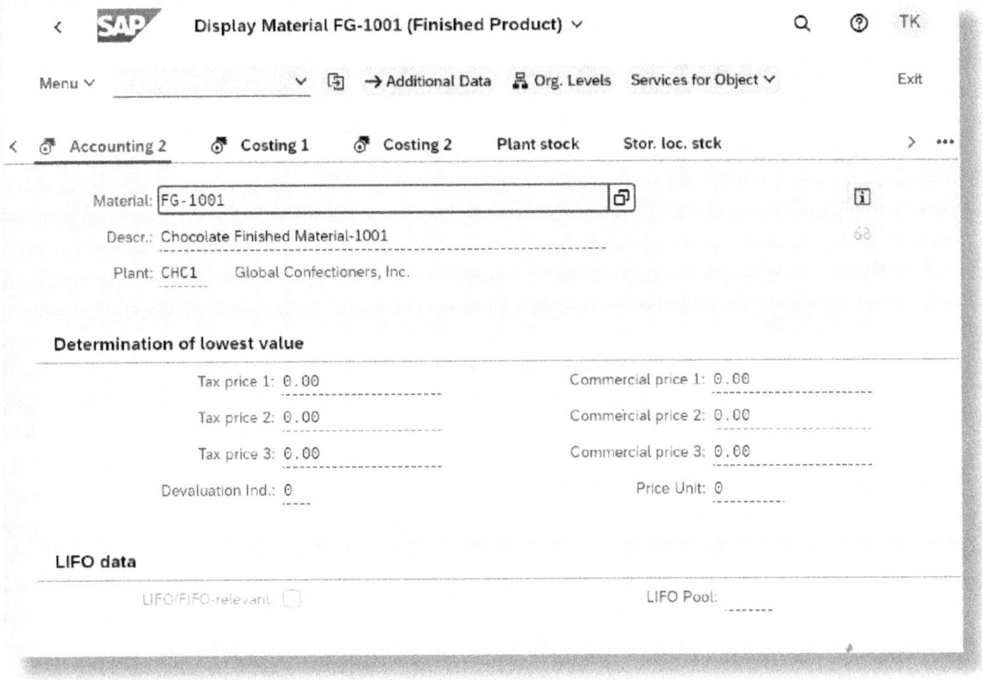


*Figure 7.2: Display Material—Accounting 2 tab*

TAX PRICE 1 is the price at which the material is valuated for tax purposes. This price can be determined with different standard cost estimates, or it can be set manually.

COMMERCIAL PRICE 1 is the price at which the material is valuated for commercial purposes. This price can be determined with different standard cost estimates, or it can be set manually.

Special costing variants and rules are applied when calculating the costs used for updating these fields.

### Costing 1 tab

Figure 7.3 shows the COSTING 1 tab.

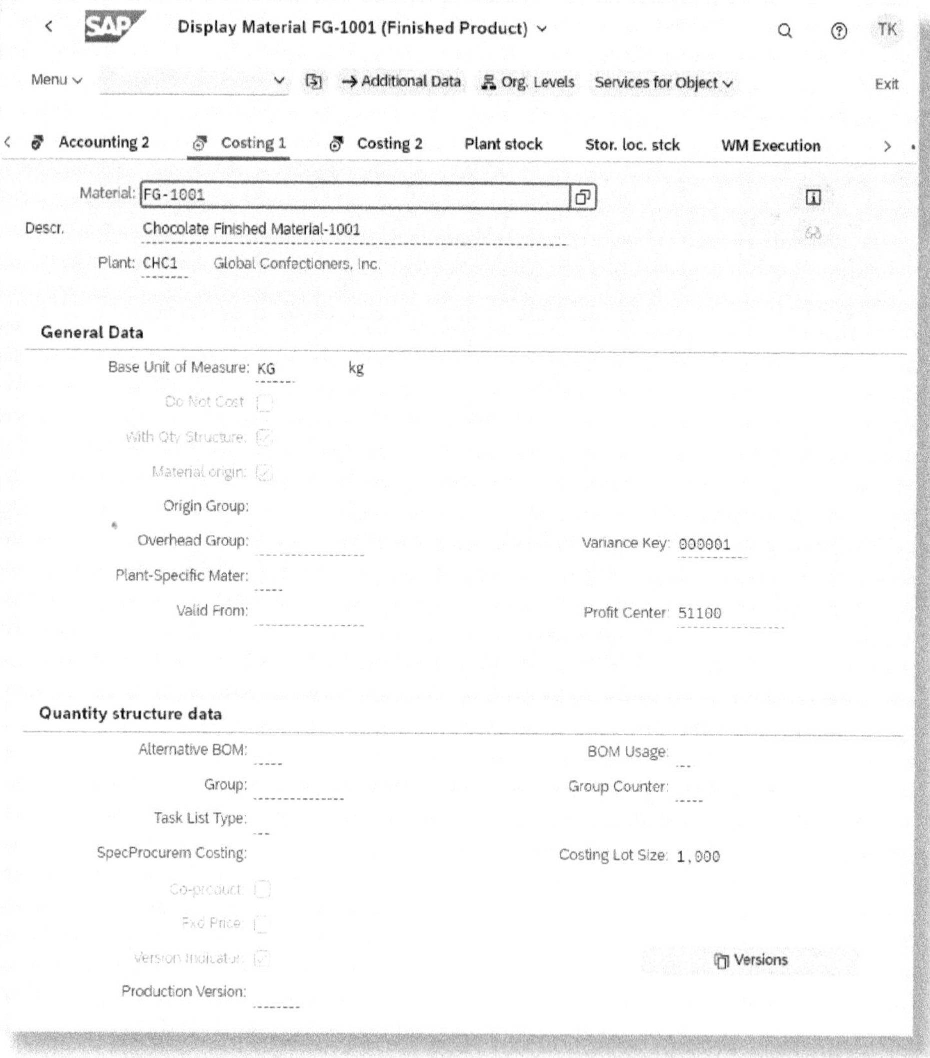


*Figure 7.3: Display Material—Costing 1 tab*

The DO NOT COST checkbox determines whether a cost estimate can be created for a material. Material will not be costed if this checkbox is selected.

The WITH QTY STRUCTURE checkbox determines the type of cost estimate that is used to update the standard cost of the material. If selected, cost estimates using the CREATE MATERIAL COST ESTIMATES app are used. Otherwise, the system uses cost estimates developed with manually entered cost items, without referring to standard quantity structures such as recipes, routes, and BOMs (CREATE UNIT COST ESTIMATE SINGLE app).

The MATERIAL ORIGIN checkbox helps to analyze material costs during reporting by providing material number details in accounting documents.

The ORIGIN GROUP setting is used to break costs down below a cost component level. Origin groups are assigned to cost components so that costing can be viewed at this level. An origin group overrides the assigned account when determining the cost component for the material cost.

Variances can only be calculated for orders for which a VARIANCE KEY has been maintained. All produced materials must have a variance key. One standard value should be defined for the variance key.

The OVERHEAD GROUP is a key that defines which overhead basis/formula will be applied to the material while carrying out the standard cost estimate.

**Overhead group for freight**

An overhead group of 10% freight on raw materials, 8% freight on packaging materials, and 3% cost on other supplies can be set up to include estimated freight in standard costs.

The PROFIT CENTER field identifies the responsible department, location, or product line of a business unit—depending on the profit center design implemented. A profit center for transactional data, including process order, purchase order, and sales order will be derived from this assignment in the material master.

The COSTING LOT SIZE is the quantity used for cost estimates. The costing lot size must be the same or greater than the price unit on the accounting screen.

## Costing 2 tab

Figure 7.4 shows the COSTING 2 tab.

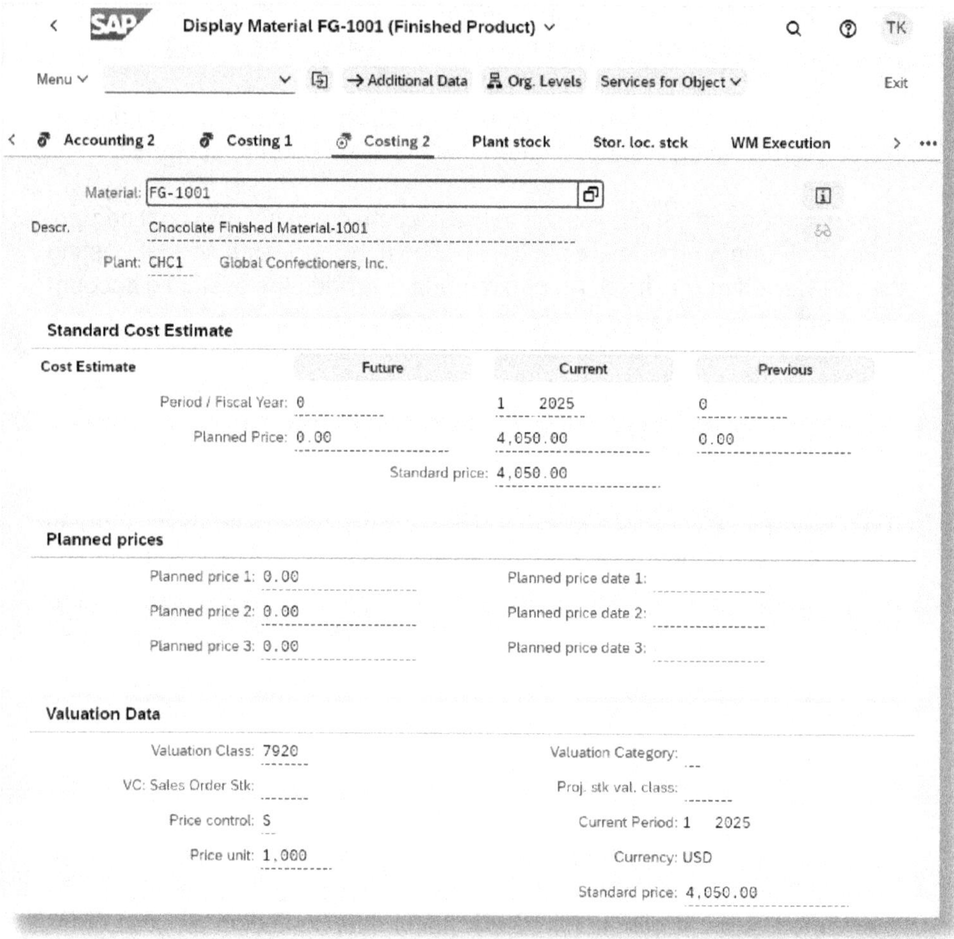


*Figure 7.4: Display Material—Costing 2 tab*

The marked cost estimate is stored in the FUTURE: PLANNED PRICE field. This field is updated when the *mark cost estimate* step is performed in the RELEASE MATERIAL COST ESTIMATES app or he MANAGE COSTING RUNS app—it cannot be updated directly in the material master.

The released cost estimate is stored in the CURRENT: PLANNED PRICE field (the value in this field is also updated in the STANDARD PRICE field). Both of these fields are updated during the *release cost estimate* step in the RELEASE MATERIAL COST ESTIMATES app or the MANAGE COSTING RUNS app—it cannot be updated directly in material master.

The previously released cost estimate is stored in the PREVIOUS: PLANNED PRICE field. This field is updated when a new cost estimate is released. Similar to future and current planned prices, this field cannot be updated directly in the material master.

**Updating cost estimates in the material master**

Future, current, and previous planned price fields cannot be updated directly in the material master. They are updated when the cost estimate mark/release step is performed in either the RELEASE MATERIAL COST ESTIMATES app or the MANAGE COSTING RUNS app.

PLANNED PRICE 1 is a manually set price that overrides other prices for externally procured material if configured in the valuation variant access sequence. PLANNED PRICE 2 and PLANNED PRICE 3 are treated in the same manner.

PLANNED PRICE DATE 1 is the date from which the planned price is effective (relevant to the valuation date in the costing run).

## 7.3.2 Settings impacting product costs—not directly owned by finance

### Basic data 1 tab

Figure 7.5 shows the BASIC DATA 1 tab.

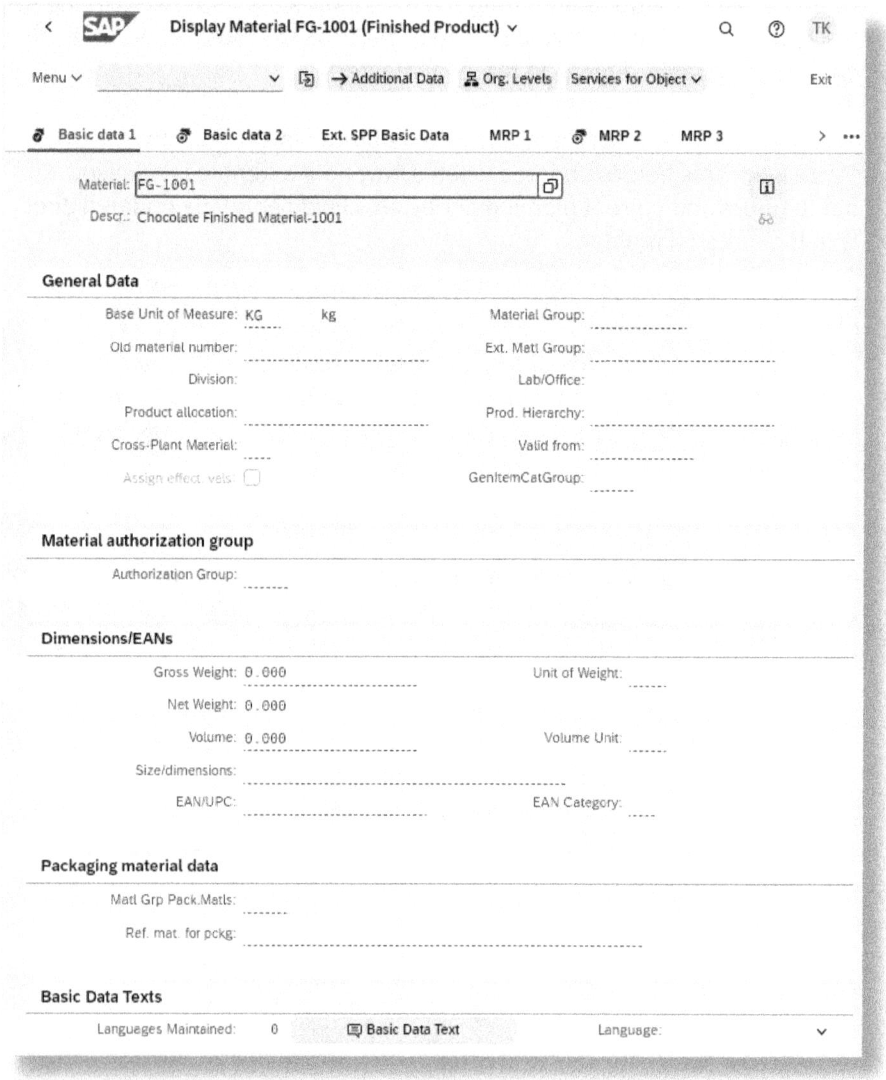


*Figure 7.5: Display Material—Basic data 1 tab*

The BASE UNIT OF MEASURE indicates the unit in which the cost will be presented in the costing and accounting tabs. The base unit of measure requires careful consideration at the design stage because it cannot be changed once it has been set up and dependent transactions have been carried out.

**Base unit of measure—example**

Companies such as GCI need to consider how finished products, such as chocolate bars, should be maintained. Should it be in grams or kilograms, or by the case? Should the aluminum foil used to wrap the chocolate be maintained in meters, centimeters, feet, or inches? These are valid questions and provide examples of the kinds of important decisions that need to be made at the early stages of system implementation. A significant amount of downstream master data, transaction data, and processes depend on the decision regarding which base unit of measure to use. Once a material is used for transactions, it is very difficult to change its unit of measure.

**Alternative units of measure**

Consider a finished material that is created with *cases* as the base unit of measure; however, there is also a need to track the weight of the material in *kilograms*. SAP software provides an *alternative units of measure* feature, where you can maintain a conversion from the alternative units (kg) to the base unit of measure (cases).

Units of measure belonging to the same dimension do not need to be maintained as alternative units. For example, if a material is created with a base unit of measure of kilograms, there is no need to maintain conversion from kilograms to grams at the material master level. The system will automatically derive the conversion as 1,000 grams to a kilogram because they both belong to the dimension *mass*. However, a conversion of this material from kilograms to cubic feet or cubic meters will need to be maintained as an alternative unit, because cubic feet and cubic meters belong to the dimension *volume*.

*Material status* is used to determine which transactions are allowed for the given material status. The CROSS-PLANT MATERIAL status, maintained in the BASIC DATA 1 tab, applies to all plants.

The PLANT-SPECIFIC MATER (plant-specific material) status on the MRP 1 and COSTING 1 plant tabs override the status on the BASIC DATA 1 tab.

The PROD. HIERARCHY (product hierarchy) on the BASIC DATA 1 tab is an alphanumeric character string used to structure product characteristics; for example, AA-BBB-CCCC-DD-E. The product hierarchy design has an impact on Margin Analysis and sales reporting.

### MRP 2/Costing 1 tabs

The MRP (materials requirement planning) tabs are important with regard to planning. There are several fields that influence costing.

The material status is used to determine which transactions are allowed for a particular material status. The CROSS PLANT MATERIAL status, maintained under basic data, applies to all plants. The plant-specific material status on the plant tabs (MRP 1 and COSTING 1) overrides the status on the basic data tabs.

The SPECIAL PROCUREMENT setting specifies how the material is procured (purchased, transferred, manufactured, etc.). On the MRP 2 tab, this is used by the planning team to identify the preferred sourcing method. This can be left blank, or it can have a two-character special procurement key ID assigned. If left blank, the system uses the default behavior of the procurement type (F for external purchase or E for in-house manufacturing). This key drives both planning and costing functionalities.

On the COSTING 1 tab, it is possible to maintain an override value using the SPECPROCUREM COSTING field (see Figure 7.3). If this is left blank, then cost estimates look to the value maintained in MRP 2. If there is a value in this field, the cost estimate will use this value regardless of the value maintained in MRP 2.

The options for special procurement keys include:

- 10 Consignment
- 20 External procurement
- 30 Subcontracting (external manufacturing)
- 40 Stock transfer (procurement from alternate plant)
- 45 Stock transfer from plant to MRP area
- 50 Phantom assembly
- 52 Direct production/collective order

- 60 Planned independent requirements
- 70 Reservation from alternate plant
- 80 Production in alternate plant

Additional special procurement keys can be defined in configuration. For example, if two different materials are procured by stock transfer from separate plants, two different stock transfer special procurement keys will be required. These keys are alphanumeric and can use letters and numbers interchangeably.

### MRP 2 tab

Figure 7.6 shows the material master MRP 2 tab.

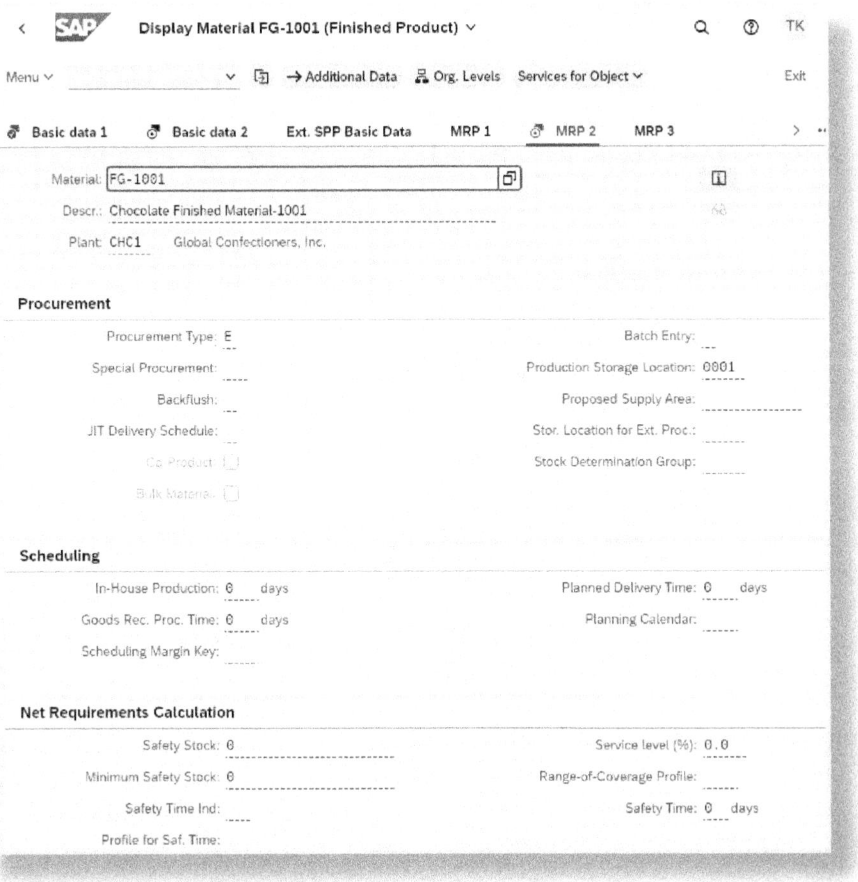


*Figure 7.6: Display Material—MRP 2 tab*

The PROCUREMENT TYPE field indicates whether a product is purchased (F), produced in-house (E), or both (X). This field is important from both an MRP and a costing perspective. If a material is flagged as F, the costing run will look for the purchase price. If the material is flagged as E, the costing run will look for a BOM/master recipe for the costs. If the field is flagged as X, then the costing run program will first try to cost the material as in-house. If in-house costing is not successful, then the material will be costed as procured.

The BACKFLUSH field can be populated in the material master. It influences whether a component material will be issued directly (exact quantity consumed will be specifically entered) or defaulted from a BOM standard. Two backflush options are possible:

1. Always backflush.
2. Work center decides whether to backflush.

If option 1 is selected, then the default value in the BOM will be used for consumption. If option 2 is selected, or if the field is left blank, then the backflush rule can be set at the individual routing/recipe stage.

## 7.4 Bill of material

A *bill of material* is a detailed list of components needed to make up a semi-finished good (SFG) or finished good (FG). The list contains the object number, quantity, and unit of measure of each component. The components are known as BOM items.

A product can be manufactured using one or more different BOMs depending on the different production methods. Each set of BOMs is called an *alternative BOM*.

BOMs are plant-specific (where the same finished material can be produced using different components in different plants).

USAGE 1 BOM applies to MRP, as well as production, and can also be optionally used for costing. USAGE 6 BOM applies to costing. Having these different BOMs in use means dual maintenance (e.g., usage 1 BOM needs to be maintained for production and usage 6 BOM needs to be maintained for costing).

BOM for usage 1 drives planning requirements. Demand creates dependent requirements that drive the replacement of components and bulk materials.

A *phantom material*, which is contained within a BOM, is not costed and contains no inventory. It is used purely for ease of maintaining certain groups of components.

Figure 7.7 shows the MAINTAIN BILL OF MATERIAL app for header material FG-1001 for which there is one component material—RAW-1001.

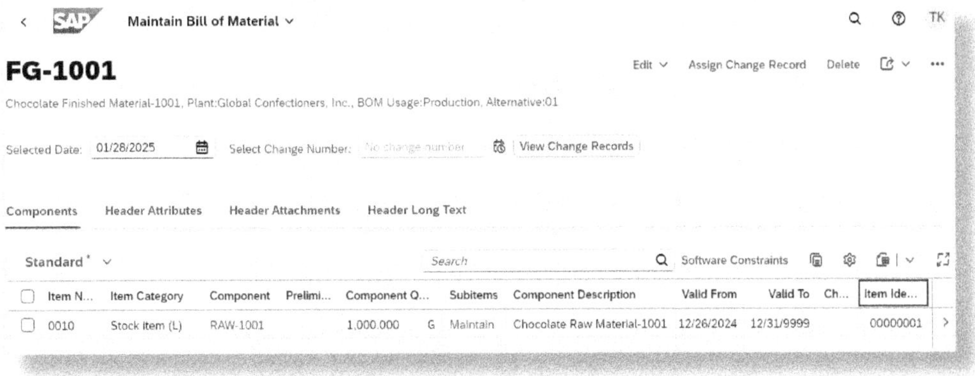


*Figure 7.7: "Maintain Bill of Material" app—bill of material items*

Figure 7.8 shows the COSTING RELEVANCY settings on the STATUS/LONG TEXT tab at BOM item level.

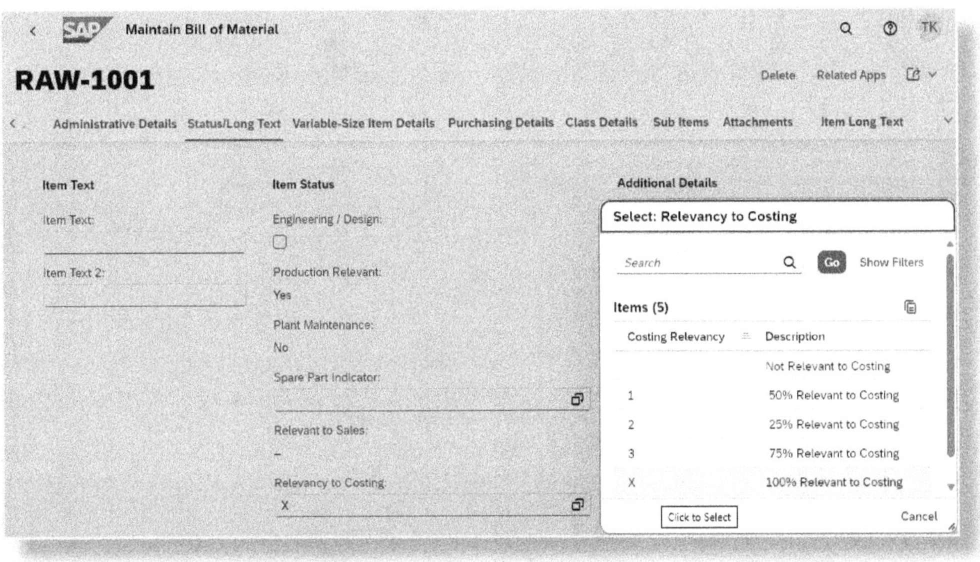


*Figure 7.8: "Maintain Bill of Material" app—BOM costing relevancy flag*

## 7.5 Work center/resource

A *resource* (or *work center* in the case of discrete or repetitive manufacturing) represents a processing area, individual machine, a group of machines, or an entire production line. Every operational production step is carried out as a production resource. Production resources are linked to cost centers to define cost calculation and reporting and are created at plant level.

Figure 7.9 shows the COSTING tab in the DISPLAY RESOURCE app. The default entries under ACTIVITY TYPE are maintained with a costing formula.

The CREATE WORK CENTER, CHANGE WORK CENTER, and DISPLAY WORK CENTER apps are used to maintain work centers in discrete manufacturing.

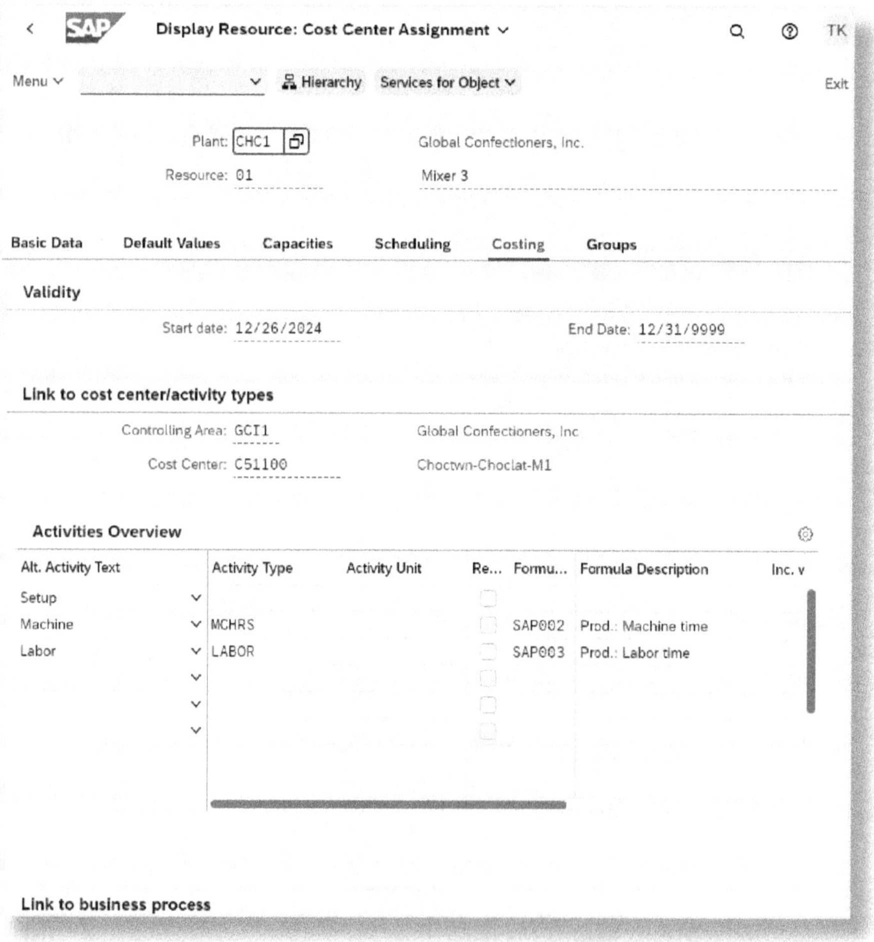


*Figure 7.9: "Display Resource" app—resource Costing tab*

## 7.6 Routing/master recipe

A *master recipe* is required for every SFG or FG produced and is a combination of BOM and routings (operation steps). It consists of a header and several operations. Each operation is performed on a resource.

A production version is used to link a BOM alternative to a routing (operation) so that the master recipe design is complete. This is very important when a product has multiple BOMs and multiple routings.

A recipe definition has various tabs:

- RECIPE HEADER tab—contains the product name, SKU, valid scalable quantities, and QA requirements (inspection plans).
- OPERATIONS tab—contains the manufacturing process, setup, check-in materials, fill product, etc., as well as resource and cost information for each operation.
- MATERIALS tab—(BOM) contains material numbers and exact proportions.
- ADMINISTRATIVE DATA tab—enables change control (version, effective dates).

Figure 7.10 shows the OPERATIONS tab in the MANAGE MASTER RECIPES app. This defines the steps required to manufacture the product.

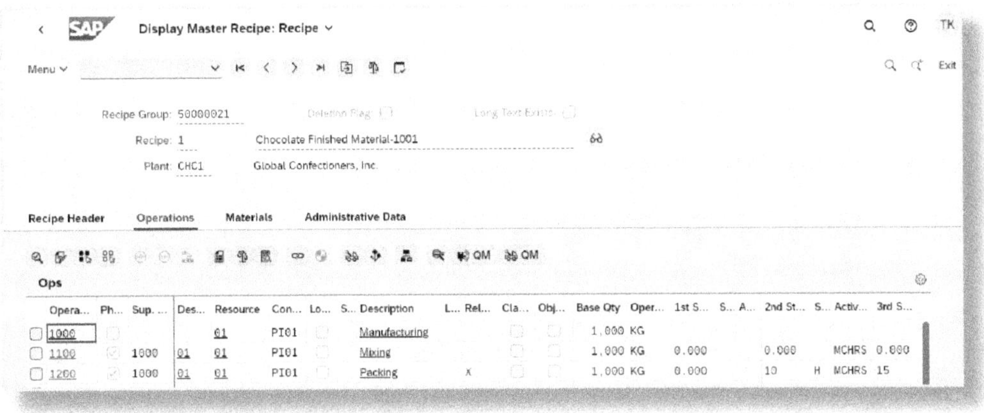


*Figure 7.10: "Manage Master Recipes" app—recipe Operations tab*

**Routings in discrete and repetitive manufacturing**

Discrete manufacturing uses routings instead of recipes. Routings are similar to recipes but with simpler structures. They use work centers instead of resources to define a specific step or operation. The MANAGE ROUTINGS app is used for maintaining these quantity structures.

Figure 7.11 shows OPERATION details.

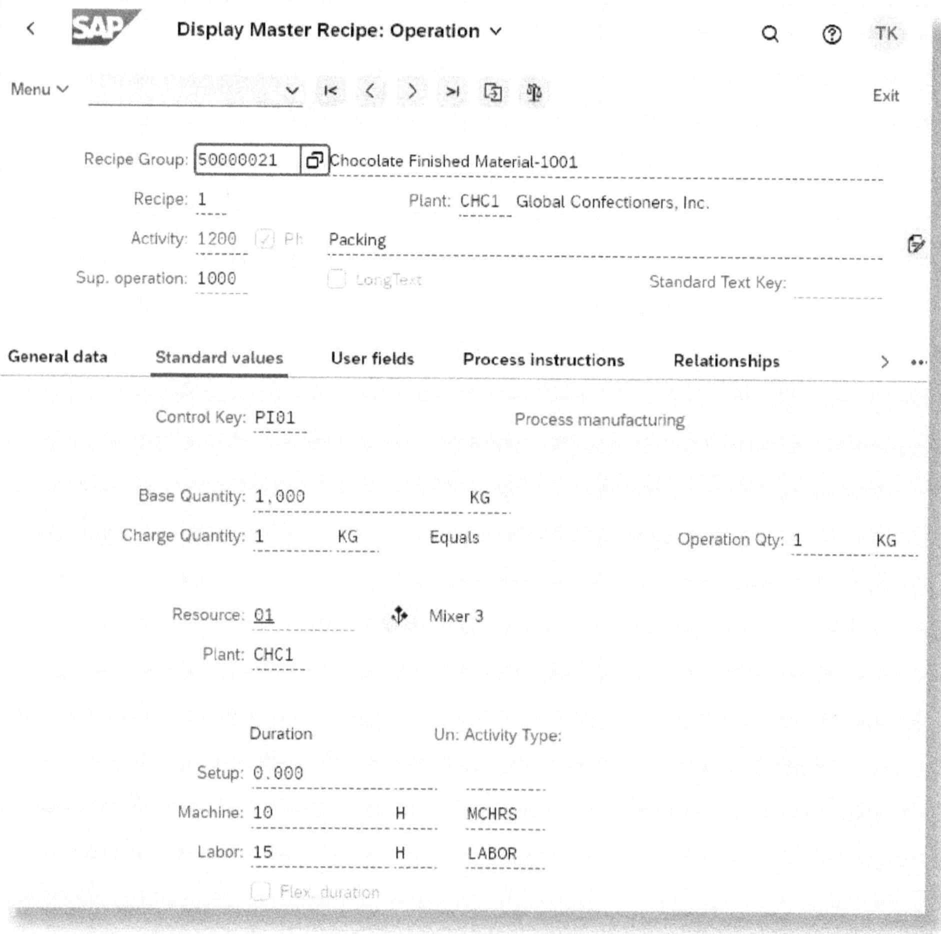


*Figure 7.11: "Manage Master Recipes" app—Operation details*

As shown in the screenshot, it takes 10 MACHINE hours and 15 LABOR hours at RESOURCE 01 to produce 1,000 KG of this product. These hours are represented by activity type. For example, three workers usually staff this machine, but there is a plan to staff only two workers. The recipe will need to be updated to reflect this change—10 hours of labor instead of 15 hours.

> **Production versions**
>
> Production versions are required by the system for planning and production reporting. A production version links a specific recipe or routing to a bill of materials alternative. The combination defines how the product is made.

## 7.7 Rolled-up costs during costing

Product costing elements are as follows:

- Costing variant—determines various strategies for costing.
- Activity type—determines which quantity rate will be used for absorbing direct and indirect costs (labor, equipment, etc.).
- Cost component—determines how costs will be summarized.
- Costing sheet—determines how overhead costs will be added.
- Cost estimate—holds planned costs for a material or process order.
- Costing run—enables costing of multiple materials at the same time.

### 7.7.1 Costing variant

A *costing variant* is a repository of specific business rules that contains all the control parameters for costing, including parameters that control how cost estimates are executed and the material prices or activity prices that are used to valuate the costing items.

In material costing (costing with and without quantity structure), the costing variant determines the following:

- Costing type—where this costing will be used
- Valuation variant—what will be used for costing

- Date control—what dates will be used for valuation and quantity structure
- Quantity structure determination ID—what BOM/master recipe will be used for costing, production, etc.
- Transfer control—whether components will be re-costed, or will pass on their existing roll-up cost

Figure 7.12 shows COSTING VARIANT configuration using transaction OKKN.

The menu path is: TOOLS • CUSTOMIZING • IMG • SPRO EXECUTE PROJECT • CONTROLLING • PRODUCT COST CONTROLLING • PRODUCT COST PLANNING • MATERIAL COST ESTIMATE WITH QUANTITY STRUCTURE • DEFINE COSTING VARIANTS.

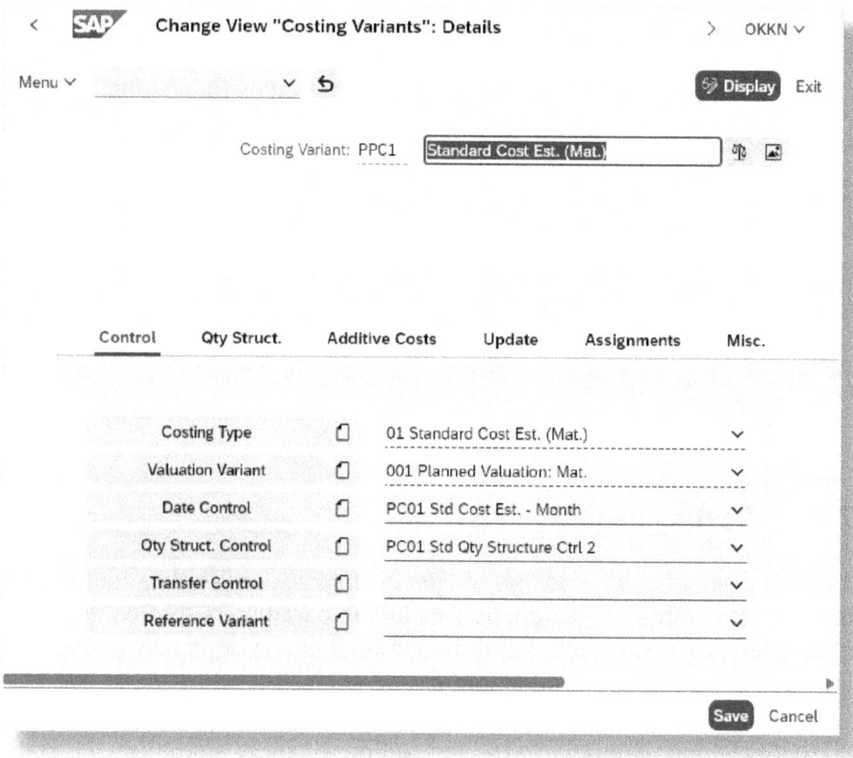


*Figure 7.12: OKKN—Costing variant*

### 7.7.2 Valuation variant

A *valuation variant* defines how the material, activities, subcontractors, and overhead surcharges will be valued using strategy sequences for each; for example, first use 1, if it has no value, use 2, etc.

- Material valuation—price from purchasing info record
- Activities—plan price for the period
- Subcontractors—net purchase order price
- External processing—effective price from quotation
- Overhead—costing sheet PP-PC1

Figure 7.13 shows the VALUATION VARIANT configuration (transaction OKK4).

The menu path is: TOOLS • CUSTOMIZING • IMG • SPRO EXECUTE PROJECT • CONTROLLING • PRODUCT COST CONTROLLING • PRODUCT COST PLANNING • MATERIAL COST ESTIMATE WITH QUANTITY STRUCTURE • COSTING VARIANT: COMPONENTS • DEFINE VALUATION VARIANTS. It is also accessible from costing variant transaction OKKN.

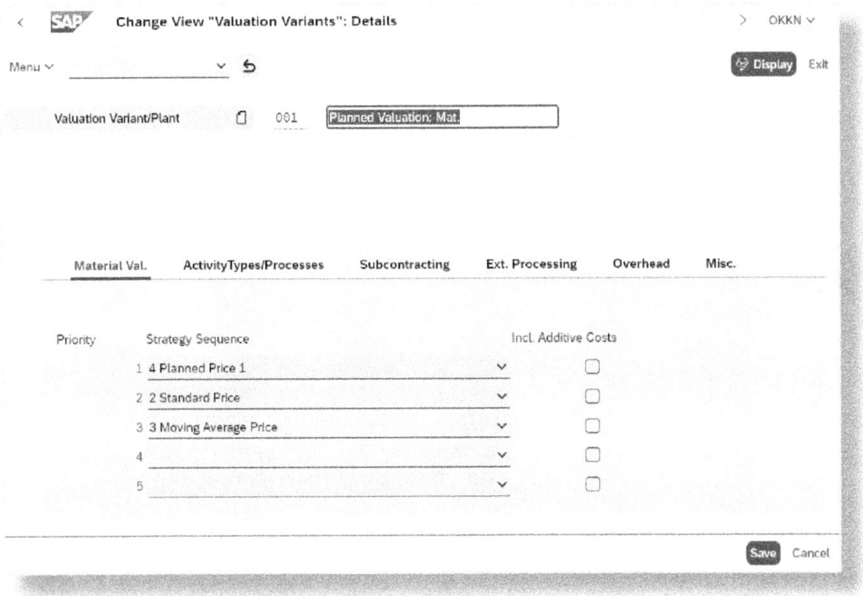


*Figure 7.13: OKK4—Valuation variant*

### 7.7.3 Costing sheet

A *costing sheet* is used to allocate indirect overhead to a product.

A specified percentage of overhead is applied to the product based on material issues or labor activity charges on the production order.

Cost centers with indirect overheads are credited.

Examples of overhead calculation include:

- Inbound freight cost as a percentage of base material cost.
- $/kilogram based on weight of material.
- $/kilogram based on weight of material for specific origin group.
- $/hour based on hours spent (use of overhead rates can give similar results to that of using activity type, but it uses a different vehicle for absorbing costs).

Figure 7.14 shows COSTING SHEET configuration (transaction KZS2).

The menu path is: TOOLS • CUSTOMIZING • IMG • SPRO EXECUTE PROJECT • CONTROLLING • PRODUCT COST CONTROLLING • PRODUCT COST PLANNING • BASIC SETTINGS FOR MATERIAL COSTING • OVERHEAD • DEFINE COSTING SHEETS. It is also accessible from costing variant transaction OKKN.

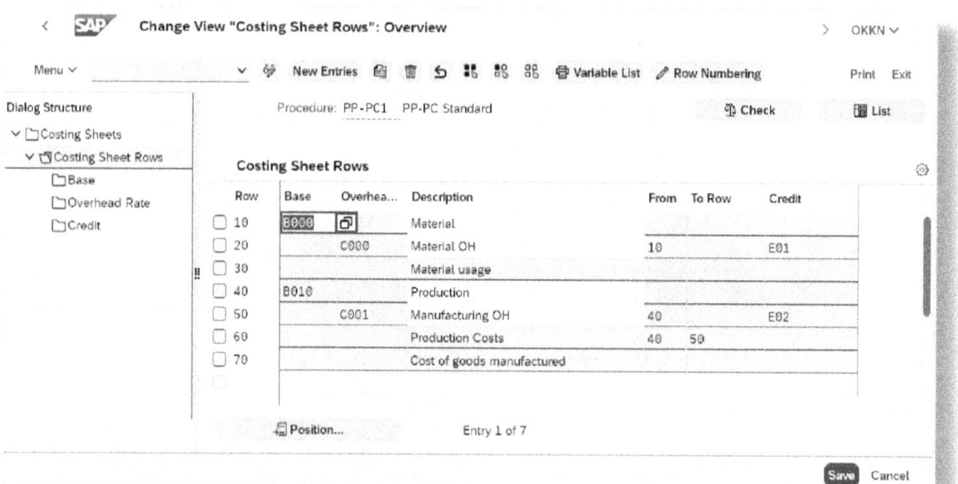


*Figure 7.14: KZS2—Costing sheet*

## 7.7.4 Cost estimate

A *cost estimate* is the planned cost of a production cost carrier. It utilizes the BOM and routing (quantity structure) to arrive at the planned cost, which can be transferred to the material master as a planned price to be utilized in product costing to valuate the material. The costing variant determines which cost estimate to consider for the standard cost estimate.

Figure 7.15 shows the COSTING DATA tab in the CREATE MATERIAL COST ESTIMATES app.

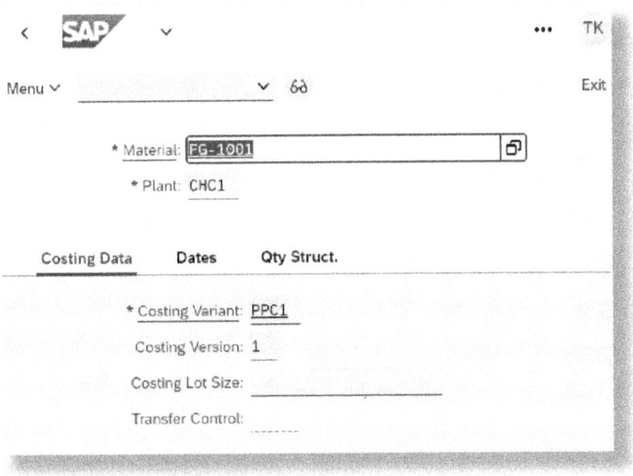


*Figure 7.15: "Create Material Cost Estimates" app—Costing Data tab*

Figure 7.16 shows the DATES tab in the CREATE MATERIAL COST ESTIMATES app.

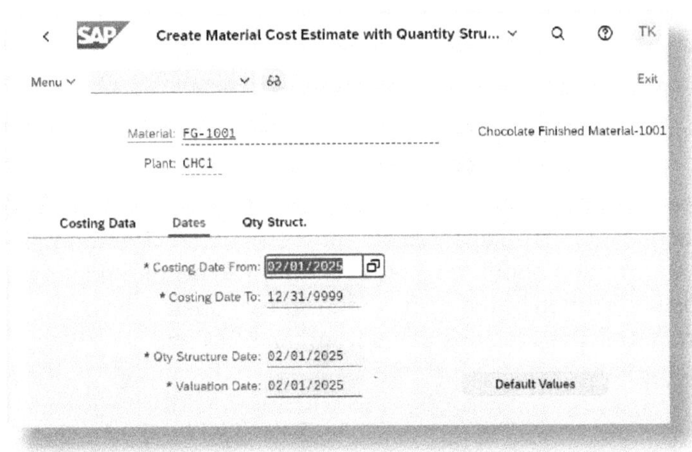


*Figure 7.16: "Create Material Cost Estimates" app—Dates tab*

**☛ Dates in cost estimate**

COSTING DATE FROM cannot be in the past for a standard cost estimate that is released to material master. Validity dates of the BOM and routing/recipe used for costing depend on the QTY STRUCTURE DATE (quantity structure date). Material and activity prices depend on the VALUATION DATE selected in the cost estimate selection screen.

Figure 7.17 shows the results of the cost estimate calculation.

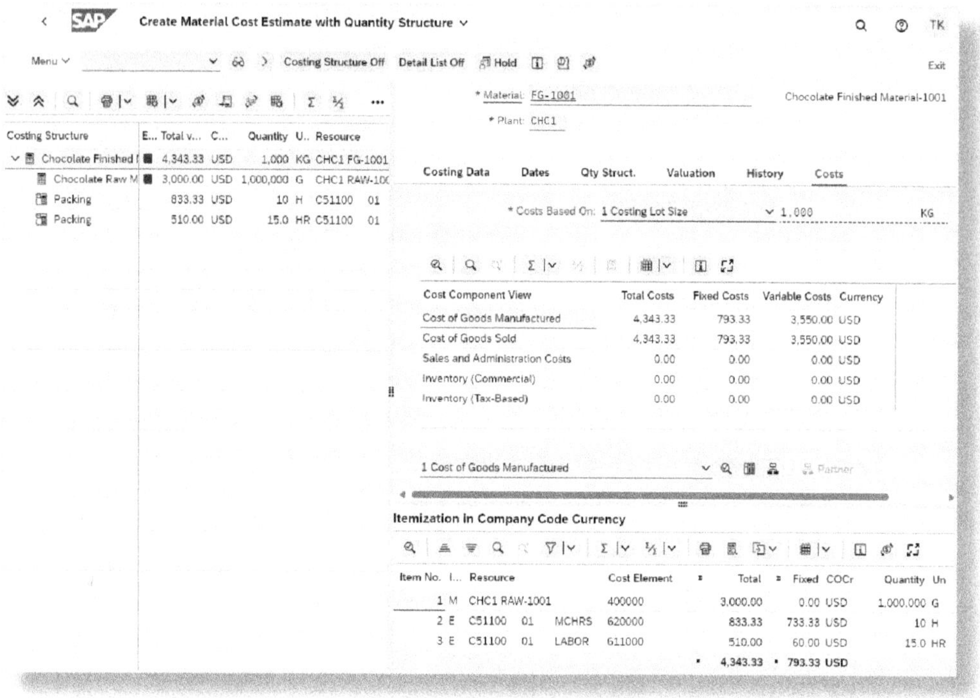


*Figure 7.17: "Create Material Cost Estimates" app—results*

The fully exploded COSTING STRUCTURE is on the left. This shows costs broken down by each level in the supply chain for the material. The top right section shows information about the cost estimate. The bottom right section contains the itemization of the costs at the current costing level. For a manufactured material, this includes costs from the BOM and activity type costs picked up from the recipe.

Once the cost estimate has been reviewed and validated for accuracy, cost estimates are *marked* and *released* (RELEASE MATERIAL COST ESTIMATES Fiori app).

A marked standard cost estimate is transferred to the material master record as the future standard price on the COSTING 2 tab of the material master.

A released standard cost estimate is transferred into the material master record as the current standard price.

When a cost estimate is released for another period, the previously maintained current planned price is moved to the previous planned price field, thereby allowing a historical view of the price from within the material master.

> **! Cost estimate release**
>
> Releasing an incorrect cost estimate could result in incorrect financial postings. It is not possible to release another cost estimate for the same period unless reorganization is performed. If a cost estimate is released for a second time in the current period, there could be issues interpreting the results of the actual costing run for that material in the period. It is very important that a cost estimate is thoroughly reviewed before releasing the cost.

## 7.7.5 Costing run

A *costing run* enables you to cost multiple materials at the same time. It reproduces the entire process of costing a product with a BOM. It can be executed in background mode for large volumes of materials. The MANAGE COSTING RUNS Fiori app is used to create and execute the costing run.

Costing results can be used to mark and release several standard cost estimates at once. Mark and release steps are built into the mass costing run (unlike CREATE MATERIAL COST ESTIMATES individual costing, where mark and release steps are performed using a different app—RELEASE MATERIAL COST ESTIMATES).

Figure 7.18 shows a costing run processed by the MANAGE COSTING RUNS app.

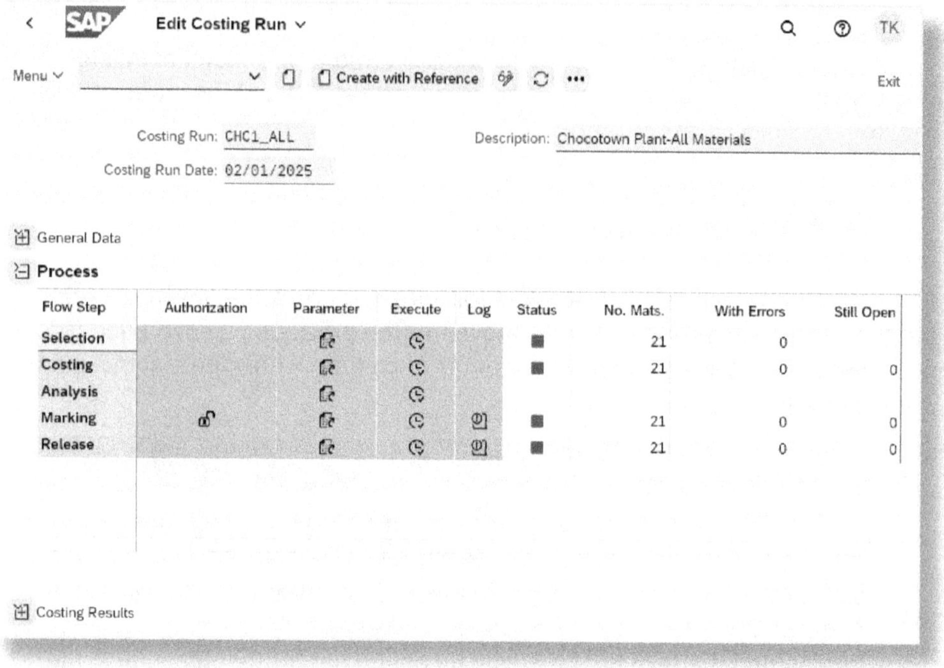


*Figure 7.18: "Manage Costing Runs" app—Costing run processing*

There are five costing run steps that are used for updating standard costs:

1. The SELECTION step defines the materials to be costed. It also sets up the order in which the materials are to be costed in order to optimize how the cost estimates are created.

2. The COSTING step uses the order defined in the previous step to generate cost estimates for each of the materials selected.

3. The ANALYSIS step generates a report that can be referenced to review the costing results for all the materials. This enables you to check the accuracy of the results before performing the steps that make the costs the new standard for the materials.

4. The MARKING step assigns the future standard for the materials for the fiscal period defined in the costing run.

5. The RELEASE step makes the future costs that were assigned during MARKING to become the new standard. This can only be done during the period defined by marking.

Most organizations have a pre-defined frequency for costing—monthly, quarterly, or annually. Costing runs often need to be repeated to meet this costing frequency.

The MANAGE COSTING RUNS app offers a *repeat costing run* feature, which enables a costing run to be executed on a monthly, quarterly, or yearly basis, without having to manually create the run each time.

## 7.8 Cost components

The cost of a product is usually made up of material, labor, overhead, and subcontract costs. *Cost components* enable cost breakdowns using predetermined categories/buckets. The origin for each cost component needs to be defined, which is usually a cost element range group associated with that component.

Figure 7.19 shows COST COMPONENT configuration (transaction OKTZ).

The menu path is: TOOLS • CUSTOMIZING • IMG • SPRO EXECUTE PROJECT • CONTROLLING • PRODUCT COST CONTROLLING • PRODUCT COST PLANNING • BASIC SETTINGS FOR MATERIAL COSTING • DEFINE COST COMPONENT STRUCTURE.

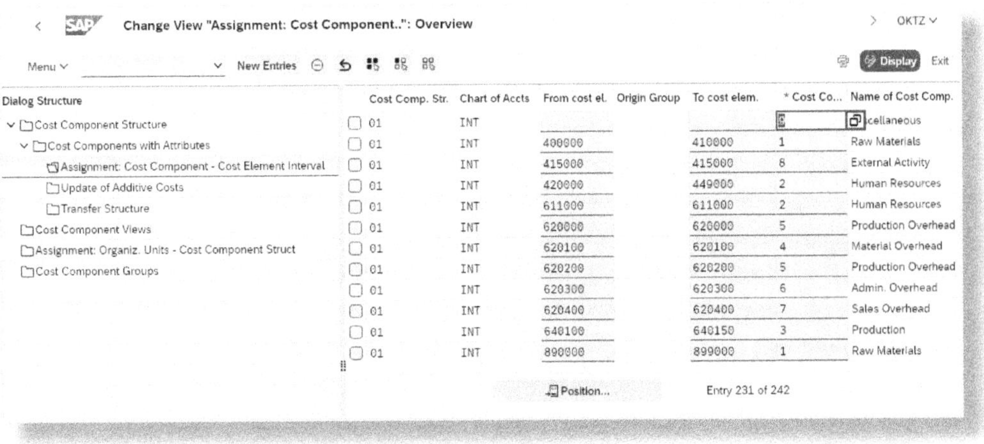


*Figure 7.19: OKTZ—Cost component setup*

The maximum number of cost components that can be used is 120 if there is no need to distinguish between fixed and variable costs for a specific cost component. If a cost component is defined to show both fixed and variable costs, then two slots are required, thereby reducing the total number of cost components available. As a general rule, when more cost components are defined, it becomes more difficult to get a good picture of the cost breakdown. Understanding how the costs are going to be classified is an important step when setting up a new system.

> **40 or 120 cost components?**
>
> Alex was under the impression from his earlier investigations into SAP that only 40 cost components were allowed. Originally, SAP provided for only 40 in the system, but he learned that as of On-Premise edition 1909, the maximum number has been increased to 120.

Figure 7.20 shows results of the COST COMPONENT view in the DISPLAY MATERIAL COST ESTIMATES app. Cost component 1 (RAW MATERIALS) includes only the costs associated with the BOM component. Cost component 2 (HUMAN RESOURCES) is associated with the LABOR activity type assigned in the recipe. Cost component 5 (PRODUCTION OVERHEAD) includes all the MCHRS costs.

**Cost Components in Company Code Currency**

| CC... | Name of Cost Comp. | Overall | Fixed | Variable | Currency |
|---|---|---|---|---|---|
| 1 | Raw Materials | 3,000.00 | | 3,000.00 | USD |
| 2 | Human Resources | 510.00 | 60.00 | 450.00 | USD |
| 3 | Production | | | | USD |
| 4 | Material Overhead | | | | USD |
| 5 | Production Overhead | 833.33 | 733.33 | 100.00 | USD |
| 8 | External Activity | | | | USD |
| 9 | Miscellaneous | | | | USD |
| | | **4,343.33** | **793.33** | **3,550.00** | **USD** |

*Figure 7.20: "Display Cost Estimates" app—Cost estimate cost component view*

## 7.9 Reporting in product cost planning

For reference, Alex created a table which listed important transactions relating to product costing (see Figure 7.21).

**Master data apps and transactions**

| Material master | Transaction / Fiori app | Purpose |
|---|---|---|
| Create | Create Material | Creates a new material or extends a material to another plant |
| Change | Change Material | Changes material settings |
| Display | Display Material | Displays the material settings |
| List | MM60 (transaction) | List of materials |
| **Bill of materials** | **Transaction / Fiori app** | **Purpose** |
| Create / Change / Display | Maintain Bill of Material | Maintain BOMs |
| Where used list | Find BOM for Component | List the BOMs that contain a specific material |
| Display exploded BOM | Display Multilevel BOM Explosion | Lists BOM components including all components of sub-assemblies |
| **Work centers (discrete manufacturing)** | **Transaction / Fiori app** | **Purpose** |
| Create / Change / Display | Manage Work Centers | Data maintenance for work centers for discrete manufacturing |
| List | CR05 (transaction) | Changes a work center |
| Cost center assignment | CR06 (transaction) | Displays work center settings |
| **Routings (discrete manufacturing)** | **Transaction / Fiori app** | **Purpose** |
| Create / Change / Display | Manage Routings | Maintain routings for discrete manufacturing |
| **Resources (process manufacturing)** | **Transaction / Fiori app** | **Purpose** |
| Create | Create Resource | Creates a new resource for use in recipes |
| Change | Change Resource | Changes a resource |
| Display | Display Resource | Displays resource parameters |
| Where used list | CA81 (transaction) | Lists the recipes which use a specific resource |
| **Master recipes (process manufacturing)** | **Transaction / Fiori app** | **Purpose** |
| Create / Change / Display | Manage Master Recipes | Maintain recipes for process manufacturing |
| Recipe list | C251 (transaction) | List of recipes |
| **Production version** | **Transaction / Fiori app** | **Purpose** |
| Create / Change / Display / Delete | Manage Production Versions | Maintenance of production versions and assignment to materials |

**Product costing apps and transactions**

| Cost Estimate | Transaction / Fiori app |
|---|---|
| Create | Create Material Cost Estimates |
| Display | Display Material Cost Estimates |
| Mark and release | Release Material Cost Estimates |
| Costing run | Manage Costing Runs |

| Costing reports | Transaction / Fiori app |
|---|---|
| List of material cost estimates | Costing Run Results |
| Variances between costing runs | Costing Run Comparison |
| | |
| | |

| Configuration | Transaction / Fiori app |
|---|---|
| Costing variant | OKKN (transaction) |
| Valuation variant | OKK4 (transaction) |
| Costing sheet | KZS2 (transaction) |
| Cost components | OKTZ (transaction) |

| Other costing options | |
|---|---|
| Additive costs | Create Additive Costs |
| Mixed costing – procurement alternatives | Edit Procurement Alternatives |
| Mixed costing – mixing ratios | Change Mixing Ratios |
| | |

*Figure 7.21: Product costing apps and transactions*

# 8 Production planning and controlling—where everything in the plant is clearly visible

*"Manufacturing is more than just putting parts together. It's coming up with ideas, testing principles, and perfecting the engineering, as well as final assembly."*

—James Dyson

**Because of the tightly integrated nature of the SAP Enterprise Resource Planning (ERP) system, it is important that controllers are aware of everything that happens in the production planning area. Much what production planning does (or at times, does not do) affects controlling, therefore good insight into shopfloor transactions is key to understanding the impact on the plant's financial performance.**

Before production planning can begin creating transactions, there are controlling prerequisites that have to be set up:

- The material and its components must have standard costs set up.
- The activities used in routing/recipe must have activity costs set up.

Regular production planning and shopfloor execution activities can begin once these prerequisites have been met.

## 8.1 Creating a process order

MRP controllers usually use an MRP run to create orders. Orders can be created directly from the CREATE PROCESS ORDER app. Various steps such as scheduling, material availability check, order release, and preliminary costing are performed.

Production orders use the CREATE PRODUCTION ORDER app. There are differences between production orders and process orders, but the data flow and behind-the-scenes accounting and controlling impact is similar.

A process order is created for a material and plant combination for a given order type. The order type determines what kind of production can be carried out (e.g., PI01 for a finished material, PI11 for a semi-finished material, PI99 for R&D trials, and PI98 for rework orders, etc.) and what settlement rule will be adopted for the order.

Figure 8.1 shows the initial screen of the CREATE PROCESS ORDER app.

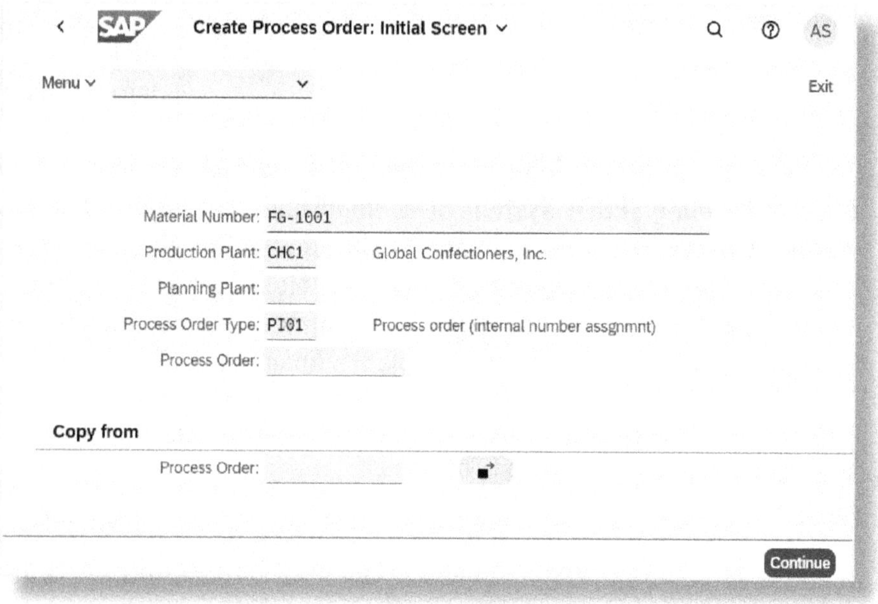


*Figure 8.1: "Create Process Order" app—Initial Screen*

Components are pulled from the BOM and operations are pulled from the master recipe. Depending on the design, shopfloor personnel can make modifications to process orders. However, as far as possible, it is best practice to keep the master data accurate and up to date in order to prevent problems during shop-floor execution. After the material, plant, and order type have been entered, the next screen shows the process order header screen (see Figure 8.2).

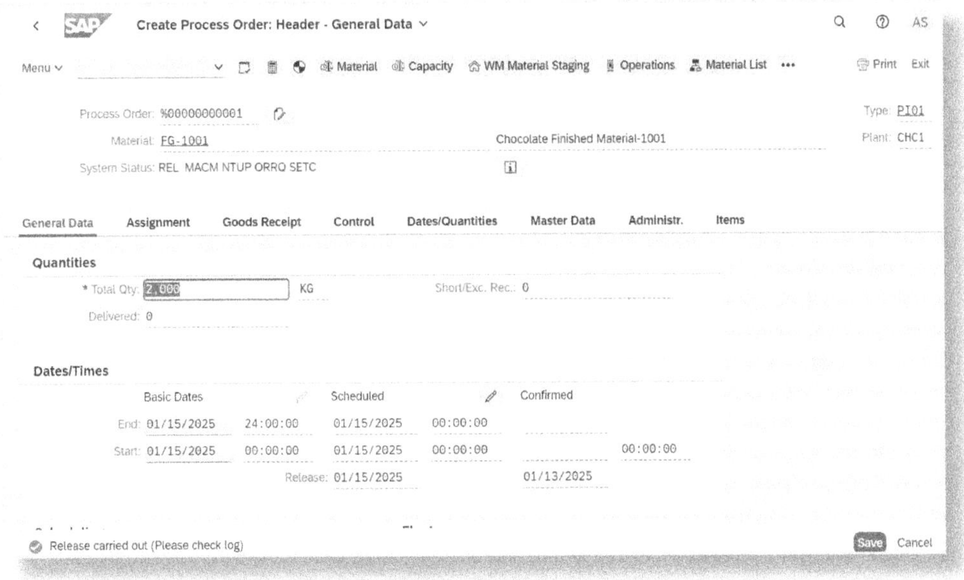


*Figure 8.2: "Create process order" app*

A settlement rule is created for the process order, depending on the order type used. Figure 8.3 shows settlement of the order to the material. This means that any variances that occur in this process order will be settled (transferred) to the material.

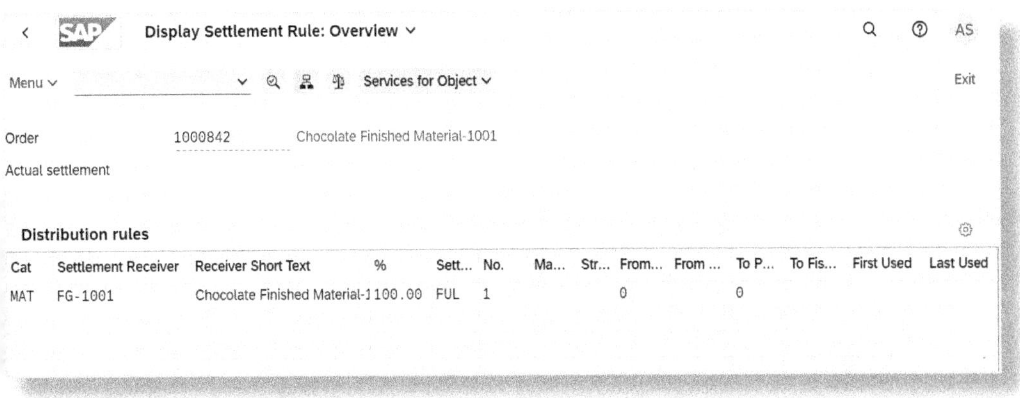


*Figure 8.3: Process order settlement rule*

The settlement rule determines how the variances in the order will be handled. The most widely used settlement rule is to settle to the material (used for regular production). Other options include settlement to cost center (used for R&D trials), GL account, and project/ WBS element (used for capital projects).

> **No financial postings at order creation stage**
>
> No financial postings are made at the time of order creation. Material reservations are created, but until these materials are issued, there are no financial postings. The order starts receiving actual costs when one or more of the following events occur: goods issue, confirmation, and/or goods receipt.

## 8.2 Goods issue

Shopfloor personnel can start recording process order transactions once the MRP controller has released the order. An order receives the first set of actual costs when issue of goods (components) occurs.

*Goods issue* is a posting in the system that records the issuance of inventory into a CO object (process order, internal order, or cost center). Goods issue is usually performed using the POST GOODS MOVEMENT app (see Figure 8.4).

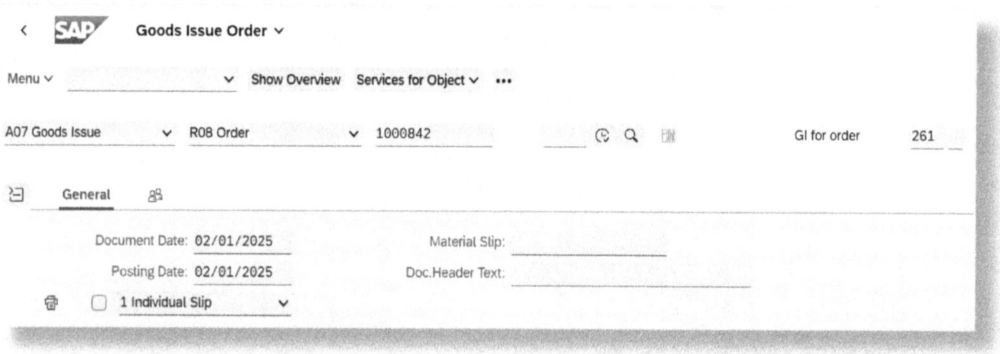


*Figure 8.4: "Post Goods Movement" app—Goods issue, initial screen*

*Movement type* 261 is used for goods issue on production/process orders. A reversal (or cancellation) of goods issue to order uses movement type 262.

Movement types are fundamental to the materials management module, and together with valuation class, it drives the financial postings that occur for a given transaction.

The actual quantity of raw material spent on the order can be entered, if available (see Figure 8.5).

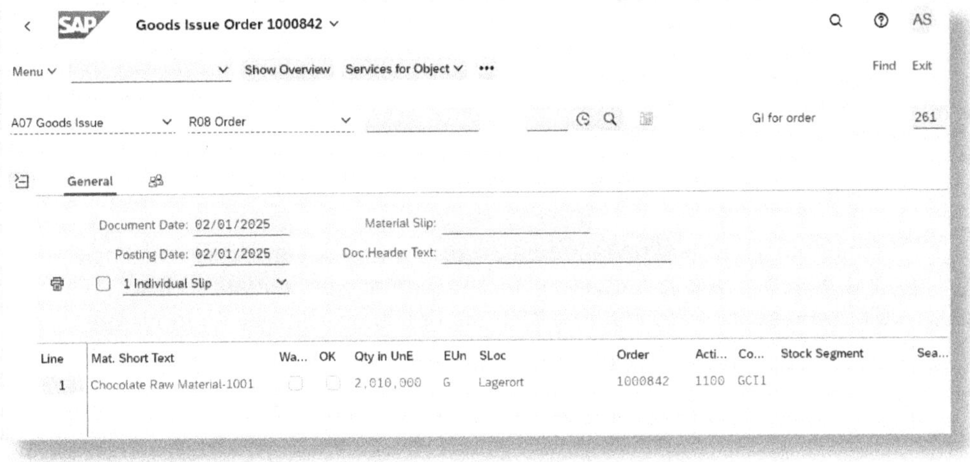


*Figure 8.5: "Post Goods Movement" app—goods issue quantity*

*Direct issue* occurs when the actual quantity is entered. *Backflushing* occurs when the default quantity proposed by the bill of material is consumed on the order. This implies that there will be no variance on the order, given that the actual quantity is the same as the standard quantity. Backflush, or not, is therefore a very critical design decision that needs to be carefully evaluated at the project implementation phase. Most organizations try to achieve a balance of data-capture accuracy (direct issue) and data-capture efficiency (backflushing).

The system provides a material document number once the goods issue transaction has been saved (see Figure 8.6). The material, quantity consumed, plant, storage location, batch number, order, movement type, etc. from this material document can be reviewed.

*Figure 8.6: "Post Goods Movement" app—Goods issue material document*

This material document usually creates accounting documents in the background, based on the system setup for movement type, valuation class, and type of transaction (see Figure 8.7). Valuation class, along with movement type, influences many of these financial postings.

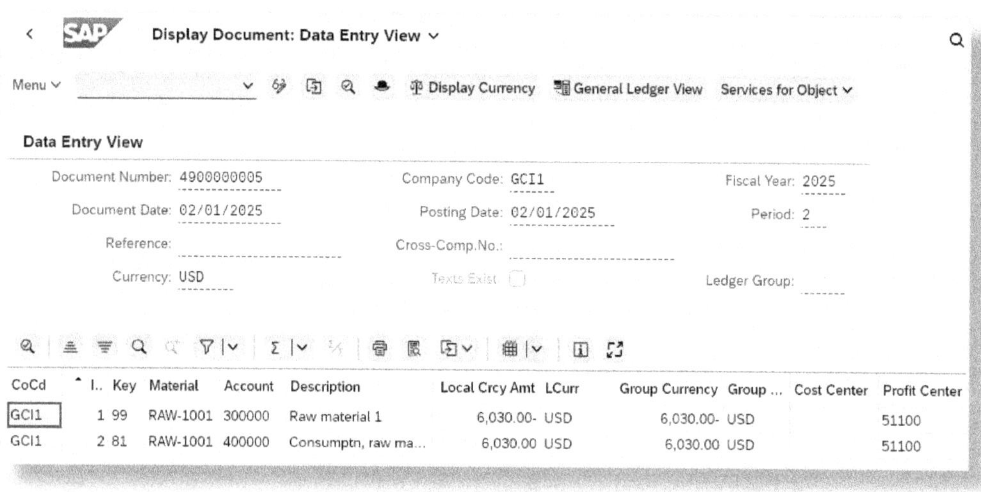


*Figure 8.7: "Post Goods Movement" app—Goods issue accounting document*

> **Accounting impact at time of goods issue**
>
> At the time of goods issue, the system credits the INVENTORY-RAW MATERIAL GL account, and debits the MATERIAL CONSUMPTION GL account and process order.

Transactions performed on process orders are immediately reflected in either the PRODUCTION COST ANALYSIS app or the ANALYZE ORDER app. The report shown in the ANALYZE ORDER app is also available from order processing in the CHANGE PROCESS ORDER and DISPLAY PROCESS ORDER apps. The process order *Open Detail* page provides a good overview of the costs posted on the process order, including comparisons of plan versus actual and target versus actual. Goods issue postings are recorded on the debit side of the process order (see Figure 8.8).

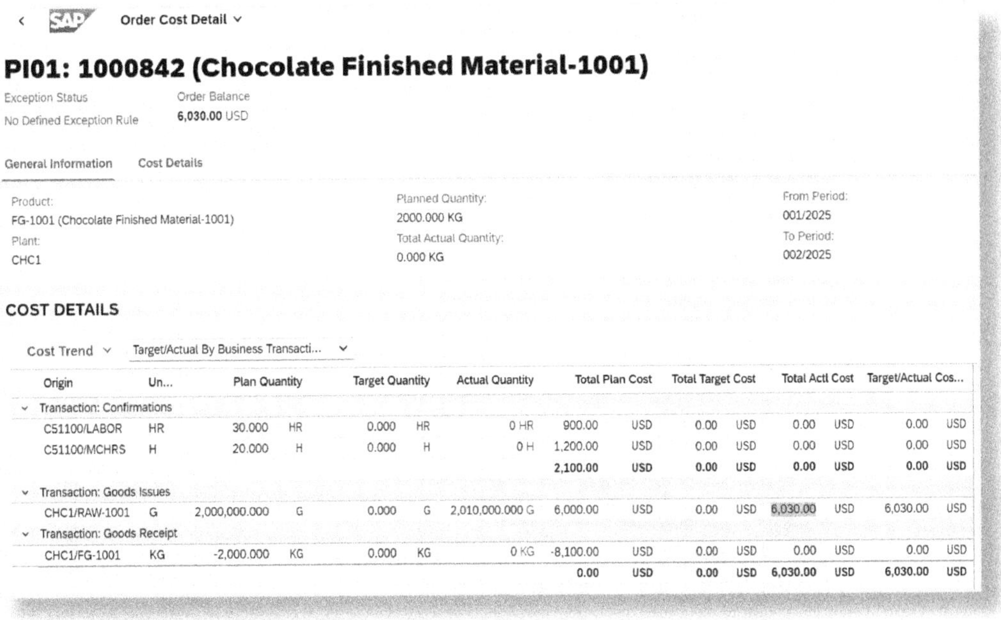


| Origin | Un... | Plan Quantity | | Target Quantity | | Actual Quantity | Total Plan Cost | | Total Target Cost | | Total Actl Cost | | Target/Actual Cos... | |
|---|---|---|---|---|---|---|---|---|---|---|---|---|---|---|
| Transaction: Confirmations | | | | | | | | | | | | | | |
| C51100/LABOR | HR | 30.000 | HR | 0.000 | HR | 0 HR | 900.00 | USD | 0.00 | USD | 0.00 | USD | 0.00 | USD |
| C51100/MCHRS | H | 20.000 | H | 0.000 | H | 0 H | 1,200.00 | USD | 0.00 | USD | 0.00 | USD | 0.00 | USD |
| | | | | | | | **2,100.00** | **USD** | **0.00** | **USD** | **0.00** | **USD** | **0.00** | **USD** |
| Transaction: Goods Issues | | | | | | | | | | | | | | |
| CHC1/RAW-1001 | G | 2,000,000.000 | G | 0.000 | G | 2,010,000.000 G | 6,000.00 | USD | 0.00 | USD | 6,030.00 | USD | 6,030.00 | USD |
| Transaction: Goods Receipt | | | | | | | | | | | | | | |
| CHC1/FG-1001 | KG | -2,000.000 | KG | 0.000 | KG | 0 KG | -8,100.00 | USD | 0.00 | USD | 0.00 | USD | 0.00 | USD |
| | | | | | | | **0.00** | **USD** | **0.00** | **USD** | **6,030.00** | **USD** | **6,030.00** | **USD** |

*Figure 8.8: "Production Cost Analysis" app—Process order costs after goods issue*

## 8.3 Confirmation

A *confirmation* is a document that records the work that has been done for an operation. *Operations* are production steps that can have materials or activities assigned to them.

Once the goods are issued to the order, it is time to record the number of hours to manufacture the product for that order.

A confirmation is usually performed using the CONFIRM PROCESS ORDER PHASE app for single phases and operations (see Figure 8.9), or using transaction CORK for order-wide confirmations.

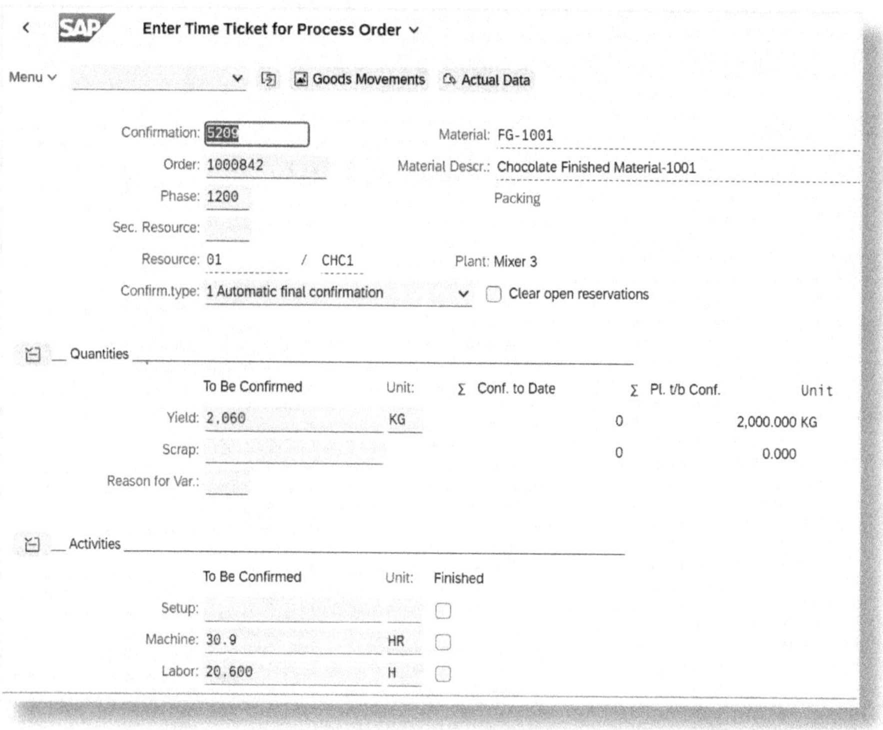


*Figure 8.9: Process order confirmation*

The confirmation transaction transfers activity quantities from the process order. The defaults on the CONFIRM PROCESS ORDER PHASE screen are 30 hours for machine time and 20 hours for labor, for a production quantity of 2,000 hours. However, this was manually updated to the actual time spent (30.90 hours) for machine time and (20.600 hours) for labor.

The confirmation records the activity quantity on the order. The actual activity spent on the order can be entered, if available. If a goods movement is associated with the confirmation, the quantity of the goods movement can also be entered or overridden as part of the confirmation process.

The cost impact of a confirmation transaction is displayed concurrently on the process order (see Figure 8.10).

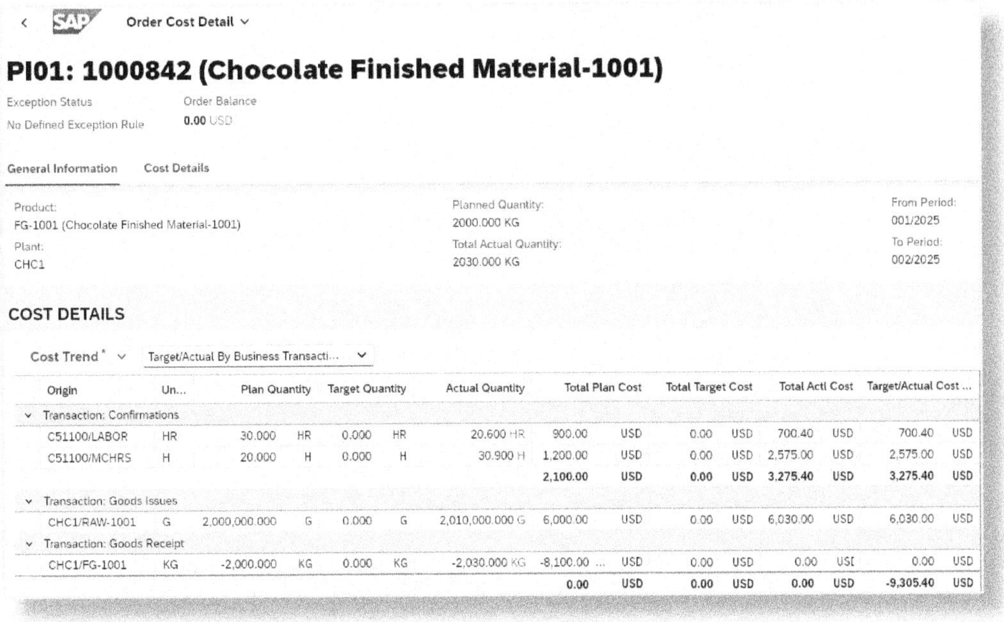


| Origin | Un... | Plan Quantity | | Target Quantity | | Actual Quantity | Total Plan Cost | | Total Target Cost | | Total Actl Cost | | Target/Actual Cost ... | |
|---|---|---|---|---|---|---|---|---|---|---|---|---|---|---|
| Transaction: Confirmations | | | | | | | | | | | | | | |
| C51100/LABOR | HR | 30.000 | HR | 0.000 | HR | 20.600 HR | 900.00 | USD | 0.00 | USD | 700.40 | USD | 700.40 | USD |
| C51100/MCHRS | H | 20.000 | H | 0.000 | H | 30.900 H | 1,200.00 | USD | 0.00 | USD | 2,575.00 | USD | 2,575.00 | USD |
| | | | | | | | **2,100.00** | **USD** | **0.00** | **USD** | **3,275.40** | **USD** | **3,275.40** | **USD** |
| Transaction: Goods Issues | | | | | | | | | | | | | | |
| CHC1/RAW-1001 | G | 2,000,000.000 | G | 0.000 | G | 2,010,000.000 G | 6,000.00 | USD | 0.00 | USD | 6,030.00 | USD | 6,030.00 | USD |
| Transaction: Goods Receipt | | | | | | | | | | | | | | |
| CHC1/FG-1001 | KG | -2,000.000 | KG | 0.000 | KG | -2,030.000 KG | -8,100.00 ... | USD | 0.00 | USD | 0.00 | USI | 0.00 | USD |
| | | | | | | | **0.00** | **USD** | **0.00** | **USD** | **0.00** | **USD** | **-9,305.40** | **USD** |

*Figure 8.10: Process order costs after confirmation*

Confirmation postings are recorded on the debit side of a process order. Looking at the quantities displayed in the report, even though the plan quantity was 20 hours of labor and 30 hours of machine hours, in the end, labor time was 20.6 hours and machine time was 30.9 hours.

The cost center and order are both impacted during an activity confirmation on the order. An order is debited with the activity quantity (and value), whereas the cost center is credited. The cost center plan/actual comparison report S_ALR_87013611 displays this information immediately upon confirmation (see Figure 8.11).

| Cost Centers: Actual/Plan/Variance | Date: 02/13/2025 | Page: 2 / 3 |
|---|---|---|
| | | Column: 1 / 2 |
| Cost Center/Group | C51100 | Choctwn-Choclat-M1 |
| Person responsible: | Carl | |
| Reporting period: | 2 to 2 2025 | |

| Cost Elements | Act. Costs | Plan Costs | Var.(Abs.) | Var.(%) |
|---|---|---|---|---|
| 473000 Postage w/o phone | | 450.00 | 450.00- | 100.00- |
| 481000 Estim. depreciation | | 6,000.00 | 6,000.00- | 100.00- |
| * Debit | | 29,500.00 | 29,500.00- | 100.00- |
| 611000 Labor Hours | 700.40- | 17,000.00- | 16,299.60 | 95.88- |
| 620000 Machine Hours | 2,575.00- | 12,500.00- | 9,925.00 | 79.40- |
| * Credit | 3,275.40- | 29,500.00- | 26,224.60 | 88.90- |
| ** Over/Underabsorption | 3,275.40- | | 3,275.40- | |

*Figure 8.11: Cost center report after confirmation*

> **Accounting impact on confirmation**
>
> At the time of activity confirmation, the system credits the activity type secondary cost element in the cost center and debits the activity type secondary cost element in the process order.

## 8.4 Goods receipt

*Goods receipt (GR)* is a posting in the system that shows the production of goods.

A goods receipt is usually performed using the POST GOODS RECEIPT FOR PROCESS ORDER Fiori app (see Figure 8.12).

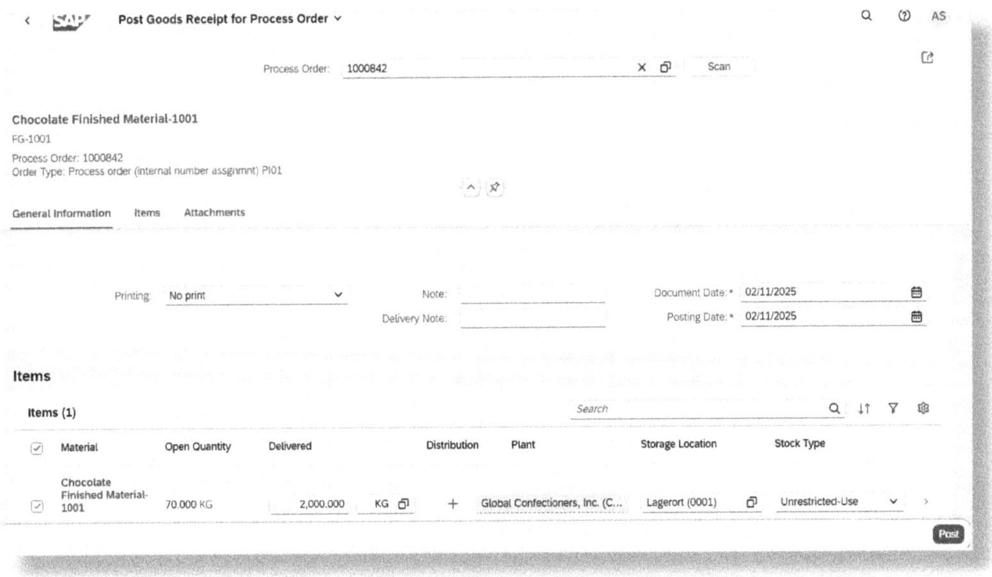


*Figure 8.12: "Post Goods Receipt for Process Order" app—initial screen*

Movement type 101 is used for goods receipts on production/process orders. A reversal (or cancellation) of a goods receipt to order is carried out using movement type 102.

In the example in Figure 8.13, the actual production was 2,060 KG, even though the process order contained a plan to produce 2,000 KG. The additional quantity of 60 KG is often referred to as *over delivery*. Plan costs for this order are calculated based on the plan quantity of 2,000 KG, but the target costs for the order are calculated based on the actual quantity of 2,060 KG.

As with goods issue, a goods receipt transaction also creates a material document (see Figure 8.14). The material, quantity produced, plant, storage location, batch number, order, movement type, etc., from the material document can be reviewed.

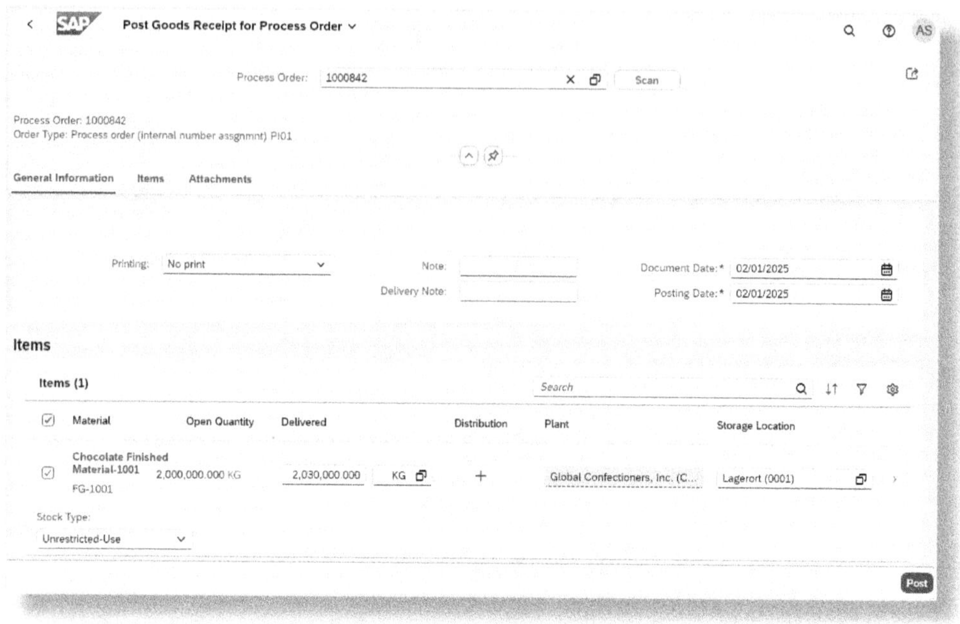


*Figure 8.13: "Post Goods Receipt for Process Order" app—quantity screen*

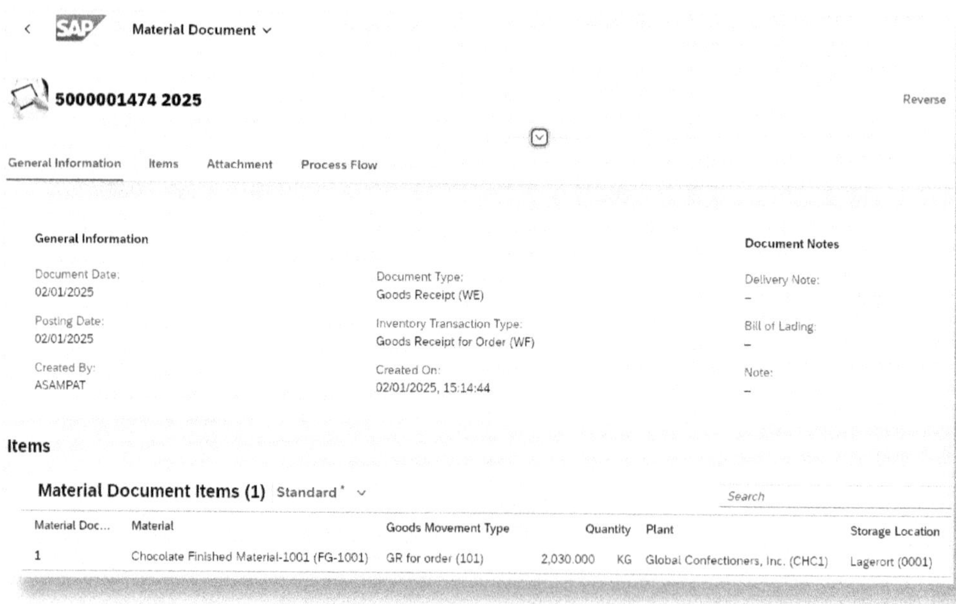


*Figure 8.14: Material Document—goods receipt*

Similarly, for this material document, accounting documents are created in the background, based on the system setup for movement type, valuation class, and type of transaction (see Figure 8.15).

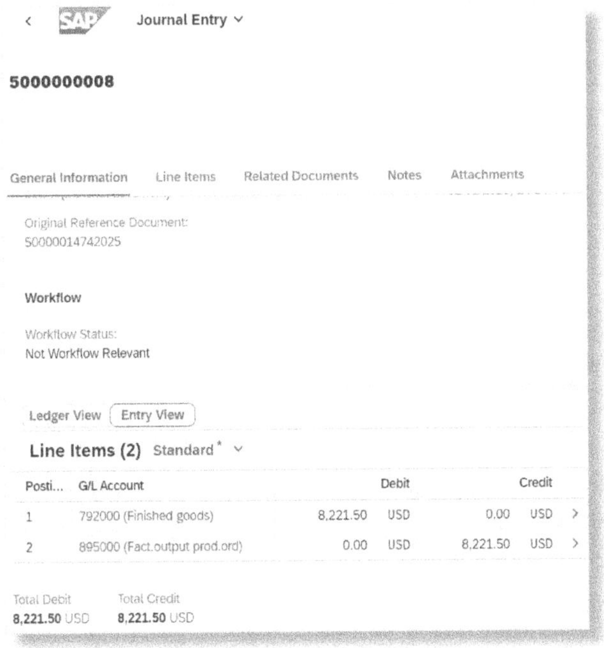


*Figure 8.15: Goods receipt accounting document*

The goods receipt transaction records the production on a process order by posting the quantity and value on the credit side to the process order (see Figure 8.16).

The target quantity and cost are also updated and adjusted for the actual production quantity.

> **Accounting impact at time of goods receipt**
>
> At the time of goods receipt, the system credits the factory output production (also known as production value) GL account and process order, and debits the inventory GL account.

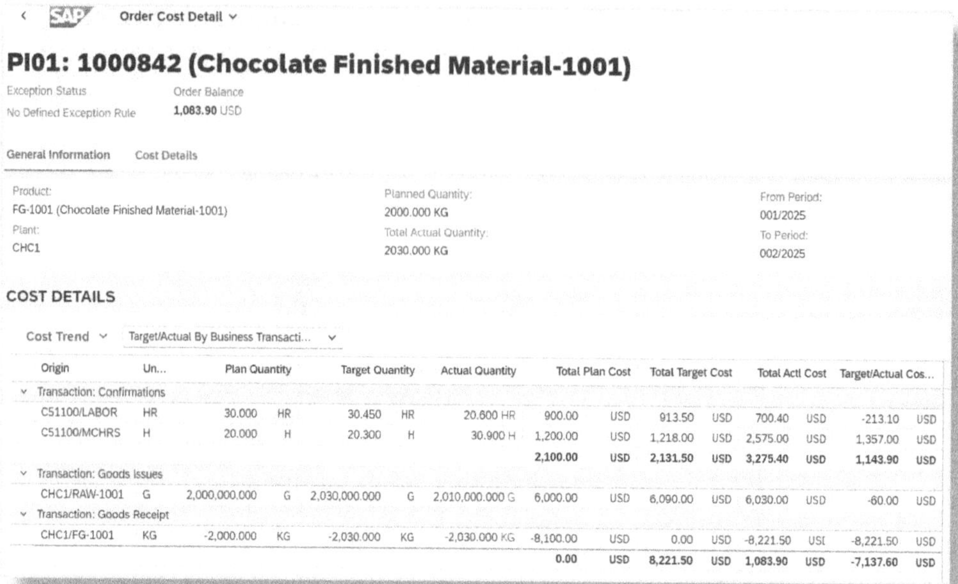


*Figure 8.16: Production cost analysis —process order costs after goods receipt*

Alex summarized the list of transactions for production planning and controlling (see Table 8.1).

| Fiori app / Transaction code | Description |
|---|---|
| Create Process Order | Process order creation |
| Change Process Order | Process order changes |
| Display Process Order | Process order display |
| Production Cost Analysis | Display process order costs |
| Create Production Order | Production order creation |
| Post Goods Movement | Enter goods issue for an order |
| Post Goods Movement or Material Documents Overview | Material document display |
| Manage Journal Entries | Accounting document display |
| Confirm Process Order Phase/ transaction CORK | Enter confirmation |
| Post Goods Receipt for Production Order | Enter goods receipt from a manufacturing order |
| Post Goods Movement | Enter any goods movement |

*Table 8.1: Apps and transactions for production planning and controlling*

# 9 Month-end closing—the organization's status report

*"Month end is approaching—keep calm and carry on accounting."*
—Anonymous

**"Month-end is approaching," Bob said to Alex. "You should know the steps that we perform in finance during this time. We have been doing this every month for several years now. The steps include process order WIP, variance, settlement, and analysis."**

**Alex could relate—at FLW, materials, production, and finance performed coordinated tasks during the last few days of the month, and the activities continued into the first few days of the new month.**

## 9.1 Cycle count and distribution of usage variances

The physical inventory count (also known as cycle count) is performed by materials and shopfloor personnel. Depending on whether there was a net increase or net decrease in the physical inventory versus system inventory, a gain or loss is posted on the income statement.

Whereas cycle count is more of a shopfloor and/or warehouse activity, there are finance and internal control implications that result from these transactions. Finance should therefore be aware of the process. Additionally, some organizations want to spread cycle count differences to production/ process orders that ran in the recent past. This process is supported by the *distribution of usage variances (DUV)* functionality found in SAP software. DUV is executed using the DISTRIBUTION OF INVENTORY DIFFERENCES app.

Process orders are settled at month end. Depending on their status, some orders may be incomplete and need to be carried forward to the next month. Completed orders qualify for variance calculation, whereas incomplete orders are treated as work-in-process.

## 9.2 Process order status

The system assigns various statuses to an order in the course of the order's lifecycle. For example, order status CRTD (created) is set at the time of order creation, REL (released) is set at the time of release, PDLV (partially delivered) at the time of partial delivery, DLV (delivered) at the time of final delivery, and TECO (technically complete) at the time of technical completion. The order status determines what type of business transactions are allowed and therefore plays an important role in the order lifecycle.

The status for an order can be reviewed in the PRODUCTION COST ANALYSIS app by clicking on the ORDER STATUS hyperlink. Alternatively, in the DISPLAY PROCESS ORDER app, click on the "status" button . Figure 9.1 shows various statuses set for a sample order.

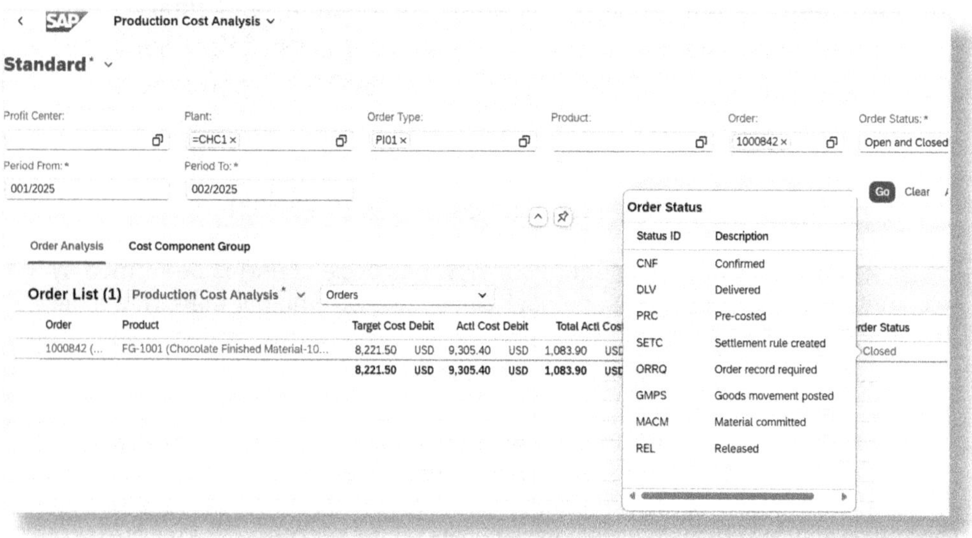


*Figure 9.1: Production Cost Analysis —Order status display*

From a finance perspective, the important statuses include:

- REL (released)—this status is set when an order is released. It allows all actual and committed values to be posted to the order.
- PRC (pre-costed)—indicates that a plan cost estimate exists for an order.
- PDLV (partially delivered)—this status is set during goods receipt if only part of the planned quantity has been delivered.

- DLV (delivered)—this status is set if either the planned quantity of an object has been delivered, or if the delivery completed indicator has been set during goods receipt.
- TECO (technical completion)—this means ending a production order from a logistical viewpoint. This function is typically used if the execution of an order has to be stopped prematurely, or if the order could not be executed in the required manner and open requirements for the order (reservations, capacities, etc.) need to be deleted.
- VCAL (variances calculated)—this status is set by the system when there are calculated variances for an order.
- RESA (results analysis carried out)—this status is set by the system when you have performed a WIP calculation for an order.

**Completed versus incomplete orders**

*Completed orders* are orders where the system status is either DLV (delivered) or TECO (technically completed), or both.

*Incomplete (WIP) orders* are orders where costs have been posted against them, but the system status is neither DLV (delivered), nor TECO (technically complete).

## 9.3 Work in progress

Incomplete orders (also referred to as WIP orders) are processed using the following apps:

- CALCULATE WORK IN PROCESS – COLLECTIVE app—WIP mass processing
- CALCULATE WORK IN PROCESS ORDER – SINGLE app—WIP individual processing

Previously calculated WIP can be displayed with the following transactions:

- KKAQ—WIP mass display
- KKAY—WIP individual display

Figure 9.2 shows the selection screen in the CALCULATE WORK IN PROCESS – COLLECTIVE app.

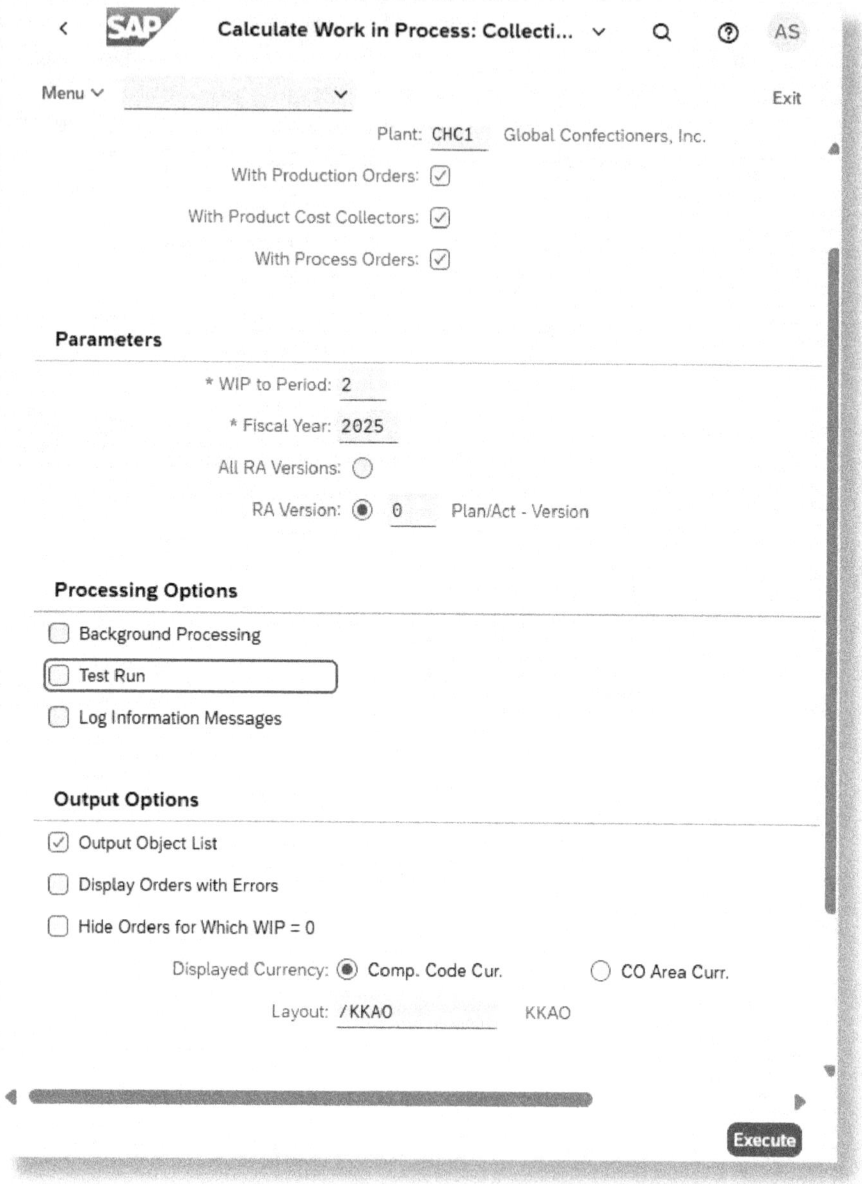


*Figure 9.2: WIP collective processing selection screen*

Figure 9.3 shows the results screen for WIP calculation in the CALCULATE WORK IN PROCESS COLLECTIVE app.

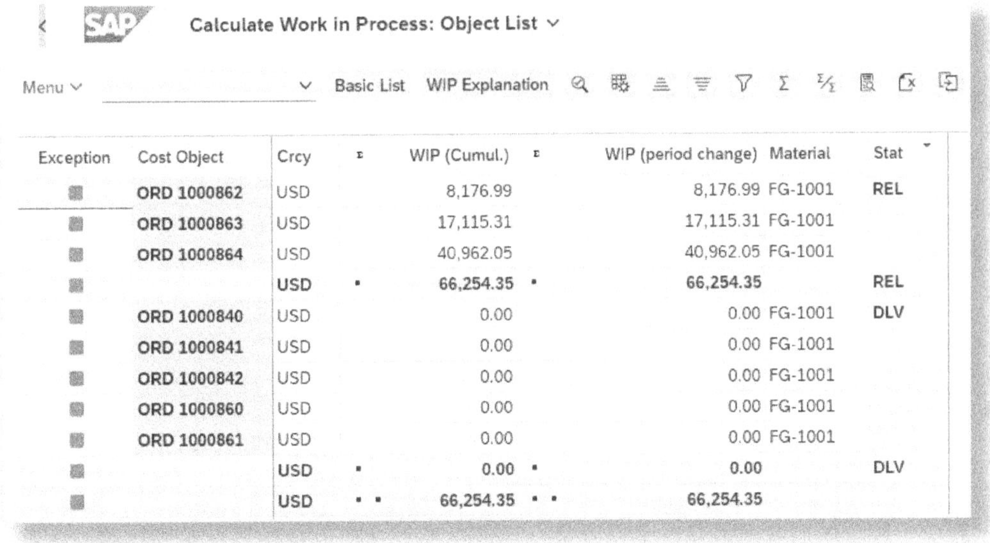


| Exception | Cost Object | Crcy | Σ | WIP (Cumul.) | Σ | WIP (period change) | Material | Stat |
|---|---|---|---|---|---|---|---|---|
| | ORD 1000862 | USD | | 8,176.99 | | 8,176.99 | FG-1001 | REL |
| | ORD 1000863 | USD | | 17,115.31 | | 17,115.31 | FG-1001 | |
| | ORD 1000864 | USD | | 40,962.05 | | 40,962.05 | FG-1001 | |
| | | USD | • | 66,254.35 | • | 66,254.35 | | REL |
| | ORD 1000840 | USD | | 0.00 | | 0.00 | FG-1001 | DLV |
| | ORD 1000841 | USD | | 0.00 | | 0.00 | FG-1001 | |
| | ORD 1000842 | USD | | 0.00 | | 0.00 | FG-1001 | |
| | ORD 1000860 | USD | | 0.00 | | 0.00 | FG-1001 | |
| | ORD 1000861 | USD | | 0.00 | | 0.00 | FG-1001 | |
| | | USD | • | 0.00 | • | 0.00 | | DLV |
| | | USD | • • | 66,254.35 | • • | 66,254.35 | | |

*Figure 9.3: WIP collective processing result screen*

**! SAP's WIP process is not referring to semi-finished materials!**

Many organizations refer to semi-finished materials as "WIP materials", which can confuse SAP's WIP process with semi-finished materials. These are two different things. SAP's *WIP (work-in-process) calculation* is a process to carry forward the balance for an incomplete order, whereas *WIP materials* is an alternative term for *semi-finished materials*.

**☛ WIP calculation does not post financial entries!**

WIP calculation does not post any entries, it merely calculates the amount to be carried over into the next period as WIP. A WIP entry is posted when a settlement transaction is executed.

## 9.4 Variance calculation

Completed orders qualify for variance calculation. As the name suggests, the system calculates target versus actual variances. Targets are determined by the standard cost estimate.

Completed orders (with status DLV or TECO) are processed using the following apps:

- RUN VARIANCE CALCULATION ORDERS – BY LOT app—variance mass processing
- RUN VARIANCE CALCULATION ORDER – SINGLE app—Variance individual processing

So far, we have seen several types of costs:

- **Plan costs**—collected on the order when the order is created. They take into account the plan production quantity and are based on components pulled from usage 1 BOM and modified in the order (if permitted).
- **Actual costs**—recorded when one or more of goods issue, activity confirmation, or goods receipt occur. Note that the term *actual costs* comes with a caveat. The components quantity might be based on actual cost; material price is based on standard cost of the components and is not actual cost. Similarly, the activity quantities could be based on actual, but the price is based on the planned price of activities. It is only when the orders are revalued with actual price that the activities are valued at actual cost.
- **Target costs**—recorded when actual goods receipt and/or variance calculation is carried out. Target costs are calculated based on the released cost estimate in proportion to the actual goods receipt (production) quantity. Depending on design, a released cost estimate might have been set up based on usage 1 BOM or usage 6 BOM. Therefore, the target cost in an order might show a different number than shown in the plan costs.

Figure 9.4 shows the selection screen in the RUN VARIANCE CALCULATION ORDERS – BY LOT app.

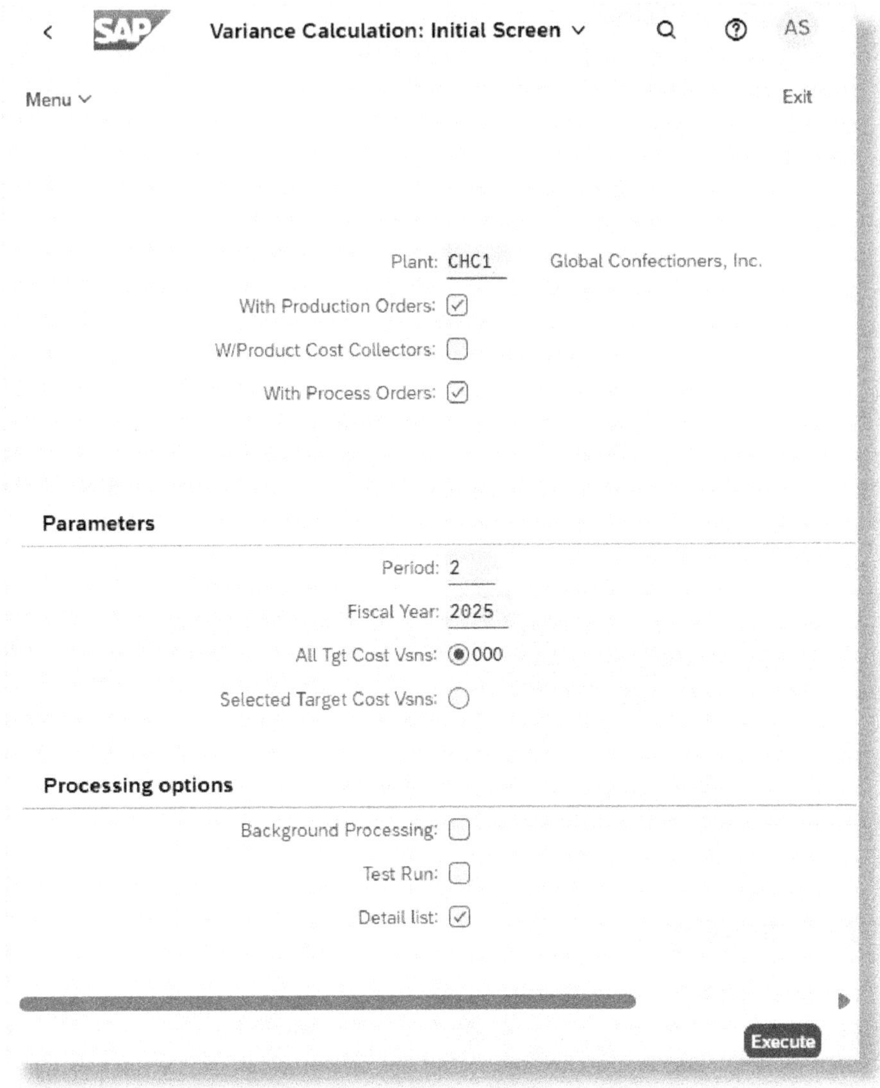


*Figure 9.4: Variance calculation selection screen*

Figure 9.5 shows the results screen.

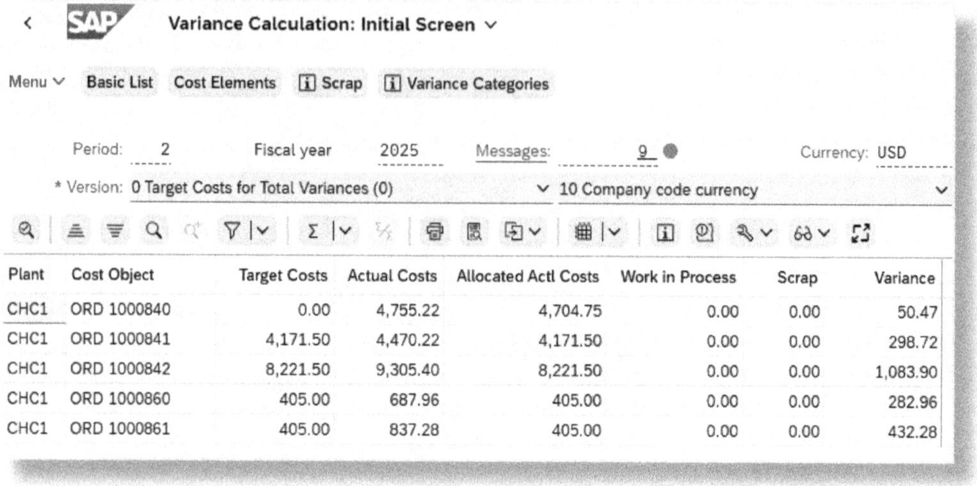


*Figure 9.5: Variance calculation result screen*

**Variance calculation does not post any financial entries!**

A variance calculation transaction does not post any entries; it merely calculates the amount of variance to be settled. Variance entry is posted when the settlement transaction is executed.

## 9.5 Settlement

Now that WIP and variance calculation have been completed, it is time to post these values to financial accounting using the settlement process. An order is settled to a specific object that is maintained in the settlement rule.

A *settlement rule* is determined by the order type and the nature of the activity/production performed on the order. While most orders settle to material, some orders might settle to either a cost center, an internal order, a GL account, or a work breakdown structure (WBS) element.

Figure 9.6 shows an example of a settlement rule where the order is settled to a material. Other possible object types are shown in the drop-down menu.

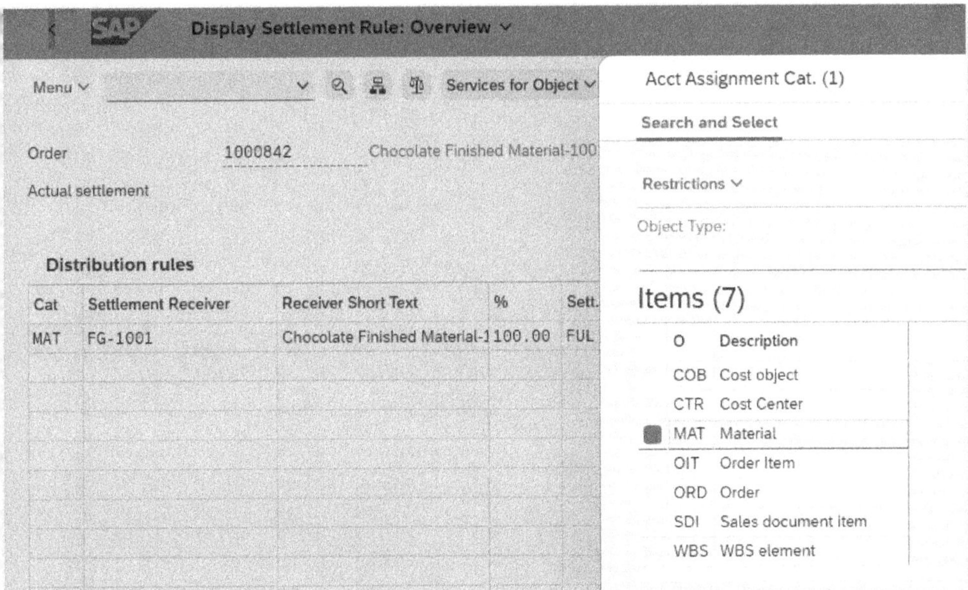


*Figure 9.6: Display process order—settlement rules*

Settlement is performed using the following apps:

- SETTLE ORDERS OPTIMIZED app—mass settlement processing.
- RUN ACTUAL SETTLEMENT ORDER – SINGLE app—individual settlement processing.

Figure 9.7 shows the selection screen.

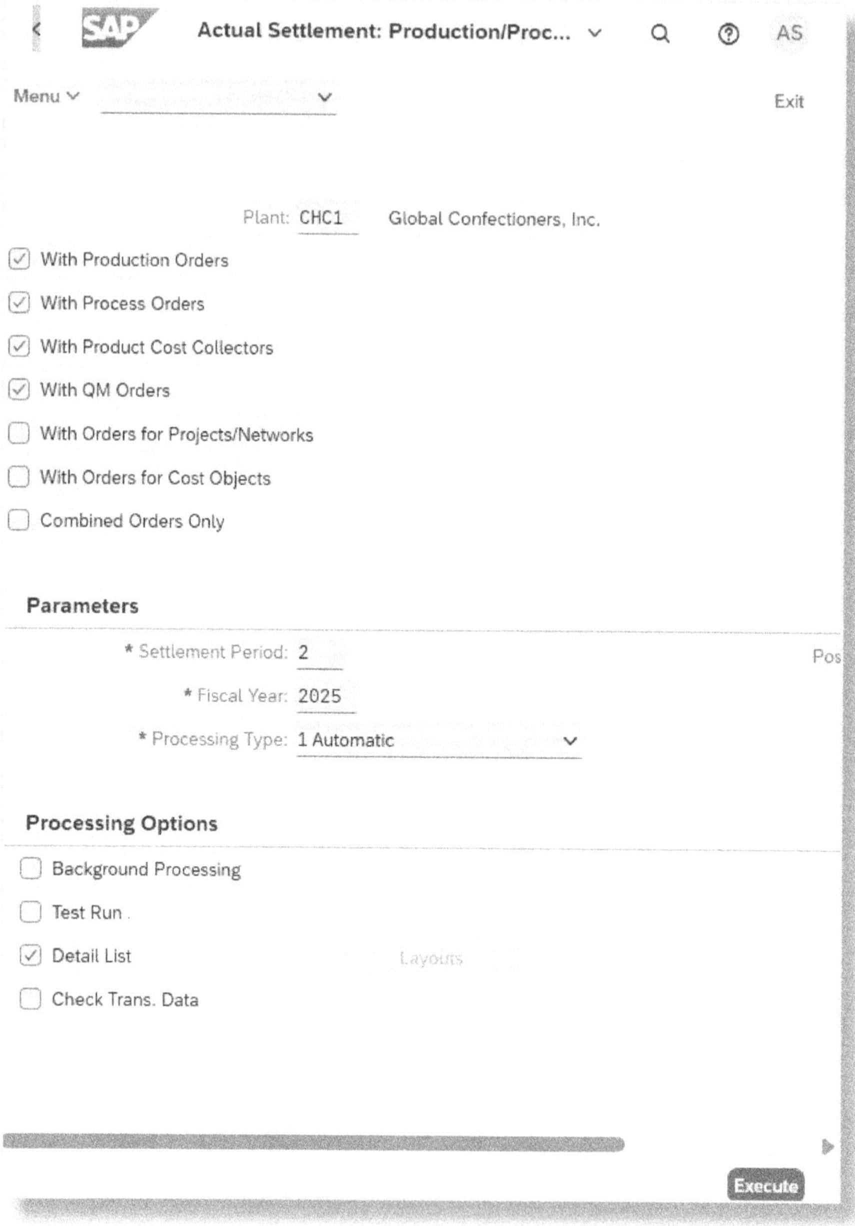


*Figure 9.7: Settlement selection screen*

Figure 9.8 shows the results screen for collective processing SETTLE ORDERS OPTIMIZED.

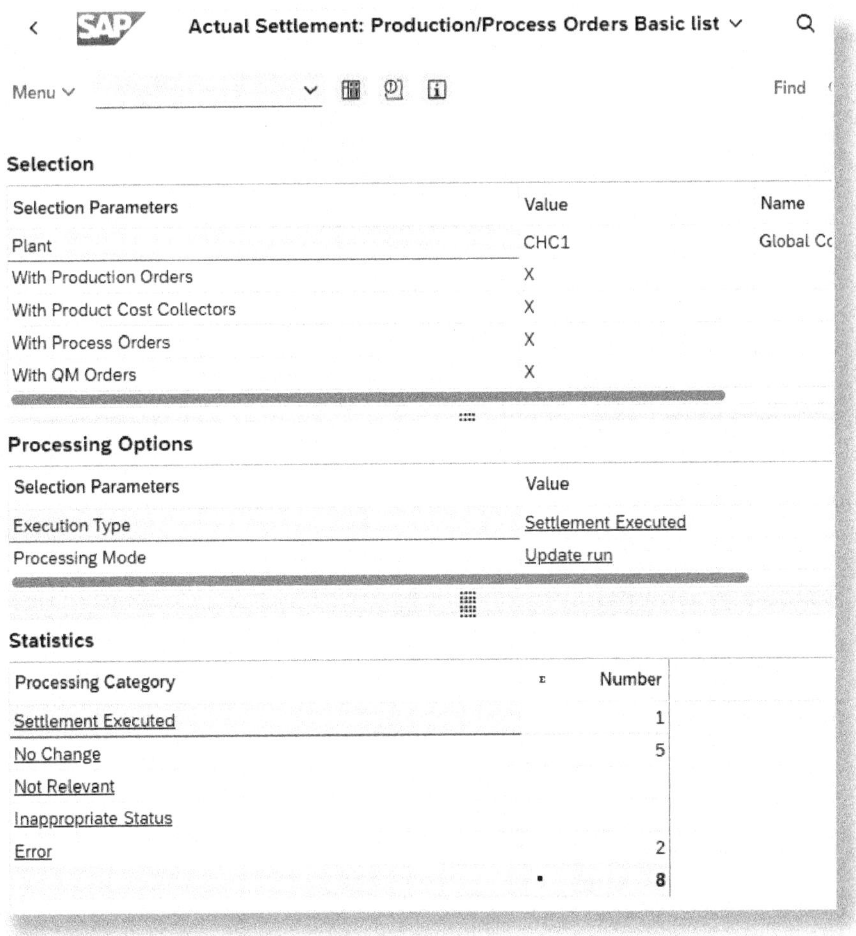


*Figure 9.8: Settlement result screen*

Figure 9.9 and Figure 9.10 show an FI document posted at the time of settlement for a completed order.

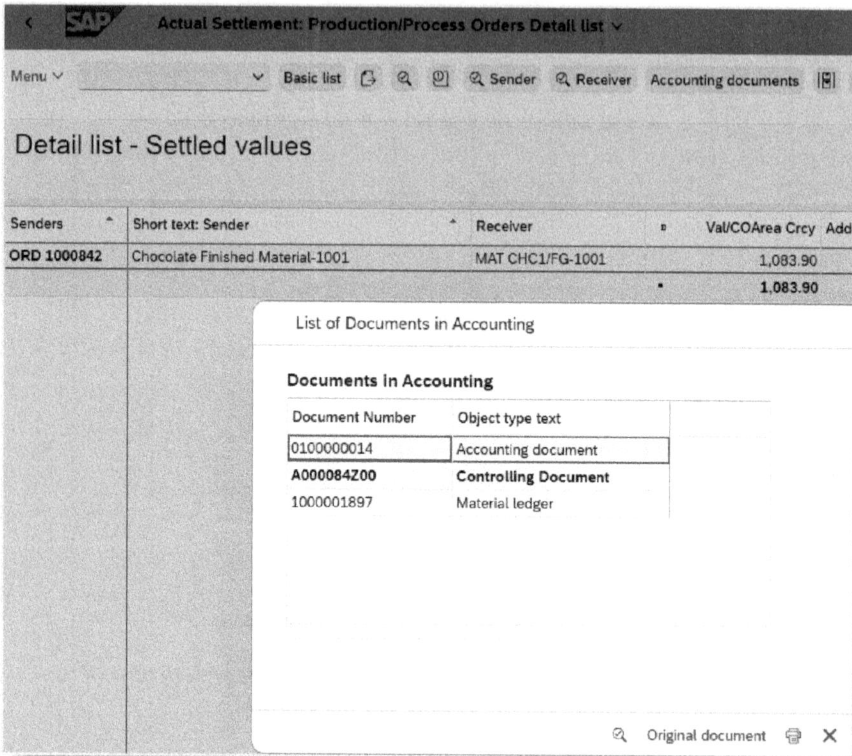


*Figure 9.9: Settlement detail list*

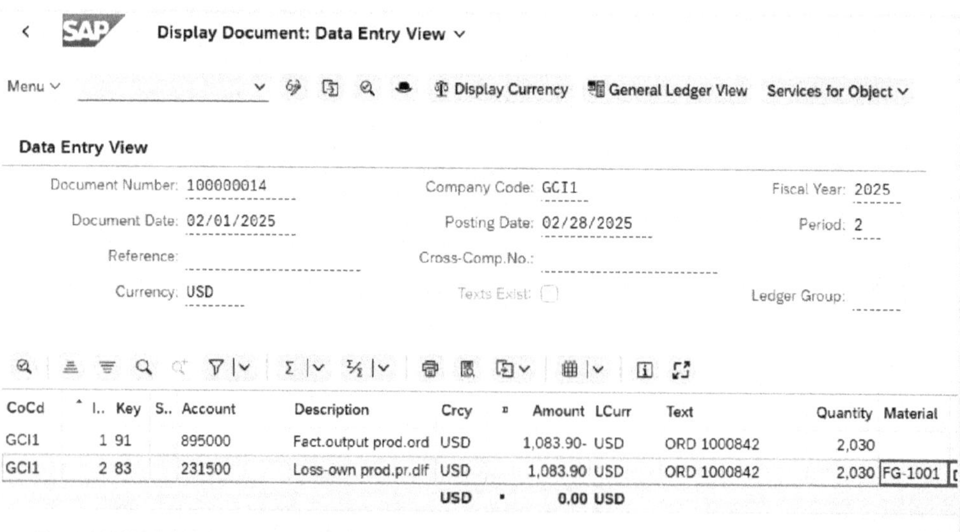


*Figure 9.10: Settlement FI document completed order*

Figure 9.11 shows the order cost display in the PRODUCTION COST ANALYSIS app and includes a new record for SETTLEMENT in the order. The order balance is now zero.

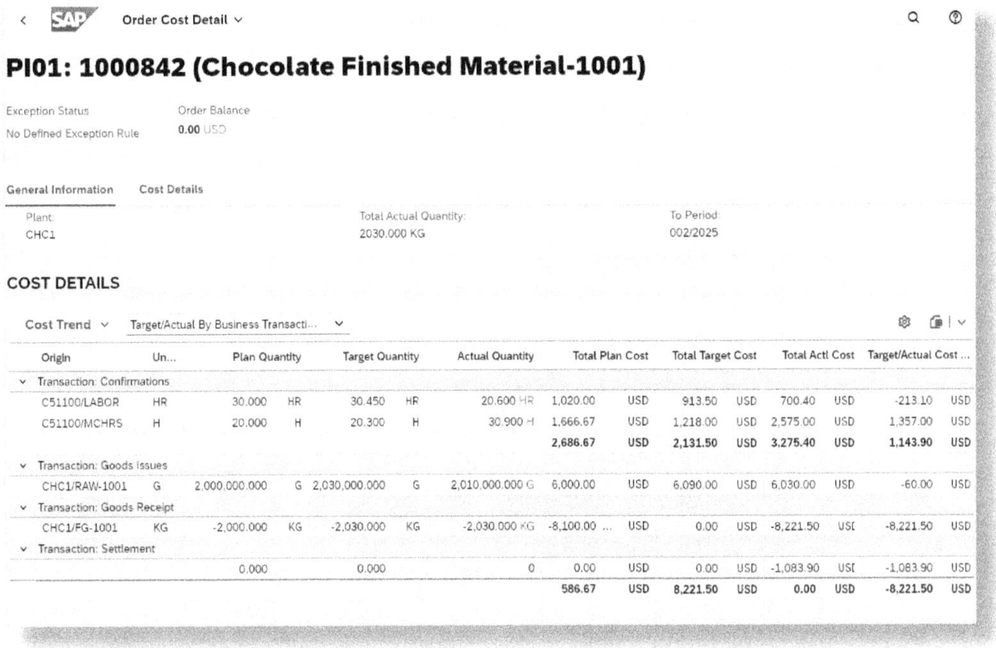

Order Cost Detail

**PI01: 1000842 (Chocolate Finished Material-1001)**

Exception Status: No Defined Exception Rule
Order Balance: 0.00 USD

General Information | Cost Details

Plant: CHC1
Total Actual Quantity: 2030.000 KG
To Period: 002/2025

COST DETAILS

Cost Trend | Target/Actual By Business Transacti...

| Origin | Un... | Plan Quantity | Target Quantity | Actual Quantity | Total Plan Cost | Total Target Cost | Total Actl Cost | Target/Actual Cost ... |
|---|---|---|---|---|---|---|---|---|
| Transaction: Confirmations | | | | | | | | |
| C51100/LABOR | HR | 30.000 HR | 30.450 HR | 20.600 HR | 1,020.00 USD | 913.50 USD | 700.40 USD | -213.10 USD |
| C51100/MCHRS | H | 20.000 H | 20.300 H | 30.900 H | 1,666.67 USD | 1,218.00 USD | 2,575.00 USD | 1,357.00 USD |
| | | | | | **2,686.67 USD** | **2,131.50 USD** | **3,275.40 USD** | **1,143.90 USD** |
| Transaction: Goods Issues | | | | | | | | |
| CHC1/RAW-1001 | G | 2,000,000.000 G | 2,030,000.000 G | 2,010,000.000 G | 6,000.00 USD | 6,090.00 USD | 6,030.00 USD | -60.00 USD |
| Transaction: Goods Receipt | | | | | | | | |
| CHC1/FG-1001 | KG | -2,000.000 KG | -2,030.000 KG | -2,030.000 KG | -8,100.00 ... USD | 0.00 USD | -8,221.50 USI | -8,221.50 USD |
| Transaction: Settlement | | | | | | | | |
| | | 0.000 | 0.000 | 0 | 0.00 USD | 0.00 USD | -1,083.90 USI | -1,083.90 USD |
| | | | | | **586.67 USD** | **8,221.50 USD** | **0.00 USD** | **-8,221.50 USD** |

*Figure 9.11: Order Cost Detail screen—costs after settlement*

> **Financial entry at WIP**
>
> WIP entry at settlement posts to the P&L and balance sheet accounts that are configured for carrying forward balances to the next month. When looking at order costs by business transaction, there are no report lines relating to order settlement. Instead, WIP cost shows up in a separate column. Order cost totals are not affected.

Figure 9.12 displays an accounting document posted for a WIP order.

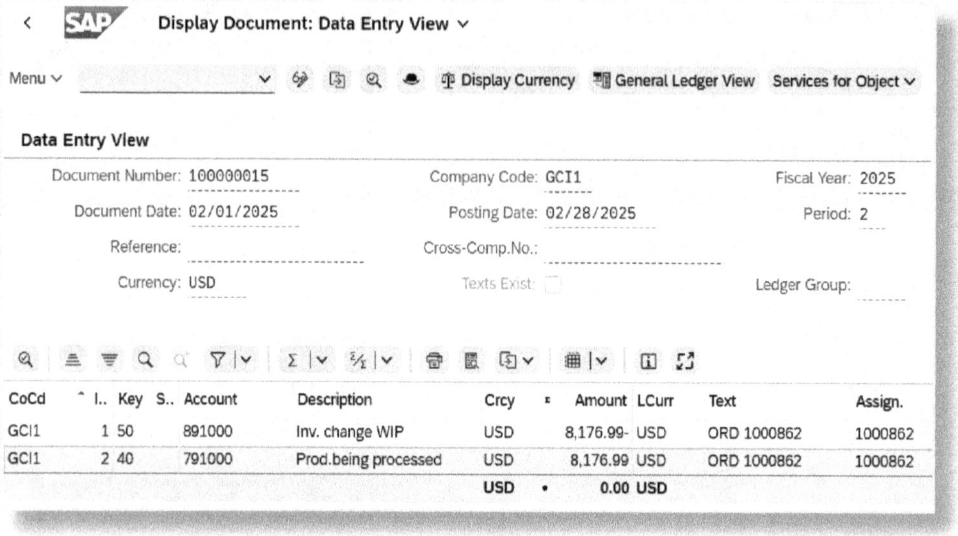


| CoCd | I.. | Key | S.. | Account | Description | Crcy | Amount | LCurr | Text | Assign. |
|---|---|---|---|---|---|---|---|---|---|---|
| GCI1 | 1 | 50 | | 891000 | Inv. change WIP | USD | 8,176.99- | USD | ORD 1000862 | 1000862 |
| GCI1 | 2 | 40 | | 791000 | Prod.being processed | USD | 8,176.99 | USD | ORD 1000862 | 1000862 |
| | | | | | | USD | 0.00 | USD | | |

*Figure 9.12: Settlement FI document WIP order*

> **WIP entry is reversed when an order is completed**
>
> WIP values are automatically reversed during the subsequent period's settlement once the orders are set to TECO/DLV status. (Orders may not always be completed in the subsequent month but might be completed after several months depending on the type of industry and the nature of the product and/or production process).
>
> An order usually has either WIP or variance posting in a particular month. An order could get both a WIP and a variance posting in the month in which an incomplete order is completed.

Variance posting in the general ledger is a two-step process. First, all production variances are bundled and posted to one price difference (PRD-PRF) account. Transaction key PRD (cost/price differences), account modifier PRF (production order settlement), and the valuation class drive the accounting entries. Transaction keys are used to determine general ledger accounts used by the system. An account modifier is used to differentiate account determinations.

Second, based on the needs of the Margin Analysis module, the total variance can be split back into the original variance categories and reposted into separate variance category accounts. The original posting is immediately reversed and distributed back into the individual categories. This enables the variance categories to not only be analyzed using CO reports, but also using general ledger reports and Margin Analysis. This setup is optional and depends entirely on data needs for financial analysis. The following prerequisites must be met:

- Produced materials are valued at the standard price.
- Variance calculation is run for production/process orders.
- Order types and their corresponding settlement profile(s) are defined to enable variance calculation.
- Price difference splitting structure is defined.

To configure production variance split, use menu path: TOOLS • CUSTOMIZING • IMG • SPRO EXECUTE PROJECT • FINANCIAL ACCOUNTING • GENERAL LEDGER ACCOUNTING • PERIODIC PROCESSING • INTEGRATION • MATERIALS MANAGEMENT • DEFINE ACCOUNTS FOR SPLITTING PRICE DIFFERENCES.

**Automate WIP, variance, settlement**

As noted earlier, WIP and variance calculations do not post any financial entries—postings occur only at time of settlement. This implies that WIP and variance can be run as many times as required. Settlement can also be run as many times as necessary, providing multiple postings for the same order are acceptable. Running these transactions daily might be overkill, so it can be run on a weekly or monthly basis. The settlement process is required at least once per fiscal period.

Online execution (also referred to as foreground mode) of WIP, variance, and settlement transactions needs to be completed at the plant/controlling area level. Another way to handle frequent runs is to set up these transactions to run as batch jobs (also referred to as background mode).

Scheduling background jobs ensures that these jobs are run automatically by the system. Background jobs create output (also known as *spool*) that can be reviewed by the business user.

In addition, these transactions can be resource intensive. Therefore, scheduling them during off-peak hours helps maintain system performance during working hours when there could be a maximum load on the system.

*Background jobs* can be set up using transaction SM36. This transaction can be controlled centrally by BASIS or the batch management team. Specific naming conventions need to be followed, depending on the company's internal processes.

Program names for background runs are:

- WIP—program SAPKKA07BG
- Variance—program RKKKS1N0
- Settlement—program RK07CO88

Variants need to be set up to ensure the jobs run for the desired selection criteria, such as plant, year, period, and parallel processing.

Background jobs can be reviewed using transaction SM37. The following sample job names have been defined for weekly settlement of orders:

- ZCO101_SAPKKA07BG_WIP_WEEKLY
- ZCO102_RKKKS1N0_VAR_WEEKLY
- ZCO103_RK07CO88_SETT_WEEKLY

## 9.6 Reporting in cost object controlling

Apart from individual order display, there are specific mass order display transactions that can be very useful for performing queries on orders:

- MONITOR PRODUCTION / PLANNED ORDERS—production order information system.
- MONITOR PROCESS / PLANNED ORDERS—process order information system.
- ANALYZE SUMMARIZATION HIERARCHY—review the combined costs of multiple orders based on a summarization hierarchy

The PRODUCTION COST ANALYSIS Fiori app provides a financial summary of orders, which enables drilldown into individual orders, as shown in Figure 9.11. Similarly, the SELECT ORDERS app provides greater control of which orders to display in the report. It also provides the ability to drill down into individual order cost details. Various columns are available. You can change the layout by clicking on the ⚙ button to select the fields that match the requirement. Figure 9.13 shows an example of some of the key fields that can be used at the top level of the PRODUCTION COST ANALYSIS report.

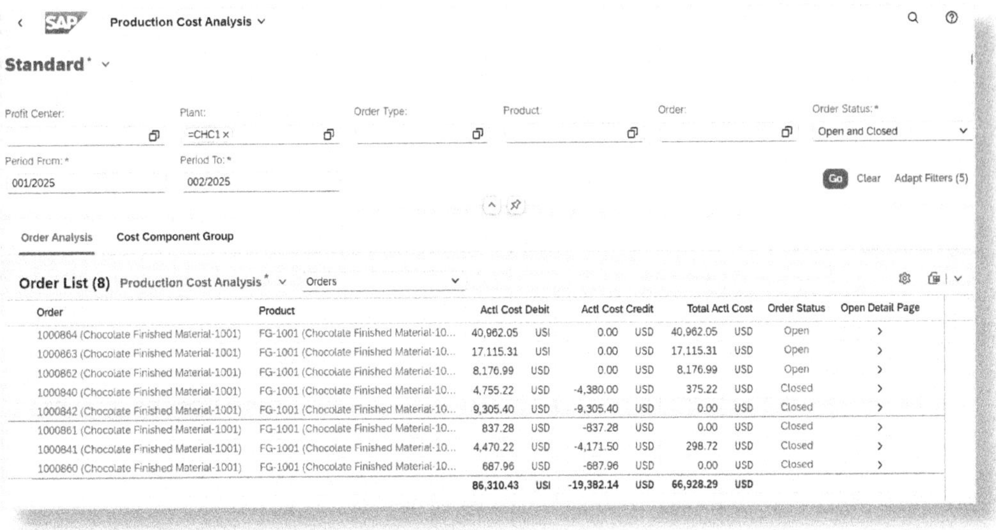


*Figure 9.13: Production Cost Analysis*

Order summarization is another powerful reporting option that is available for orders. First, a summarization hierarchy is maintained to define how the report should look. Several characteristics can be used to define the hierarchy. This includes material, profit center, plant, order type, order status, and many other order characteristics. The summarization hierarchy is maintained using transaction KKR0, under menu path: TOOLS • CUSTOMIZING • IMG • SPRO EXECUTE PROJECT • CONTROLLING • PRODUCT COST CONTROLLING • COST OBJECT CONTROLLING • SETTINGS FOR SUMMARIZED ANALYSIS/ ORDER SELECTION • MAINTAIN SUMMARIZATION HIERARCHIES.

Figure 9.14 shows a summarization report for the hierarchy company code/ plant/order type/material.

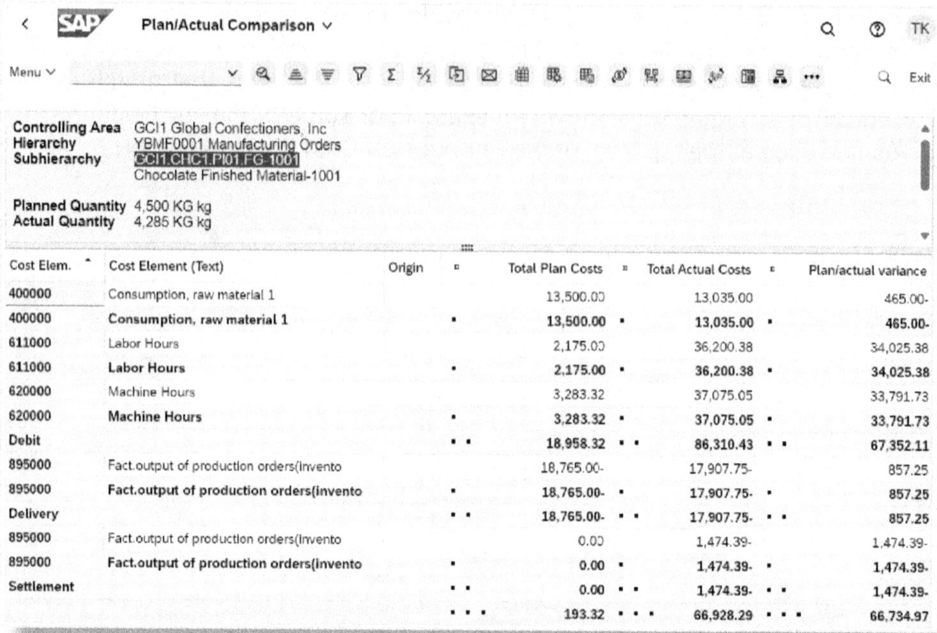


Controlling Area GCI1 Global Confectioners, Inc
Hierarchy YBMF0001 Manufacturing Orders
Subhierarchy GCI1.CHC1.PI01.FG-1001
Chocolate Finished Material-1001

Planned Quantity 4,500 KG kg
Actual Quantity 4,285 KG kg

| Cost Elem. | Cost Element (Text) | Origin | | Total Plan Costs | | Total Actual Costs | | Plan/actual variance |
|---|---|---|---|---|---|---|---|---|
| 400000 | Consumption, raw material 1 | | | 13,500.00 | | 13,035.00 | | 465.00- |
| **400000** | **Consumption, raw material 1** | | • | **13,500.00** | • | **13,035.00** | • | **465.00-** |
| 611000 | Labor Hours | | | 2,175.00 | | 36,200.38 | | 34,025.38 |
| **611000** | **Labor Hours** | | • | **2,175.00** | • | **36,200.38** | • | **34,025.38** |
| 620000 | Machine Hours | | | 3,283.32 | | 37,075.05 | | 33,791.73 |
| **620000** | **Machine Hours** | | • | **3,283.32** | • | **37,075.05** | • | **33,791.73** |
| **Debit** | | | • • | **18,958.32** | • • | **86,310.43** | • • | **67,352.11** |
| 895000 | Fact.output of production orders(invento | | | 18,765.00- | | 17,907.75- | | 857.25 |
| **895000** | **Fact.output of production orders(invento** | | • | **18,765.00-** | • | **17,907.75-** | • | **857.25** |
| **Delivery** | | | • • | **18,765.00-** | • • | **17,907.75-** | • • | **857.25** |
| 895000 | Fact.output of production orders(invento | | | 0.00 | | 1,474.39- | | 1,474.39- |
| **895000** | **Fact.output of production orders(invento** | | • | **0.00** | • | **1,474.39-** | • | **1,474.39-** |
| **Settlement** | | | • • | **0.00** | • • | **1,474.39-** | • • | **1,474.39-** |
| | | | • • • | **193.32** | • • • | **66,928.29** | • • • | **66,734.97** |

*Figure 9.14: Summarization hierarchy analysis for material FG-1001*

# 10 Actual costing and SAP Material Ledger—so this is where the actual costs reside

*"The cost of a thing is the amount of what I will call life, which is required to be exchanged for it, immediately or in the long run."*
—Henry David Thoreau

**Knowing how much a product costs is essential for accurately determining the profitability of a product. However, most decisions are based on the standard cost of the product, because it is often not easy to get an precise picture of the actual cost. Actual costing functionality provided by the Material Ledger component of SAP Controlling bridges this gap. It provides the ability to capture actual costs by tracking variances at material (product) level. This chapter provides an overview of actual costing in SAP Material Ledger.**

Bob walked into Alex's office one morning. "Hey Alex, can you help me look up the actual cost of cocoa butter for last month? Purchasing called me this morning and said that cocoa prices have been volatile for the last few months and will likely go up again. As you know, this is one of the most widely used raw materials in our products and any change in its price is going to have a far-reaching effect on our product costs. We've been asked to provide information on our budget assumption versus what we actually paid for cocoa so far this year. It's possible that we may re-establish the standard for cocoa. Can you please identify the closing inventory quantities so that we can estimate the expected revaluation?"

Alex knew where he could find the budget assumption—it was built into the standard cost of the material, and he could look it up in the MATERIAL MASTER COSTING 2 view. However, he was not sure where he could find the actual price. Alex turned to the user manual to see if he could find an answer. He found this information in the section on *Material Ledger*.

Alex noted that the material ledger provides the functionality to derive actual costs and enables revaluation of inventory to actual costs. "This is exactly the information I was looking for," Alex said to himself and continued to read through the chapter with curiosity.

## 10.1 SAP Material Ledger overview

SAP Material Ledger inventory valuation at actual cost includes the following broad steps:

- Collecting actual data during the month.
- Determining price—accumulating price differences for materials based on the type of transactions performed.
- Calculating periodic unit price at the end of the month.

SAP Material Ledger collects *material movement* data throughout the month. Material movements include goods receipts from purchase orders, goods issues to manufacturing orders, goods receipts from manufacturing orders, and goods issues to deliveries.

Price differences can result from these goods movements. For example, if a purchased material has a standard cost of 1.00 USD per unit but the purchase order price is 1.25 USD per unit, the result is a price difference of 0.25 USD per unit, which is posted to a price difference account. Likewise, when manufacturing orders are settled at the end of the month, any differences that occur because the order debits (goods issues and activity confirmations) do not match the order credits (goods receipts from the order) result in price differences for the manufactured material. These types of variances, which are associated directly with the material, are known as *single-level price differences*. The results of these differences are also pushed up to the next level in the manufacturing supply chain when the material is consumed as a part of an order, stock transport, or customer delivery. This enables the actual value of the components to be included in the actual cost of the next level material. These are known as *multi-level material price differences*.

The *periodic unit price* records the average actual cost for each material—whether procured or produced. The periodic unit price is calculated as part of the period-end closing process for multi-level material determination and includes the combination of single-level and multi-level price differences in the final actual cost of the material.

Additionally, the system calculates an *actual cost component split*. This information enables standard vs. actual or cross-period actual comparison at a more detailed level.

**Actual cost component split**

SAP Material Ledger Actual Costing calculates the breakdown of the actual cost components of labor, material, overhead, sub-contracting, etc. based on the values associated with the single-level and multi-level differences determined for the material.

**! SAP Material Ledger provides details for analysis, but not always the reasons for variances**

The SAP Material Ledger actual cost rollup is not necessarily a substitute for analysis of where and why cost differences have occurred. However, it provides a detailed level of information to efficiently drill down to postings that may have been responsible for a large abnormal/unexpected variance.

The material ledger supports up to three different currency types for valuing inventory. The currency types can point to different currencies or to different valuation views for the local or group currency types. The three valuation views are as follows.

- Legal valuation–the valuation that is used by governments to value inventory, profits, and financial transactions; currency type ending in 0
- Group valuation–the valuation used internally to show true profitability of the enterprise as a whole. Transfer pricing between company codes is automatically eliminated; currency type ending in 1
- Profit center valuation–the view that shows internal profit center performance including transfer pricing between profit centers even within the same company code; currency type ending in 2

The local currency type (10) and group currency type (30) can use these different valuation views. For example, group currency type with the group valuation view can be defined as 31, and local currency type with the profit center valuation view can be defined as 12 when configuring the allowable currencies in FINSC_LEDGER. Using currency type 10 or 30 indicates the legal valuation view.

**! Group currency and group valuation view**

It is easy to confuse group currency and group valuation. *Group currency* is the client-defined currency (transaction SCC4) and is sometimes considered to be the same as the controlling area currency. It can be assigned to all three valuation views: 30 (group, currency legal valuation), 31 (group currency, group valuation), and 32 (group currency, profit center valuation).

*Group valuation view* is a special setting for any currency type that is used for elimination of intercompany profit. For example, currency type 11 refers to local currency with the group valuation view. There is also a currency type that is defined with the controlling area.

Currency type 20 (known as controlling area currency) is obsolete and should not be used. Group currency is normally used instead of controlling area currency.

The settings for all these currency types must be defined at the company code level in FINSC_LEDGER. In order to use group valuation view or profit center valuation view, these must be defined in a currency and valuation profile in configuration. Go to TOOLS • CUSTOMIZING • IMG • SPRO EXECUTE PROJECT • CONTROLLING • GENERAL CONTROLLING • MANAGE MULTIPLE VALUATION APPROACHES/TRANSFER PRICES • BASIC SETTINGS • MAINTAIN CURRENCY AND VALUATION PROFILE.

You can use the material ledger to record inventories in up to three currencies and valuations. The use of this feature does not depend on an actual costing being used. Currency types are assigned to a material ledger type in transaction OMX2. The material ledger type is then assigned to each plant using those currencies (transaction OMX3). Bob informed Alex that GCI uses only two material ledger currencies:

- 10–local currency/legal valuation and
- 30–group currency/legal valuation.

Inventory movement valuations are posted simultaneously in both currencies without having to do a currency conversion at the time of posting. Materials are also simultaneously costed in both currencies. The ACCOUNTING 1 tab of the material shows the standard price and inventory values in all the defined material ledger currencies (see Figure 10.1).

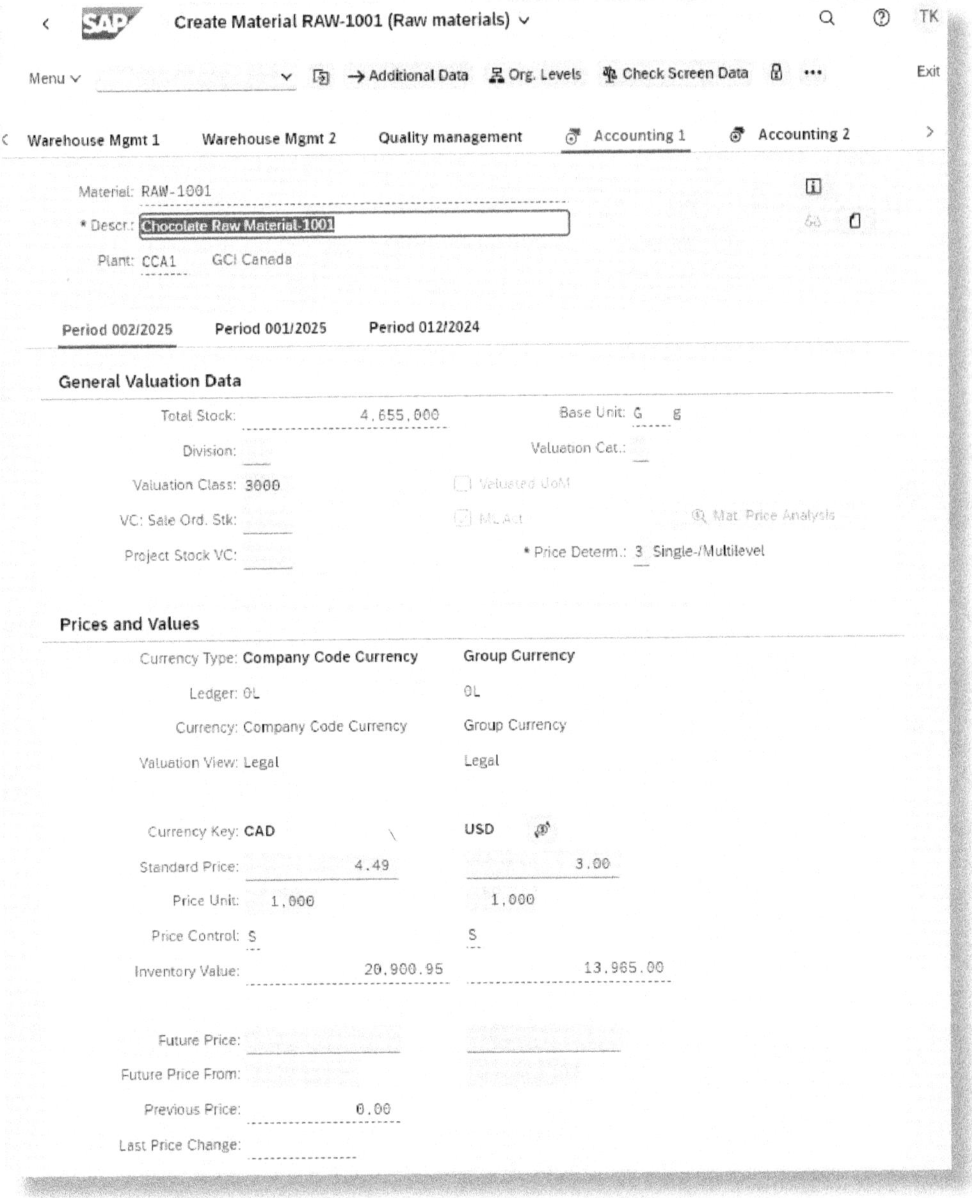

*Figure 10.1: Two currencies—Accounting 1 tab*

The price assigned to the material in CAD is 4.49 per 1,000 G, and the corresponding price in the group currency USD is 3.00 per 1,000 G.

**☛ Material ledger is mandatory—actual costing is not!**

With S/4HANA, price determination must be set to at least 2 (transaction-based) on all valuated materials. Price determination is set to 3 (single-/multilevel) only when actual costing is necessary.

So, even though the material ledger is mandatory with S/4HANA, it should be carefully noted that actual costing is not mandatory and remains optional.

## 10.2 Collecting actual data during the month

The SAP Materials Management module (in combination with the FI module) tracks goods movements and their values at standard cost, while the SAP Material Ledger tracks goods movement values at standard and actual costs. In other words, SAP Material Ledger can be considered a second set of books where each material has a record of all goods movements for actual valuation.

All relevant inventory activity from SAP is posted to the material ledger:

- Inventory movements are reflected in the material ledger as goods movement transactions occur (e.g., movement type 101 for goods receipt, 261 for goods issue, 551 for scrapping, 701 for cycle counts, 601 for sales, 201 for consumption at cost center, etc.).
- Price variances are reflected as they occur (e.g., goods receipt records standard price versus purchase order price; invoice receipt records purchase order price versus invoice price).
- Production variances are reflected at the time of process/production order settlement.
- Revaluation differences are reflected at the time of standard changes (e.g., at the beginning of the year or beginning of the month).

Figure 10.2 shows the MATERIAL PRICE ANALYSIS app.

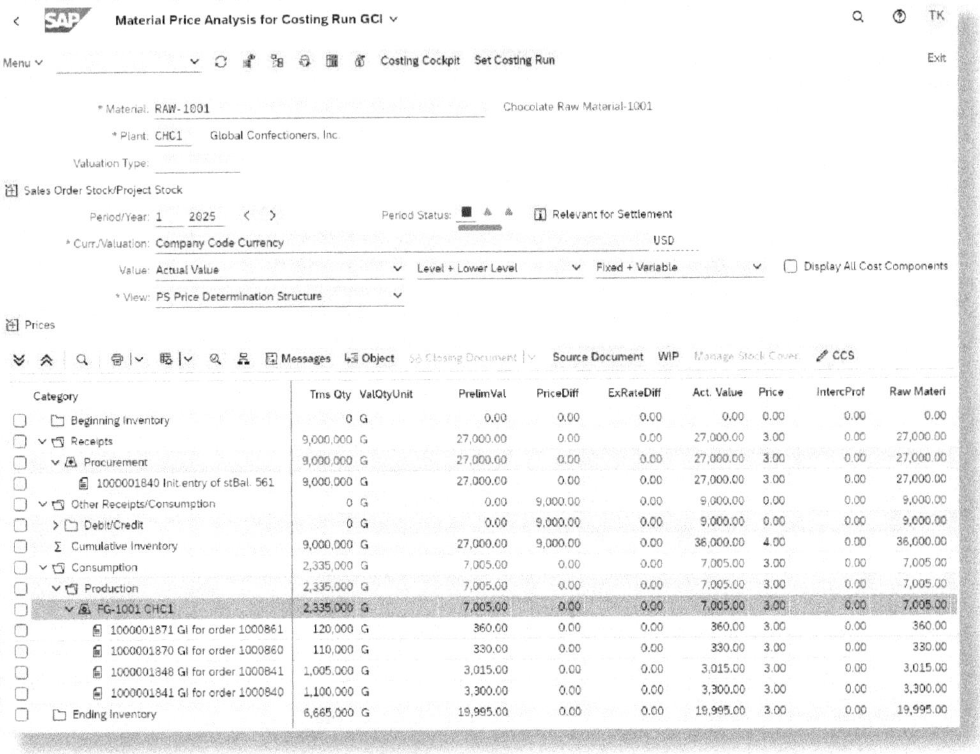


*Figure 10.2: Price analysis of raw material prior to closing SAP Material Ledger*

Material RAW-1001 had a BEGINNING INVENTORY of 0 grams. 9,000 grams were added to inventory during the month. Under CONSUMPTION, we see that 2,335 grams were consumed during the month, leaving an ENDING INVENTORY of 6,665 grams. All the transactions occurred at the standard PRICE of $3.00 per 1,000 grams. However, there is one entry under DEBIT/CREDIT for an amount of $9,000.00 that drove the actual cost up to $4.00 per 1,000 grams, as shown under CUMULATIVE INVENTORY in the report. Each goods movement transaction was reflected in this transaction. Users can navigate to the actual source document; for example, an inventory movement transaction, price change, or settlement.

Figure 10.3 shows a finished material with an opening inventory of 0 kilograms, and we can see that 2,255 kilograms were produced during the month.

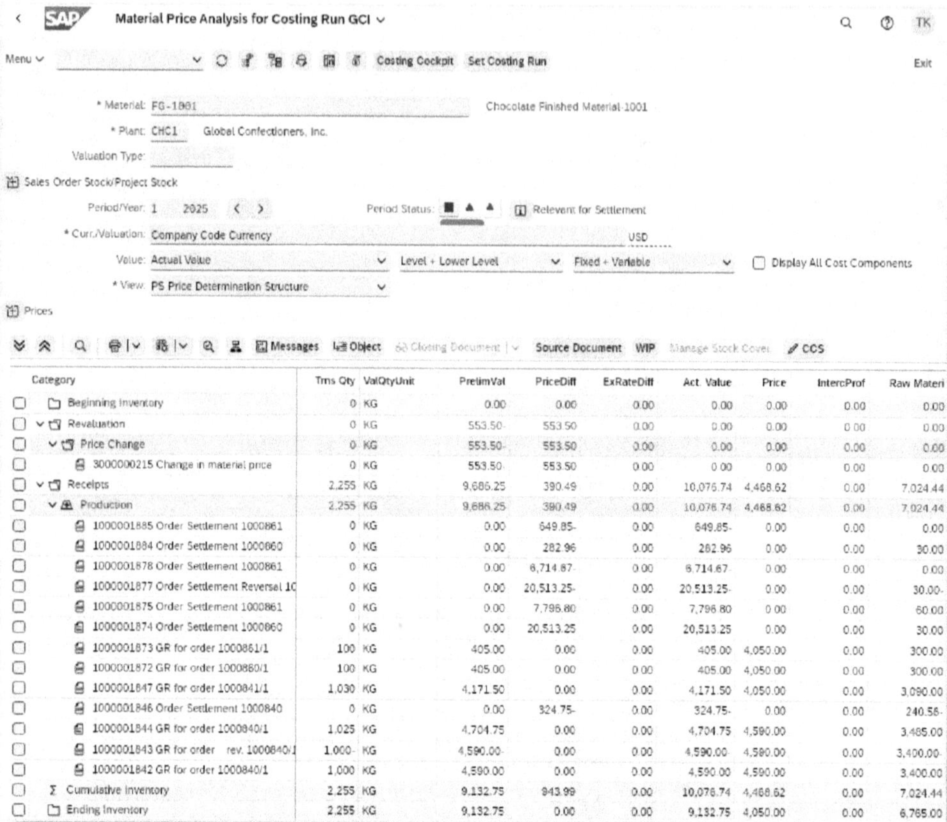


| Category | Trns Qty | ValQtyUnit | PrelimVal | PriceDiff | ExRateDiff | Act. Value | Price | IntercProf | Raw Materi |
|---|---|---|---|---|---|---|---|---|---|
| Beginning Inventory | 0 | KG | 0.00 | 0.00 | 0.00 | 0.00 | 0.00 | 0.00 | 0.00 |
| Revaluation | 0 | KG | 553.50- | 553.50 | 0.00 | 0.00 | 0.00 | 0.00 | 0.00 |
| Price Change | 0 | KG | 553.50- | 553.50 | 0.00 | 0.00 | 0.00 | 0.00 | 0.00 |
| 3000000215 Change in material price | 0 | KG | 553.50- | 553.50 | 0.00 | 0.00 | 0.00 | 0.00 | 0.00 |
| Receipts | 2,255 | KG | 9,686.25 | 390.49 | 0.00 | 10,076.74 | 4,468.62 | 0.00 | 7,024.44 |
| Production | 2,255 | KG | 9,686.25 | 390.49 | 0.00 | 10,076.74 | 4,468.62 | 0.00 | 7,024.44 |
| 1000001885 Order Settlement 1000861 | 0 | KG | 0.00 | 649.85- | 0.00 | 649.85- | 0.00 | 0.00 | 0.00 |
| 1000001884 Order Settlement 1000860 | 0 | KG | 0.00 | 282.96 | 0.00 | 282.96 | 0.00 | 0.00 | 30.00 |
| 1000001878 Order Settlement 1000861 | 0 | KG | 0.00 | 6,714.67- | 0.00 | 6,714.67- | 0.00 | 0.00 | 0.00 |
| 1000001877 Order Settlement Reversal 10 | 0 | KG | 0.00 | 20,513.25- | 0.00 | 20,513.25- | 0.00 | 0.00 | 30.00- |
| 1000001875 Order Settlement 1000861 | 0 | KG | 0.00 | 7,796.80 | 0.00 | 7,796.80 | 0.00 | 0.00 | 60.00 |
| 1000001874 Order Settlement 1000860 | 0 | KG | 0.00 | 20,513.25 | 0.00 | 20,513.25 | 0.00 | 0.00 | 30.00 |
| 1000001873 GR for order 1000861/1 | 100 | KG | 405.00 | 0.00 | 0.00 | 405.00 | 4,050.00 | 0.00 | 300.00 |
| 1000001872 GR for order 1000860/1 | 100 | KG | 405.00 | 0.00 | 0.00 | 405.00 | 4,050.00 | 0.00 | 300.00 |
| 1000001847 GR for order 1000841/1 | 1,030 | KG | 4,171.50 | 0.00 | 0.00 | 4,171.50 | 4,050.00 | 0.00 | 3,090.00 |
| 1000001846 Order Settlement 1000840 | 0 | KG | 0.00 | 324.75- | 0.00 | 324.75- | 0.00 | 0.00 | 240.56- |
| 1000001844 GR for order 1000840/1 | 1,025 | KG | 4,704.75 | 0.00 | 0.00 | 4,704.75 | 4,590.00 | 0.00 | 3,485.00 |
| 1000001843 GR for order rev. 1000840/1 | 1,000- | KG | 4,590.00- | 0.00 | 0.00 | 4,590.00- | 4,590.00 | 0.00 | 3,400.00- |
| 1000001842 GR for order 1000840/1 | 1,000 | KG | 4,590.00 | 0.00 | 0.00 | 4,590.00 | 4,590.00 | 0.00 | 3,400.00 |
| Cumulative Inventory | 2,255 | KG | 9,132.75 | 943.99 | 0.00 | 10,076.74 | 4,468.62 | 0.00 | 7,024.44 |
| Ending Inventory | 2,255 | KG | 9,132.75 | 0.00 | 0.00 | 9,132.75 | 4,050.00 | 0.00 | 6,765.00 |

*Figure 10.3: Price analysis of finished material prior to closing SAP Material Ledger*

Alex noticed price differences under the PRICEDIFF column for many of the rows. If there had been inventory quantity at the beginning of the month, a price difference would have been displayed, accounting for price differences remaining in inventory from the previous period.

## 10.3 Price determination

In normal manufacturing operations, where most materials are valued with a price control *S* (standard price), *single-level* and *multilevel* price determination is used. This is denoted as PRICE DETERM. (price determination)

ID 3 on the ACCOUNTING 1 tab of the material master. With materials such as plant maintenance supplies that are usually valued with price control *V* (moving average price), there is no requirement to roll up the differences in the next level material—*transaction based price determination* is used. This is price determination ID 2. Materials with price control *S* can also have the price determination set to 2. Those materials are not included in the actual cost calculations. Usually, price determination 2 is only assigned to *S* materials if actual costing is not enabled for the plant.

Transaction-based price determination uses the value of the material in the goods movement as the sole basis of the price. For materials with price control *V*, this includes any variances incurred as part of the goods movement. For materials with price control *S*, no differences are included as part of the final valuation of the material. Because of this:

- material is not eligible to be included in an actual costing run,
- single-level price differences cannot be included in material valuation, and
- material cannot receive multi-level price differences and it cannot allocate price differences to the next level.

The other price determination method is *single-level/multilevel price determination*. The material master uses ID 3 for price determination on the ACCOUNTING 1 tab. Two sources of differences are assigned to the material during the actual costing run:

- *Single-level price determination*—prices are calculated for each individual material:
  - Purchased material = standard price +/- price variance from purchases
  - Produced material = standard price +/- variances from process/production order
- *Multi-level price determination*—prices are calculated for the entire production stream (e.g., when rolling up all components or ingredients into a produced material):
  - Price variances from purchased ingredients
  - Production variances for manufactured ingredients

Materials using price determination 3 must use price control *S*.

## 10.4 Periodic unit price

The *periodic unit price* is the average actual cost of a material in a given period. It is calculated based on the CUMULATIVE INVENTORY line in the MATERIAL PRICE ANALYSIS app:

- Periodic unit price = (standard cost of cumulative inventory +/- variances of cumulative inventory) / cumulative inventory.

As shown in Figure 10.4, a standard cost of $3.00 was used for goods movements during the month.

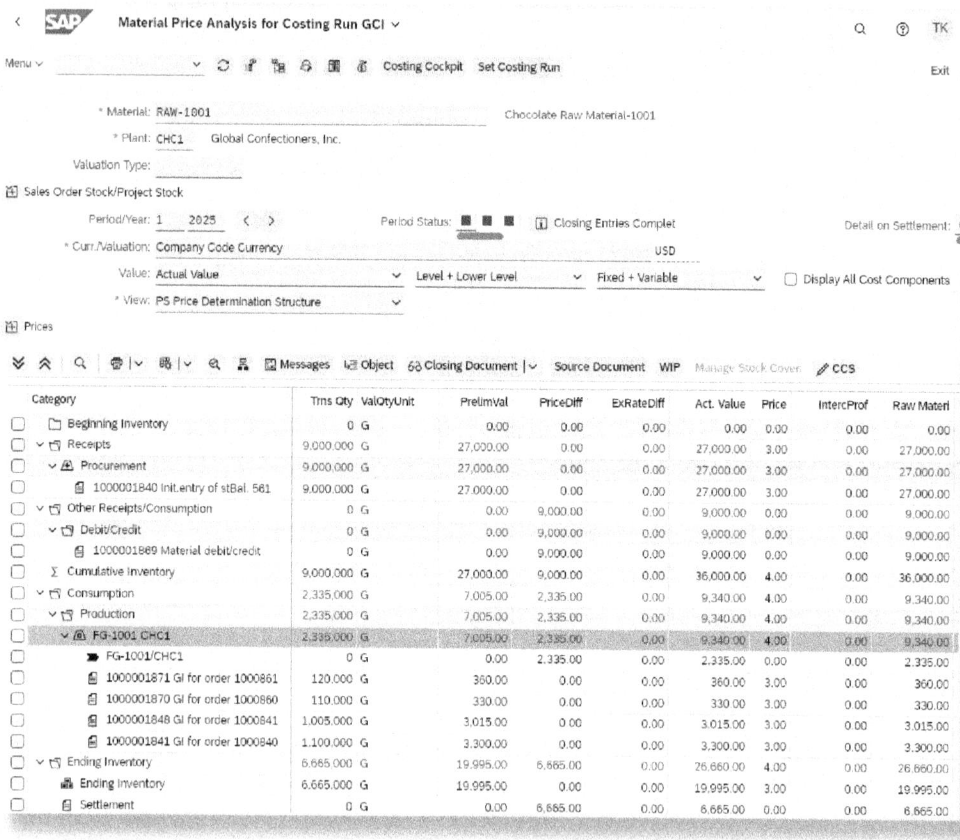


| Category | Trns Qty | ValQtyUnit | PrelimVal | PriceDiff | ExRateDiff | Act. Value | Price | IntercProf | Raw Materi |
|---|---|---|---|---|---|---|---|---|---|
| Beginning Inventory | 0 | G | 0.00 | 0.00 | 0.00 | 0.00 | 0.00 | 0.00 | 0.00 |
| Receipts | 9.000.000 | G | 27,000.00 | 0.00 | 0.00 | 27,000.00 | 3.00 | 0.00 | 27,000.00 |
| Procurement | 9,000,000 | G | 27,000.00 | 0.00 | 0.00 | 27,000.00 | 3.00 | 0.00 | 27,000.00 |
| 1000001840 Init.entry of stBal. 561 | 9.000.000 | G | 27.000.00 | 0.00 | 0.00 | 27.000.00 | 3.00 | 0.00 | 27.000.00 |
| Other Receipts/Consumption | 0 | G | 0.00 | 9,000.00 | 0.00 | 9,000.00 | 0.00 | 0.00 | 9.000.00 |
| Debit/Credit | 0 | G | 0.00 | 9,000.00 | 0.00 | 9,000.00 | 0.00 | 0.00 | 9,000.00 |
| 1000001869 Material debit/credit | 0 | G | 0.00 | 9.000.00 | 0.00 | 9.000.00 | 0.00 | 0.00 | 9.000.00 |
| Cumulative Inventory | 9,000,000 | G | 27,000.00 | 9,000.00 | 0.00 | 36,000.00 | 4.00 | 0.00 | 36,000.00 |
| Consumption | 2,335,000 | G | 7,005.00 | 2,335.00 | 0.00 | 9,340.00 | 4.00 | 0.00 | 9.340.00 |
| Production | 2,335,000 | G | 7,005.00 | 2,335.00 | 0.00 | 9,340.00 | 4.00 | 0.00 | 9,340.00 |
| FG-1001 CHC1 | 2,335,000 | G | 7,005.00 | 2,335.00 | 0.00 | 9,340.00 | 4.00 | 0.00 | 9,340.00 |
| FG-1001/CHC1 | 0 | G | 0.00 | 2.335.00 | 0.00 | 2.335.00 | 0.00 | 0.00 | 2.335.00 |
| 1000001871 GI for order 1000861 | 120.000 | G | 360.00 | 0.00 | 0.00 | 360.00 | 3.00 | 0.00 | 360.00 |
| 1000001870 GI for order 1000860 | 110.000 | G | 330.00 | 0.00 | 0.00 | 330.00 | 3.00 | 0.00 | 330.00 |
| 1000001848 GI for order 1000841 | 1,005.000 | G | 3,015.00 | 0.00 | 0.00 | 3.015.00 | 3.00 | 0.00 | 3.015.00 |
| 1000001841 GI for order 1000840 | 1.100.000 | G | 3.300.00 | 0.00 | 0.00 | 3,300.00 | 3.00 | 0.00 | 3.300.00 |
| Ending Inventory | 6.665.000 | G | 19.995.00 | 6,665.00 | 0.00 | 26,660.00 | 4.00 | 0.00 | 26.660.00 |
| Ending Inventory | 6.665.000 | G | 19.995.00 | 0.00 | 0.00 | 19,995.00 | 3.00 | 0.00 | 19.995.00 |
| Settlement | 0 | G | 0.00 | 6,665.00 | 0.00 | 6.665.00 | 0.00 | 0.00 | 6.665.00 |

*Figure 10.4: Price analysis of raw material after closing SAP Material Ledger*

A price variance of $9,000.00 for the given quantity of 9,000 grams (a variance of $1.00 per 1,000 grams) resulted in a periodic unit price of $4.00 per 1,000 grams. For the consumption of 2,335 grams, the material ledger transferred the variance of $2,335 to the next level material. Additionally, a periodic unit price of $4.00 per 1,000 grams was used to value the ENDING INVENTORY of 6,665 grams at $26,660.00 after completion of the actual costing run.

The actual value of the material at the end of period 1 has been carried over into period 2 (see Figure 10.5).

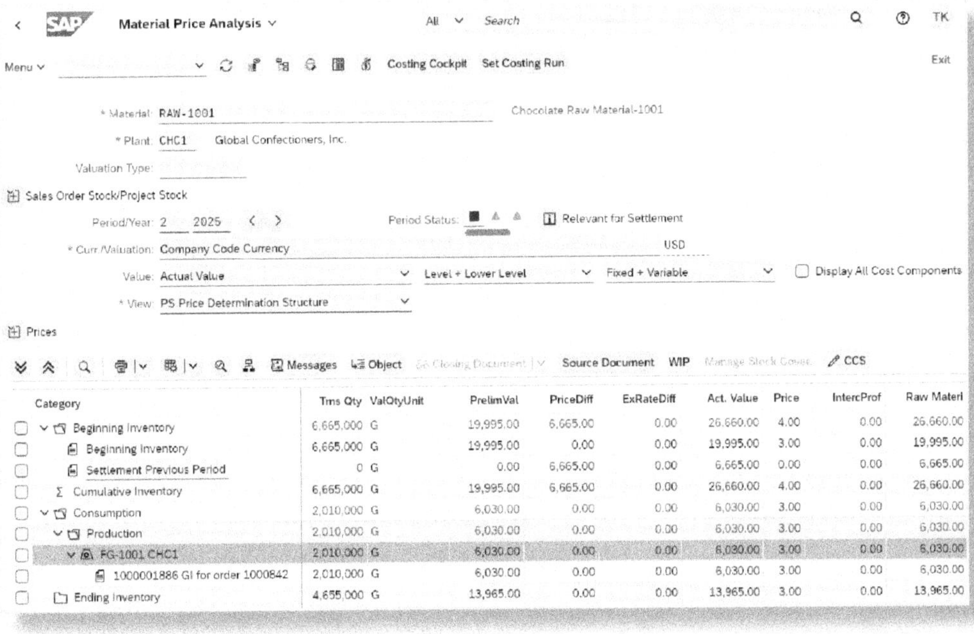


| Category | Trns Qty | ValQtyUnit | PrelimVal | PriceDiff | ExRateDiff | Act. Value | Price | IntercProf | Raw Materi |
|---|---|---|---|---|---|---|---|---|---|
| Beginning Inventory | 6,665,000 | G | 19,995.00 | 6,665.00 | 0.00 | 26,660.00 | 4.00 | 0.00 | 26,660.00 |
| Beginning Inventory | 6,665,000 | G | 19,995.00 | 0.00 | 0.00 | 19,995.00 | 3.00 | 0.00 | 19,995.00 |
| Settlement Previous Period | 0 | G | 0.00 | 6,665.00 | 0.00 | 6,665.00 | 0.00 | 0.00 | 6,665.00 |
| Cumulative Inventory | 6,665,000 | G | 19,995.00 | 6,665.00 | 0.00 | 26,660.00 | 4.00 | 0.00 | 26,660.00 |
| Consumption | 2,010,000 | G | 6,030.00 | 0.00 | 0.00 | 6,030.00 | 3.00 | 0.00 | 6,030.00 |
| Production | 2,010,000 | G | 6,030.00 | 0.00 | 0.00 | 6,030.00 | 3.00 | 0.00 | 6,030.00 |
| FG-1001 CHC1 | 2,010,000 | G | 6,030.00 | 0.00 | 0.00 | 6,030.00 | 3.00 | 0.00 | 6,030.00 |
| 1000001886 GI for order 1000842 | 2,010,000 | G | 6,030.00 | 0.00 | 0.00 | 6,030.00 | 3.00 | 0.00 | 6,030.00 |
| Ending Inventory | 4,655,000 | G | 13,965.00 | 0.00 | 0.00 | 13,965.00 | 3.00 | 0.00 | 13,965.00 |

*Figure 10.5: Material Price Analysis—Raw material for period 2*

A price difference of $6,665.00 is included in the beginning inventory shown in the SETTLEMENT PREVIOUS PERIOD line of the report. Although all movements during the period are valued at the standard $3.00 per 1,000 grams, the actual value of $4.00 from the previous period is factored into the calculation of the actual value for period 2.

When the POST CLOSE step of the actual costing run is executed, a change appears on the ACCOUNTING 1 tab of the material master. Alex compared the values for material RAW-1001 for period 2, 2025 and period 1, 2025.

Both of these periods can be viewed within the ACCOUNTING 1 tab. PERIOD 002/2025 shows the values for the current period (see Figure 10.6).

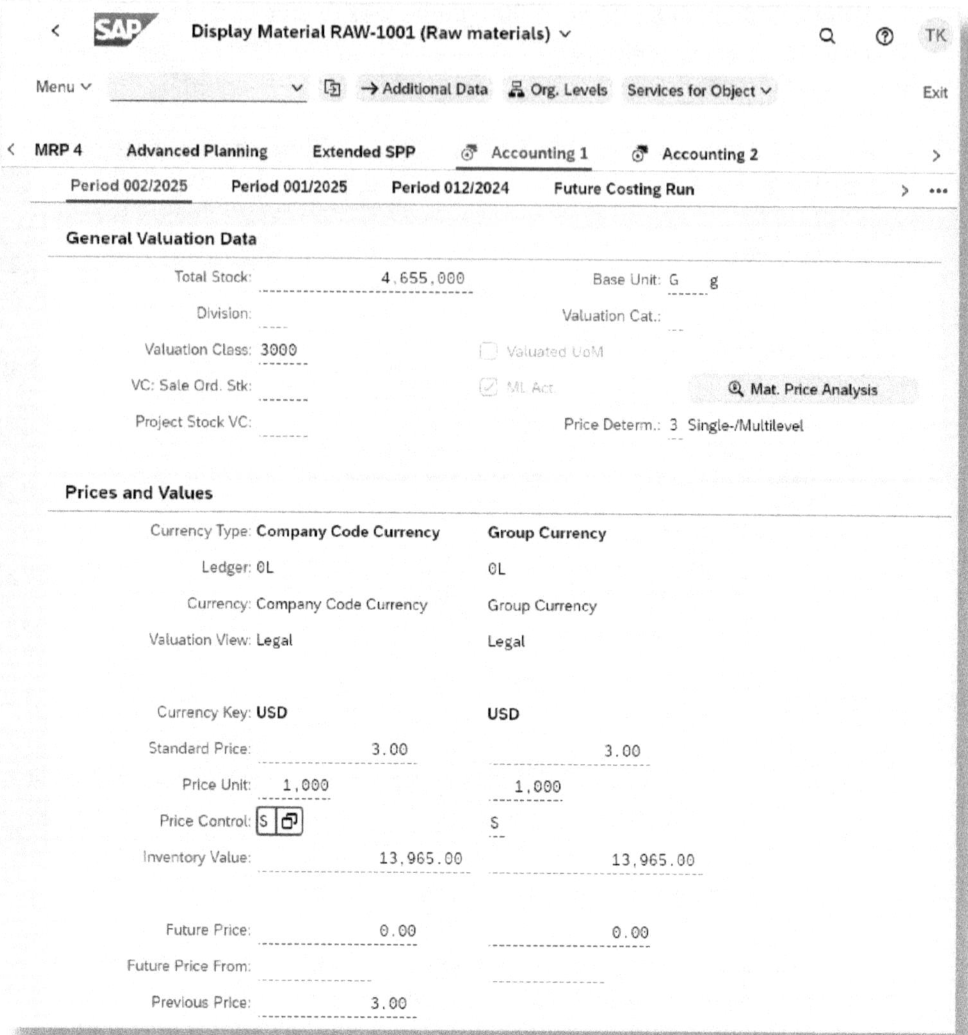


*Figure 10.6: Display Material—current period Accounting 1 tab*

Alex noted that the price control was set to *S* for standard price. He then opened the PERIOD 001/2025 tab (see Figure 10.7).

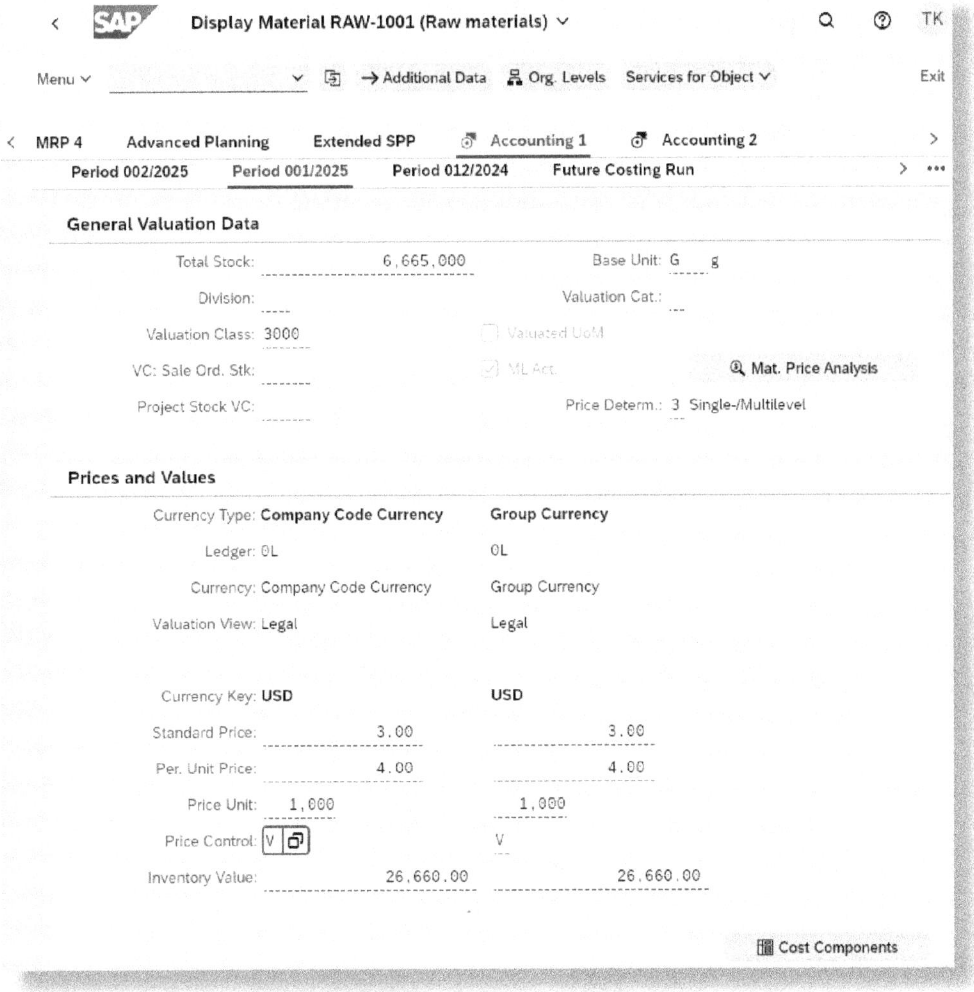

Figure 10.7: Display Material—previous period Accounting 1 tab

After the actual costing run settled the price differences, the price control was set to *V* (moving average). He asked Bob why this happened. Bob said that because the actual price was different than the standard price for the period, the price control could not be set to *S*, and after factoring in the price differences posted throughout the month, the actual price behaved more like a moving average. That is why the system set the previous period price control to *V*.

Alex also noted that in the previous period he could see the periodic unit price ($4.00 per 1,000 grams). This is not shown for the current period and is only displayed after the actual price for the period has been calculated.

Alex also looked at the price analysis for the finished material. He saw that a price difference of $2,335 was transferred from the lower level (RAW-1001) as a multi-level price difference (see Figure 10.8).

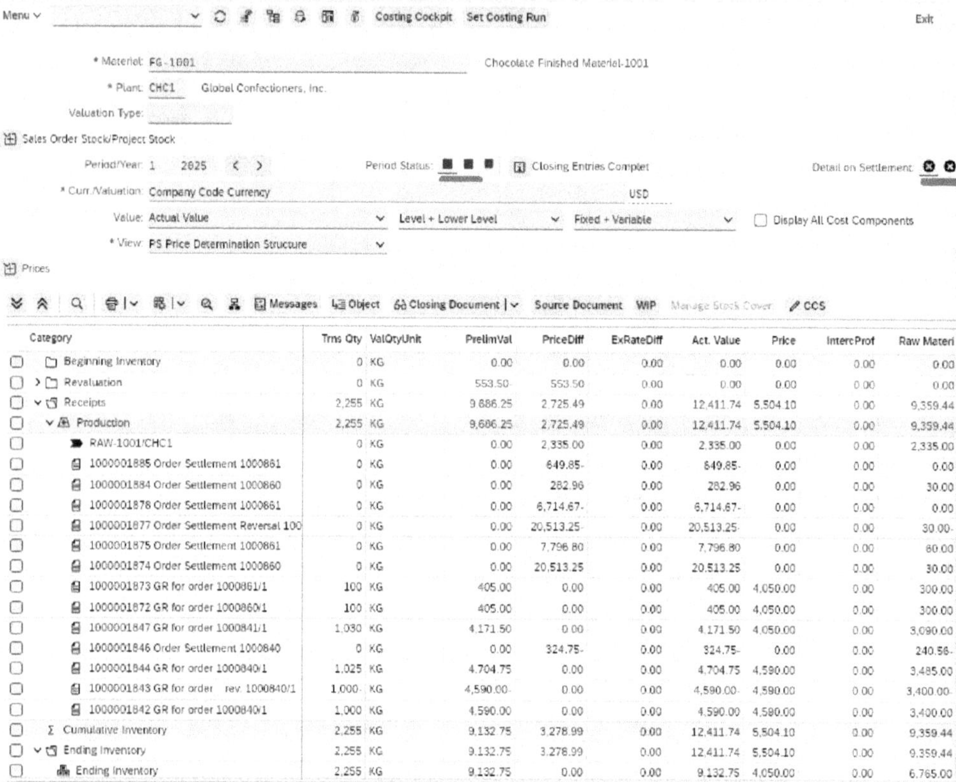


*Figure 10.8: Material Price Analysis—Price analysis finished material after SAP Material Ledger close*

In addition, variances relating to process order settlement ($2,725.49) were recorded as a single-level price difference. At the cumulative inventory level, all the variances were added up and divided by the cumulative inventory, and the periodic unit price was calculated as $5,504.10. This actual price was used to value closing inventory and transfer the revaluation of consumption to the cost center.

## 10.5 SAP Material Ledger closing cockpit

The SAP Material Ledger closing cockpit is run every month to perform actual costing using the Edit Actual Costing Runs Fiori app.

The first step is to create a costing run and assign relevant plants to the costing run. Figure 10.9 shows an example of an actual costing run for Period 1, 2025, with plant CHC1 assigned. There could be several plants attached to this costing run, depending on the material ledger footprint and business requirements.

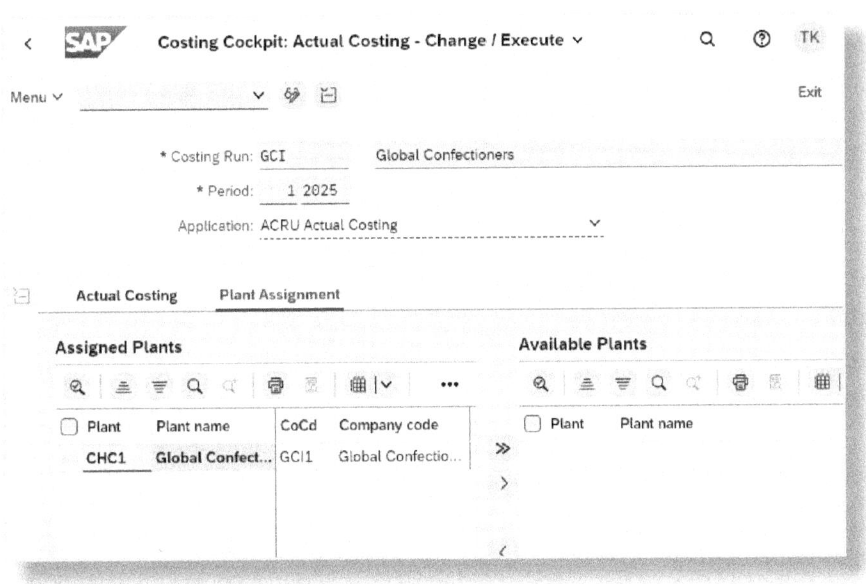


*Figure 10.9: "Edit Actual Costing Runs" app—Material Ledger closing cockpit plant selection*

> **Transparency across the value chain**
>
> For SAP Material Ledger to transfer multi-level variances (and therefore actual costs) between plants, it is essential that the plants involved in interplant goods movement are closed in the same material ledger closing run.

After selecting the plant(s), the material ledger closing cockpit requires several steps. These steps should be performed in the same sequence shown in Figure 10.10.

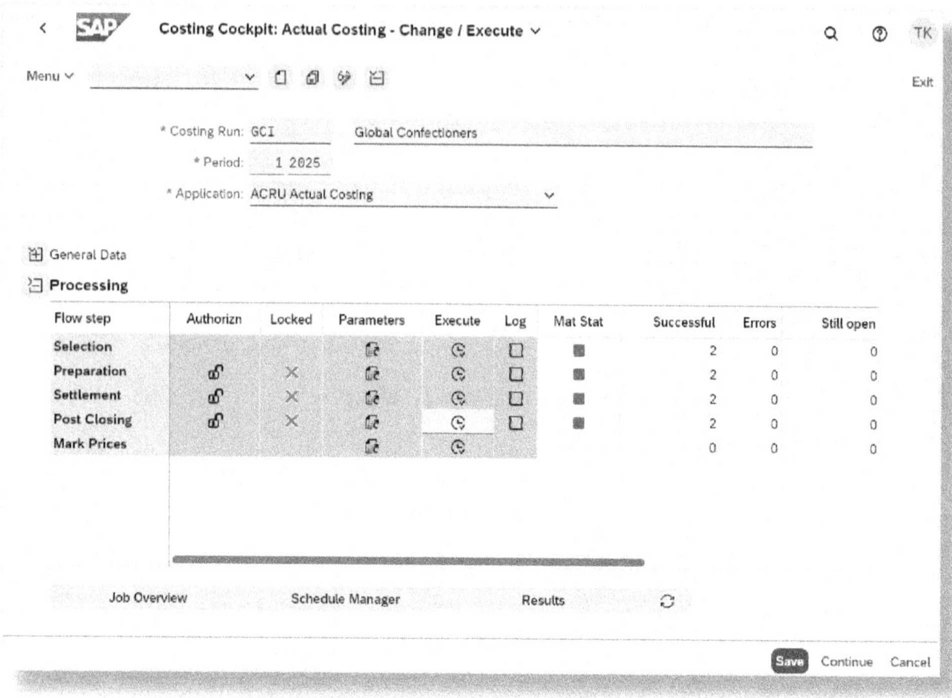


*Figure 10.10: "Edit Actual Costing Runs" app—SAP Material Ledger closing cockpit process steps*

The steps are as follows:

1. SELECTION—all materials for the given plants are selected.
2. PREPARATION—sequence of costing is established, starting with the lowest level material going all the way up to the highest-level material and goods movement.
3. SETTLEMENT—differences are determined and passed on to the next level where appropriate. Prices are calculated for each selected material.
4. POST CLOSING—all calculations performed in the previous steps are posted during this step:
    - Revaluation of consumption is posted to cost objects.
    - Inventory is revalued in FI for the period being closed.
5. MARK PRICES—this step is optional. An organization may decide not to use the periodic unit price as a standard for the upcoming month. If so, this step is skipped, and the system uses standard price for goods movement and revalues at periodic unit price only at month end.

**Actual costing calculation steps can be run multiple times**

Each of the calculation steps can be performed as many times as necessary. However, the post-closing step is performed only once in non-test mode. Reversal of the post-closing step is possible but should be carried out only when absolutely necessary.

## 10.6 Reporting in SAP Material Ledger

SAP has provided several reports that help display and analyze the results of actual costing. To make sure he was fully able to answer Bob's request, Alex made a list of useful reports, and he divided that list into reports for single materials and reports for multiple materials.

### 10.6.1 Reports for single materials

**"Material Price Analysis" app**

Alex had already looked at results using the report from the Material Price Analysis Fiori app, which was seen earlier in this chapter. He decided to list the important fields available so that he could better understand what could be seen in the report:

- TRNS. QTY—quantity in the displayed unit of measure
- VALQTYUNIT—base unit of measure
- PRELIMVAL—standard value (quantity multiplied by standard cost)
- PRICE DIFF—total variance amount
- EXRATEDIFF—variance amount associated with exchange rates
- PRICE—actual material cost per price unit (actual value / quantity)
- ACT.VALUE—prelimVal +/- price diff = actual value of the activity (quantity multiplied by periodic unit price)
- CURR—currency (local / group)
- COST COMPONENTS—displays cost broken down into the individual cost components (one column per cost component)

A great feature of this report is that Alex could scroll through multiple months of costing results to help him answer Bob's questions. See Figure 10.2, Figure 10.3, Figure 10.4, and Figure 10.5.

### Material Costs and Inventory Values report

This report tracks the value of a single material across multiple periods. An example of this report is shown in Figure 10.11. Alex was able to use this to show Bob the historical progress of the actual cocoa butter costs over several periods.

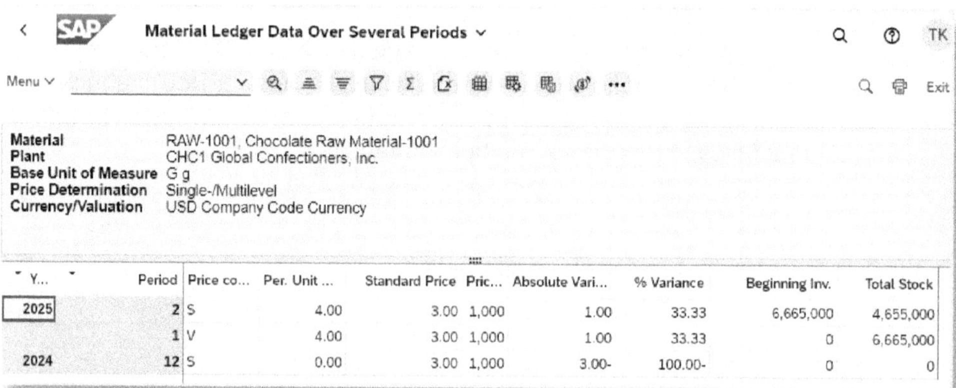


*Figure 10.11: Material Costs and Inventory Values report*

### Transaction MLCCSPD

This report shows the details of the cost component splits for the material, including both actual and standard costs (see Figure 10.12). Although the actual cost component split is shown on the MATERIAL PRICE ANALYSIS report, this provides an easy-to-read snapshot, by period, of the actual (periodic unit price) and standard values assigned to the cost components. The cost component split values can be viewed by costing lot size, price unit, period inventory quantity, and by a user-entered quantity. Alex was able to use this report for finished goods, that used cocoa butter, to show Bob the effect of the raw material prices on the finished goods.

The menu path for this transaction is ACCOUNTING • CONTROLLING • PRODUCT COST CONTROLLING • ACTUAL COSTING/MATERIAL LEDGER • INFORMATION SYSTEM • DETAILED REPORTS • COST COMPONENTS FOR PRICE.

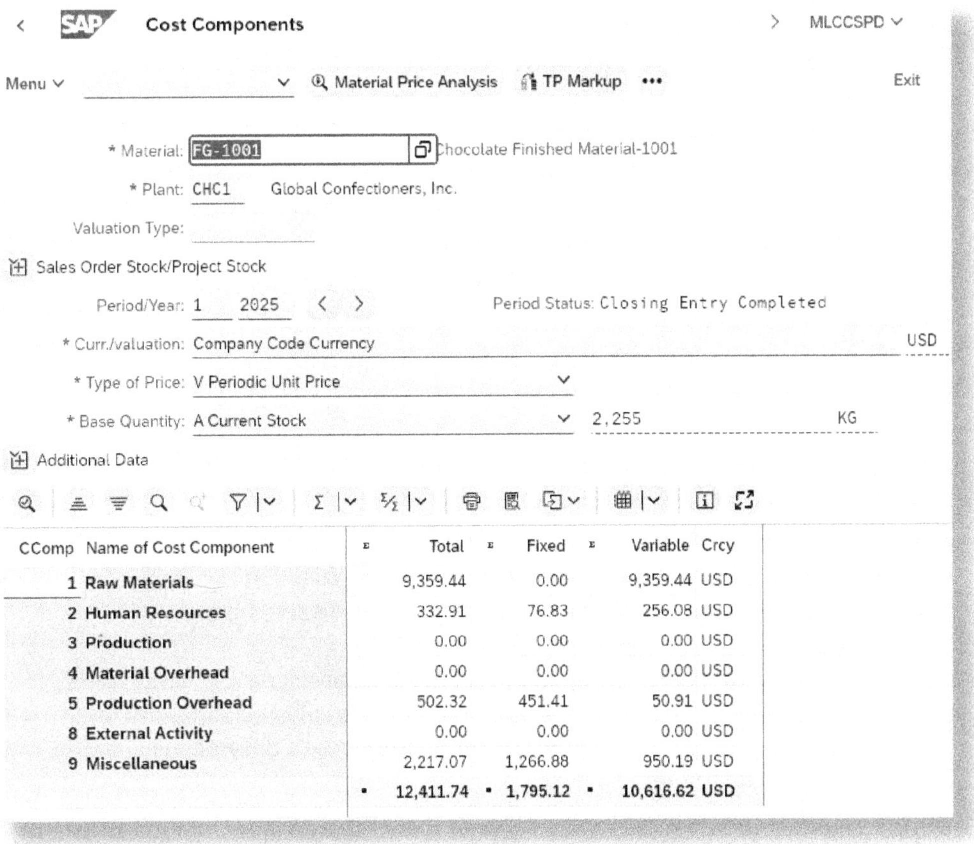


*Figure 10.12: MLCCSPD report—current stock levels*

## 10.6.2 Reports for multiple materials

### Display Actual Costing Results report

The Display Actual Costing Results report shows the prices, actual inventory values, and standard inventory values for multiple materials in a given month (see Figure 10.13). Alex was able to use this report to not only show the cocoa cost differences, but by including the main finished goods using the cocoa, he was able to show the raw material's cost impact for those goods as well.

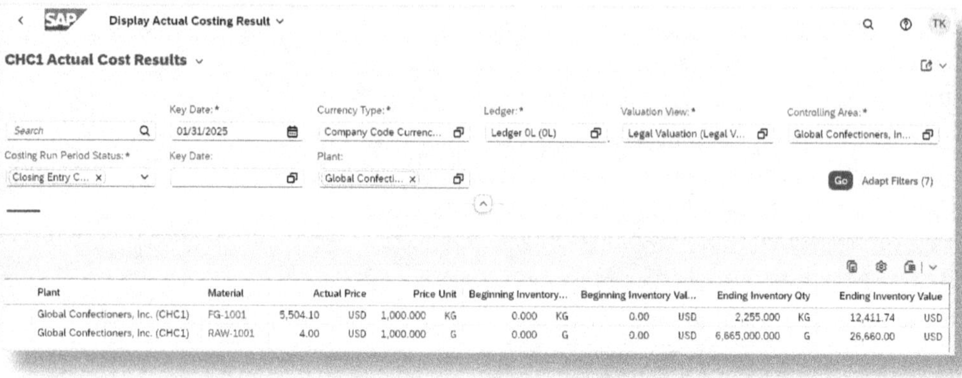


*Figure 10.13: Display Actual Costing Results report*

**Material Value Flow Monitor**

The Material Value Flow monitor is a report that is used in conjunction with the execution of the actual costing run. It helps highlight areas where cost differences are not being fully accounted for in the final results.

*Not distributed* costs are those differences which cannot be sent to the next level because the cumulative inventory of the material is less than the material quantities associated with the differences. Excess differences should not be passed on to the next level.

*Not allocated* costs are those that cannot be passed on because the next level material is not set up for actual costing. This can also be seen for activity types when the actual activity prices are defined to be allocated to manufacturing orders instead of being handled as a part of the actual costing run.

The configuration setting at GCI for processing activity type price differences tells the system to allocate activity price differences to orders, instead of allocating them as part of the actual costing run. For this reason, all differences associated with actual activity prices will not be passed directly to the material in the costing run. Figure 10.14 shows these non-allocated values for activity types MCHRS and LABOR for cost center C51100.

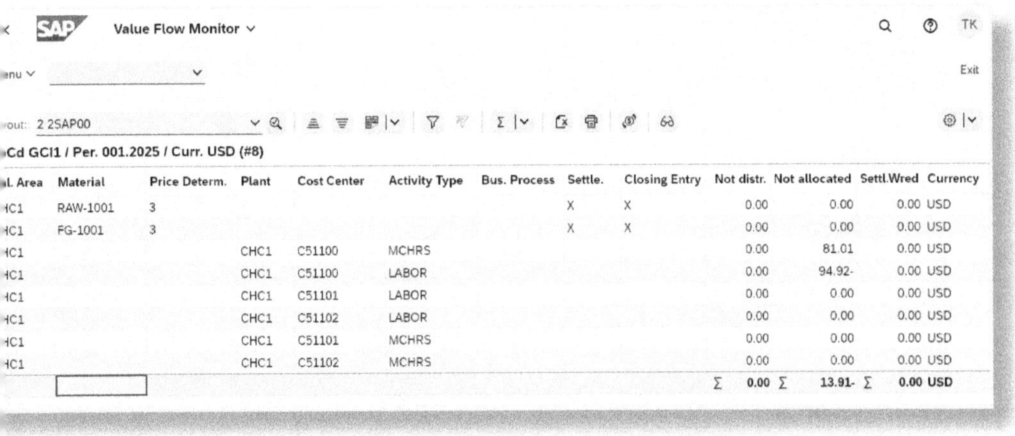

Value Flow Monitor

Cd GCI1 / Per. 001.2025 / Curr. USD (#8)

| l. Area | Material | Price Determ. | Plant | Cost Center | Activity Type | Bus. Process | Settle. | Closing Entry | Not distr. | Not allocated | Settl.Wred | Currency |
|---|---|---|---|---|---|---|---|---|---|---|---|---|
| HC1 | RAW-1001 | 3 | | | | | X | X | 0.00 | 0.00 | 0.00 | USD |
| HC1 | FG-1001 | 3 | | | | | X | X | 0.00 | 0.00 | 0.00 | USD |
| HC1 | | | CHC1 | C51100 | MCHRS | | | | 0.00 | 81.01 | 0.00 | USD |
| HC1 | | | CHC1 | C51100 | LABOR | | | | 0.00 | 94.92- | 0.00 | USD |
| HC1 | | | CHC1 | C51101 | LABOR | | | | 0.00 | 0.00 | 0.00 | USD |
| HC1 | | | CHC1 | C51102 | LABOR | | | | 0.00 | 0.00 | 0.00 | USD |
| HC1 | | | CHC1 | C51101 | MCHRS | | | | 0.00 | 0.00 | 0.00 | USD |
| HC1 | | | CHC1 | C51102 | MCHRS | | | | 0.00 | 0.00 | 0.00 | USD |
| | | | | | | | | | Σ 0.00 | Σ 13.91- | Σ 0.00 | USD |

*Figure 10.14: Material Value Flow Monitor report*

Having reviewed this report, Alex was assured that all cost differences from the cocoa were flowing up through the supply chain, and that these differences were accounted for in the finished products.

# 11 Margin (profitability) analysis—are we making any money at all?

*"There was a small typing error in our Half-Year Results Statement. For 'profit' please read 'loss'."*

—Ex – CFO.

**Alex walked into the meeting room one morning after being summoned by Bob, his manager and the plant controller at Chocotown. Bob had called an urgent meeting on short notice and wanted everyone to attend—Carl, the manufacturing manager; Dave, the inventory controller; and Erin, the finance IT support lead.**

"Corporate has been researching the profitability of the product line that we introduced last quarter," announced Bob, "and they're telling me the product is not profitable."

"That can't be right," Carl replied. "We produced the material below the standard cost and all our variances have been favorable."

"And our inventory has been under control," said Dave.

"I understand what you're saying," said Bob, "but it is not only about cost. Plus, the inventory levels don't affect profitability."

Dave was confused, "Well, I was told that I have to keep inventory in check so that our costs are lower."

Alex intervened, "That's correct, but product profitability and inventory are not directly linked. There's a cost of carrying the inventory, but this cost is more related to locking working capital."

"Alex is right," Erin interjected. "Inventory is a balance sheet item, and it doesn't directly impact product profitability. If production cost is within the expected range, then it must have to do with the selling price."

"Exactly!", Bob exclaimed, "I have been telling corporate that marketing might not be selling the product at the budgeted price."

"Then I'm off the hook!", Carl sighed with relief.

"Not really," Bob said. "The analysis of the last three months' sales is in. They found that the product was sold at the budgeted price and the cost was within the range, but where we lost money was on the promotional discounts that we gave when we launched the product."

"Oh boy!", said Carl, "Then what do we do with the three out of eight production lines that are scheduled to run this product for the next eight weeks? If you ask me to convert those back to earlier products, then we're going to need at least three days of down time. We can't afford to do that when we're already running behind on shipments. If marketing hasn't factored in promotional cost, it's not our fault here at the plant!"

"Erin, can you please provide your point of view?" Bob asked.

Alex valued Erin's opinion. After all, Erin had been in the role of finance IT support for a long time, and she knew how the SAP system worked.

"Sure, Bob," Erin said. "I believe the data that corporate is looking at is from the profitability analysis module. It collects data on sales as well as costs, and shows where we've sold how much product, in which market, in which channel, at what price, and at what discount, and so on. I believe something's going on with the new products that were introduced. Let's take a look at the system. I might not have a lot of business insight, but at least I can explain the data flow."

## 11.1 Margin Analysis—an overview

*Margin Analysis* is a sub-module of SAP Controlling that enables an organization to evaluate market segments that can be classified according to product, customer, geography, or any combination of these factors, with respect to the organization's profit or *contribution margin* (often referred to as *gross margin*).

Margin Analysis provides management with information to support internal accounting and decision making from a market-oriented point of view.

Margin Analysis creates reports using cost elements and characteristics that represent important criteria around which profitability is measured. A *profitability segment* is a collection of several characteristics. Profitability segments are automatically generated based on the set of characteristics that are available when account posting takes place. Examples of characteristics include profit center, material, sales organization, plant, customer, and other items that are important to your organization for managing profitability. This corresponds to market segments for which profitability can be reported.

Margin Analysis calculates profits according to the cost-of-sales method of accounting, where the cost of sales is compared to revenue. The emphasis is on matching costs with revenues, which allows for optimal analysis of the contribution margin.

Contribution margin is equal to sales revenues minus variable costs. This amount offsets fixed expenses and produces an operating profit for the business.

Variable costs vary in proportion to sales levels. They can include direct material and labor costs, the variable part of manufacturing overhead costs, transportation costs, and sales commission expenses.

Fixed costs remain constant (for the most part) within the projected range of sales levels. They can include facilities costs, certain general and administrative costs, and interest and depreciation expenses.

All of the above are used for a *breakeven point* calculation to identify which segments of the business are more profitable.

**Margin Analysis and costing-based CO-PA**

In the current S/4HANA environment, two different versions of profitability analysis exist side by side. Margin Analysis is directly tied to the general ledger and used to be known as *Account-Based CO-PA*. CO-PA was the original term for the profitability analysis functionality in SAP. Costing-based CO-PA is independent of the general ledger and relies on transfer structures and value fields to store data used in profitability calculations. Costing-based CO-PA provides more flexibility for data analysis than the older account-based CO-PA and is the preferred method for measuring profitability in the system. However, its main drawback is that the values in CO-PA must be reconciled to the values in the general ledger. This is not a problem with account-based CO-PA (now Margin Analysis), and the improvements that were made to it as part of the S/4HANA enhancement make this the preferred tool for understanding profitability.

## 11.2 Characteristics

Master data in Margin Analysis provides the fundamental data and content within the structures that are already determined. Master data is created when individual values are assigned to the characteristics. The combination of characteristics and values forms multidimensional profitability segments that are used as a basis for valuating operating results. The profitability segments represent the relevant market segments from the business point of view.

Characteristics created in the operating concern represent the criteria derived to provide a breakdown of operating results. SAP software contains many standard characteristics; however, if those characteristics do not satisfy reporting requirements, then user-defined characteristics can also be created. *Characteristics* are the criteria in profitability analysis according to which operating results are analyzed and differentiated sales and profit planning are performed.

**Characteristics—an example**

An organization wants to report on geography, country, region, customer channel, and product group—these will be defined as characteristics.

Within each characteristic, several possible values can be captured. For example:

- For geography—the Americas, Europe, Asia Pacific, and Africa
- For country—the United States, Canada, Mexico, Brazil, and Argentina.
- For region—Northeast, Mid-Atlantic, Midwest, Southwest, and Northwest.
- For customer channel—Direct Sales, Distributors, and Affiliates.

Characteristics are stored in the field catalog and are maintained using transaction KEA5, as shown in Figure 11.1.

The menu path is: TOOLS • CUSTOMIZING • IMG • SPRO EXECUTE PROJECT • CONTROLLING • PROFITABILITY ANALYSIS • STRUCTURES • DEFINE OPERATING CONCERN • MAINTAIN CHARACTERISTICS.

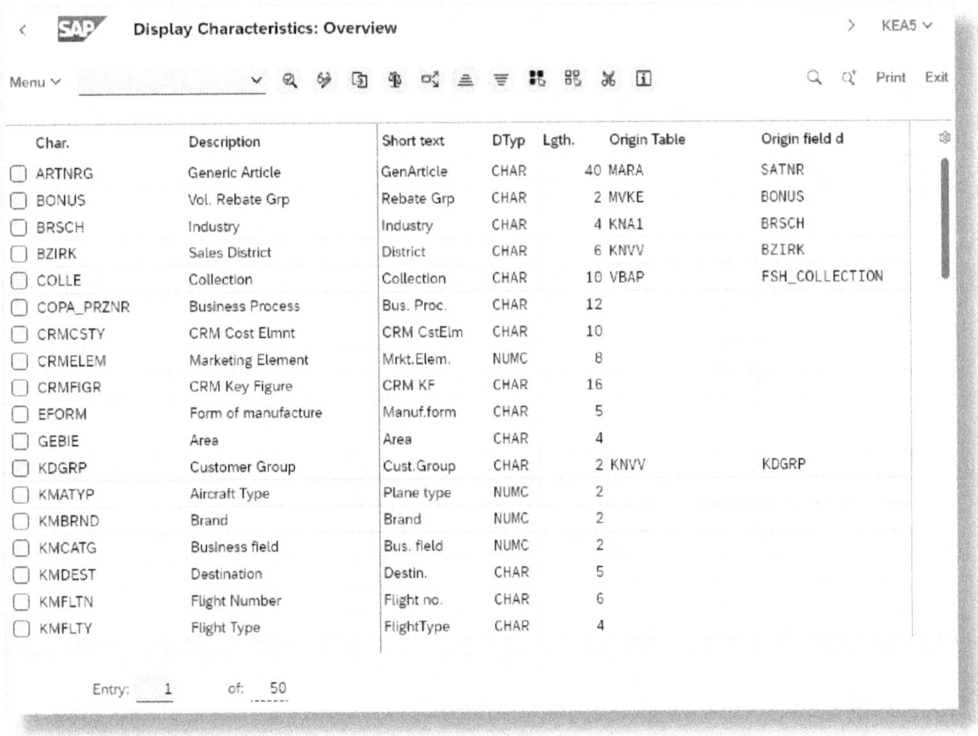

Display Characteristics: Overview

| Char. | Description | Short text | DTyp | Lgth. | Origin Table | Origin field d |
|---|---|---|---|---|---|---|
| ARTNRG | Generic Article | GenArticle | CHAR | 40 | MARA | SATNR |
| BONUS | Vol. Rebate Grp | Rebate Grp | CHAR | 2 | MVKE | BONUS |
| BRSCH | Industry | Industry | CHAR | 4 | KNA1 | BRSCH |
| BZIRK | Sales District | District | CHAR | 6 | KNVV | BZIRK |
| COLLE | Collection | Collection | CHAR | 10 | VBAP | FSH_COLLECTION |
| COPA_PRZNR | Business Process | Bus. Proc. | CHAR | 12 | | |
| CRMCSTY | CRM Cost Elmnt | CRM CstElm | CHAR | 10 | | |
| CRMELEM | Marketing Element | Mrkt.Elem. | NUMC | 8 | | |
| CRMFIGR | CRM Key Figure | CRM KF | CHAR | 16 | | |
| EFORM | Form of manufacture | Manuf.form | CHAR | 5 | | |
| GEBIE | Area | Area | CHAR | 4 | | |
| KDGRP | Customer Group | Cust.Group | CHAR | 2 | KNVV | KDGRP |
| KMATYP | Aircraft Type | Plane type | NUMC | 2 | | |
| KMBRND | Brand | Brand | NUMC | 2 | | |
| KMCATG | Business field | Bus. field | NUMC | 2 | | |
| KMDEST | Destination | Destin. | CHAR | 5 | | |
| KMFLTN | Flight Number | Flight no. | CHAR | 6 | | |
| KMFLTY | Flight Type | FlightType | CHAR | 4 | | |

Entry: 1 of: 50

*Figure 11.1: KEA5—Characteristics maintenance*

A *characteristic derivation* is an attempt to determine the characteristic values for all CO-PA characteristics in a given profitability-relevant business transaction. The characteristic values that are transferred automatically are used to determine other logically dependent characteristics. To do so, the system can access information contained in the source document, as well as information existing outside of it.

Figure 11.2 displays transaction KEDR, where characteristic derivation strategy is maintained.

The menu path is: TOOLS • CUSTOMIZING • IMG • SPRO EXECUTE PROJECT • CONTROLLING • PROFITABILITY ANALYSIS • STRUCTURES • MASTER DATA • DEFINE CHARACTERISTIC DERIVATION.

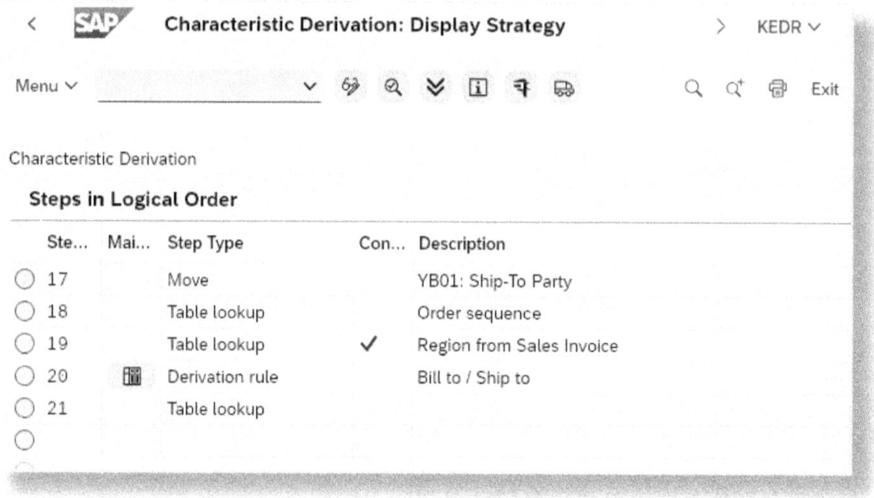


*Figure 11.2: KEDR—Characteristic derivation strategy*

Figure 11.3 shows the rule for the derivation of a ship-to customer category based on a BILL-TO PARTY.

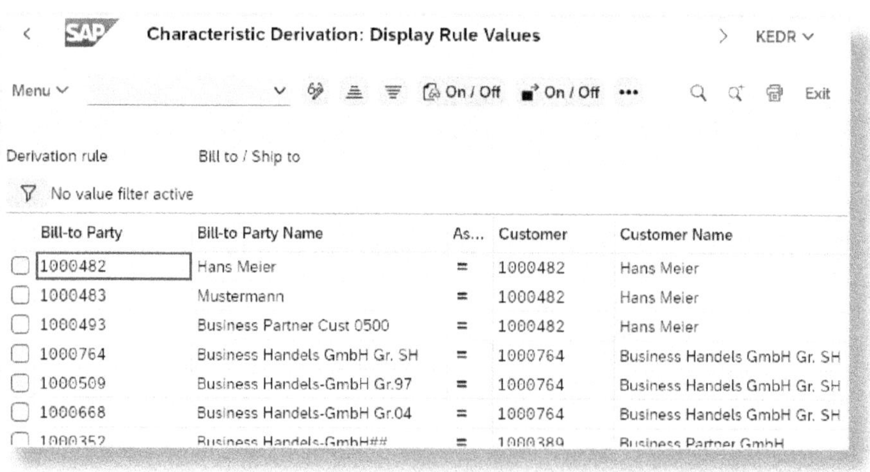


*Figure 11.3: KEDR—Characteristic rule value*

A *profitability segment* is a cost object within profitability analysis where costs and revenues are assigned. A profitability segment is defined by a combination of characteristic values. The combination of characteristic values forms multidimensional profitability segments that are used as a basis for valuating operating results. The profitability segments represent the relevant market segments from the business' perspective.

**Profitability segment—an example**

Examples of some combinations of characteristics for region or geography are as follows:

1. Americas + United States + Midwest + Distributor
2. Europe + Germany + Bavaria + Affiliate
3. Asia Pacific + Australia + New South Wales + Direct Sales
4. Africa + South Africa + Western Cape + Distributor

## 11.3 Flow of actual values from billing

Posting data from Sales and Distribution (SD) normally constitutes the most important source of information for profitability analysis.

The SD module calculates revenues during billing using a pricing mechanism. It then enters revenue in the billing document. Sales deductions are also recorded in the billing document, along with the standard cost of the goods sold.

First, however, the item is shipped to the customer. This provides information on the *cost of goods sold (COGS)*. GCI wanted to understand the contribution of the various aspects of manufacturing, such as material, labor overhead, and production overhead costs relating to the COGS amount. Alex asked Erin how the system handled this.

"Valuation using material cost estimates determines the cost of sales when a sales transaction is posted to Margin Analysis," she replied. "Quantities of products sold are multiplied by the standard costs of goods manufactured, thereby including the detailed fixed and variable cost components for the cost of goods manufactured in the individual contribution margins. There's special configuration that we do to assign accounts to the various cost components used in product costing."

This is found under menu path TOOLS • CUSTOMIZING • IMG • SPRO EXECUTE PROJECT • FINANCIAL ACCOUNTING • GENERAL LEDGER ACCOUNTING • PERIODIC PROCESSING • INTEGRATION • MATERIALS MANAGEMENT • DEFINE ACCOUNTS FOR SPLITTING THE COST OF GOODS SOLD.

"First", Eric continued, "we had to define the account we wanted to split, which in this case is the cost of goods sold account 894030. Then, we assigned the splitting accounts to this."

This configuration is shown in Figure 11.4.

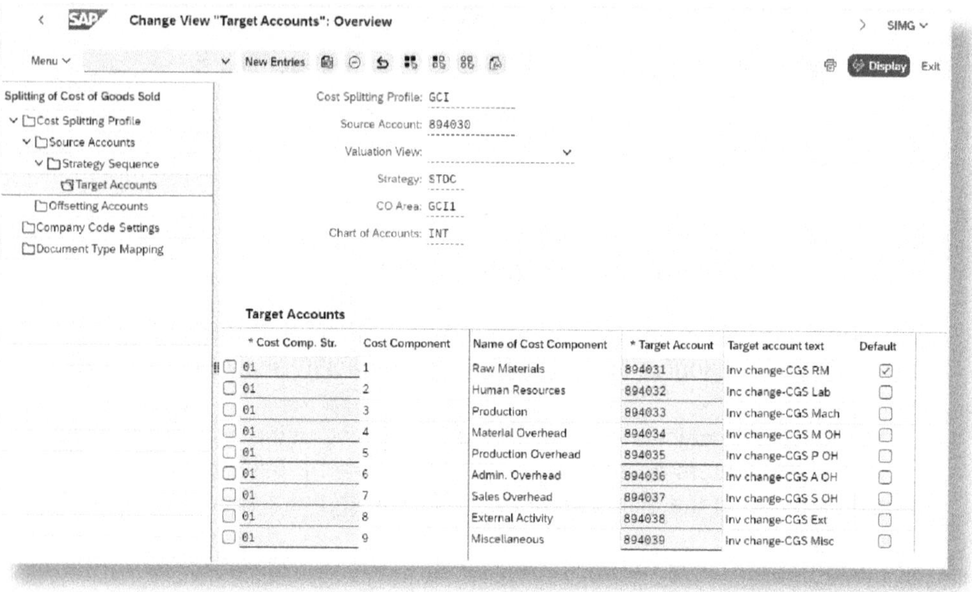


*Figure 11.4: Configuring the COGS split accounts*

"We then assigned the splitting structure to the GCI company codes. Now, when a 601 movement for a post goods issue to a customer is processed during shipping, the system first posts a document crediting inventory and debiting the COGS account."

Erin showed Alex the initial posting (see Figure 11.5).

"And, because we have enabled COGS splitting, another journal entry is made to reverse the COGS posting and to reassign the costs to the individual cost component accounts."

Alex reviewed the splitting journal entry (see Figure 11.6).

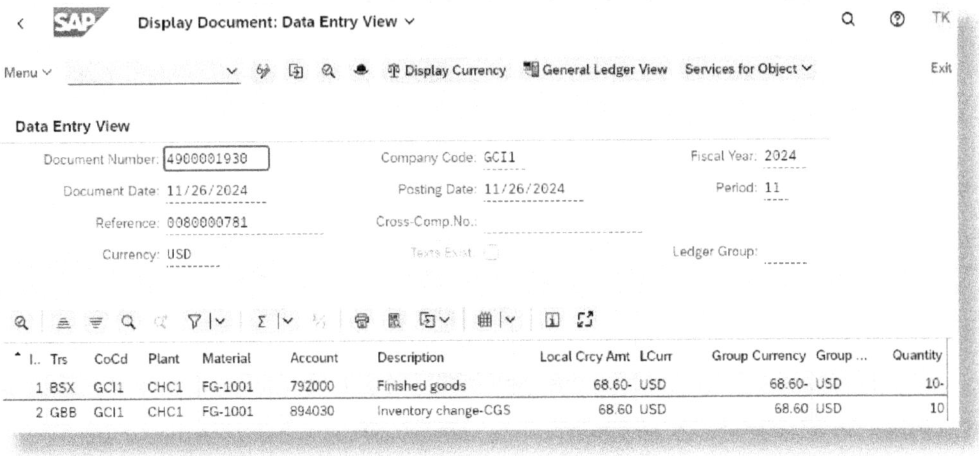


*Figure 11.5: Initial posting of COGS on shipment*

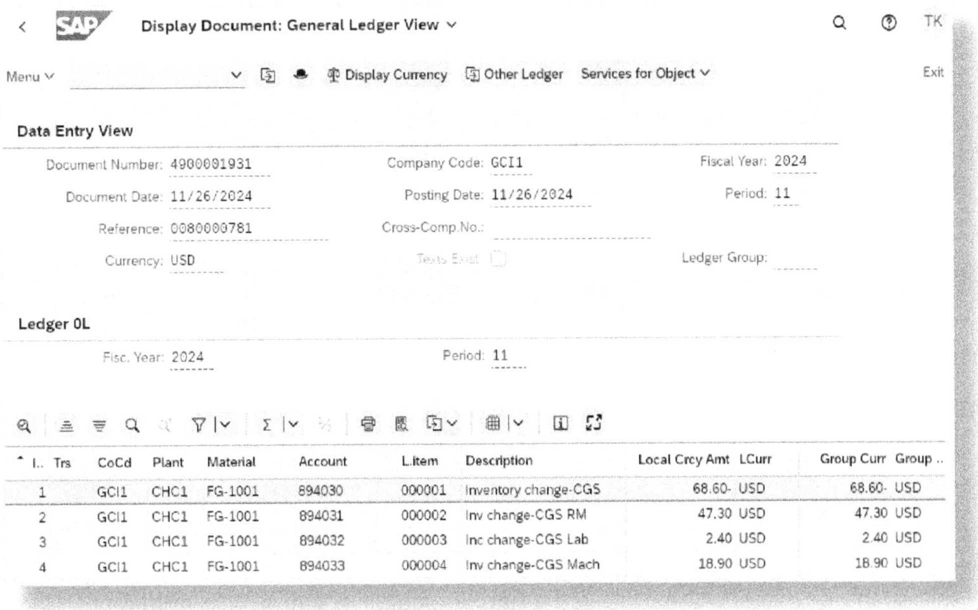


*Figure 11.6: Reversal of COGS and splitting by cost component*

"So that's how we get the proper granularity for understanding how the various components factor into the cost of goods sold," he told Erin, as he made notes about the process.

Sales order pricing is determined by special pricing procedures that are utilized when a product is ordered and entered into the system. These pricing procedures are made up of pricing conditions that not only represent the sales price, but also additional debits and credits, such as discounts, which apply to the amount that the customer will pay for the product. When a billing document is created, these conditions are made available and can be used when looking at the profitability of the product.

Documents with billing errors are recorded and can be seen in the MANAGE BILLING DOCUMENTS app. These errors need to be corrected, and the billing document should then be manually processed using the app's *post billing document* function after drilling into the details of the document. Assuming the underlying problem has been resolved, this function creates the journal entry assigned to the appropriate profitability segment.

**! Matching the COGS and revenue**

Billing errors recorded in the MANAGE BILLING DOCUMENTS app should be monitored periodically—at a minimum at period end—to ensure that costs and revenue match for each sales order.

## 11.4 Flow of actual values from FI and CO

Any relevant financial posting will derive as many characteristics as possible for assigning the posting to a profitability segment. However, some postings are so generic that certain characteristics cannot be derived. This leads to a summarized posting that does not provide enough detail to be useful in understanding the impact on specific market segments.

Alex wanted to know how GCI handled costs associated with freight and advertising, where it was not possible to directly associate costs with a given sales order line item, much less with a particular material.

Bob informed him, "Alex, we use a function called *top-down distribution* to allocate those types of costs to more detailed segments. Top-down distribution is a function in the MANAGE ALLOCATIONS app, and we use it during period-end closing activities to assign greater granularity to these costs. This is the same app that can be used for cost center assessments and distributions. Let me give you an example on the whiteboard to show you how we can assign the cost of freight to the customer to individual materials."

Bob drew the diagram shown in Figure 11.7.

**Costs without product dimension**

| Co. Code | Profit Ctr | Account | Account Name | Product | Amount |
|---|---|---|---|---|---|
| GCI1 | 51100 | 192100 | Freight | | 5,000 |
| GCI1 | 51100 | 477100 | Advertising | | 2,000 |
| GCI1 | 51200 | 192100 | Freight | | 3,000 |
| GCI1 | 51200 | 477100 | Advertising | | 1,500 |

**Costs associated with COGS posting**

| Co. Code | Profit Ctr | Account | Account Name | Product | Amount |
|---|---|---|---|---|---|
| GCI1 | 51100 | 894030 | COGS | FG-1001 | 20,000 |
| GCI1 | 51100 | 894030 | COGS | FG-1002 | 30,000 |
| GCI1 | 51100 | 894030 | COGS | FG-1003 | 10,000 |
| GCI1 | 51100 | 894030 | COGS | FG-1004 | 40,000 |
| GCI1 | 51200 | 894030 | COGS | FG-2001 | 12,000 |
| GCI1 | 51200 | 894030 | COGS | FG-2002 | 18,000 |
| GCI1 | 51200 | 894030 | COGS | FG-2003 | 6,000 |

**Result of top down distribution**

| Co. Code | Profit Ctr | Account | Account Name | Product | Amount |
|---|---|---|---|---|---|
| GCI1 | 51100 | 192100 | Freight | FG-1001 | 1,000 |
| GCI1 | 51100 | 192100 | Freight | FG-1002 | 1,500 |
| GCI1 | 51100 | 192100 | Freight | FG-1003 | 500 |
| GCI1 | 51100 | 192100 | Freight | FG-1004 | 2,000 |
| GCI1 | 51100 | 477100 | Advertising | FG-1001 | 400 |
| GCI1 | 51100 | 477100 | Advertising | FG-1002 | 600 |
| GCI1 | 51100 | 477100 | Advertising | FG-1003 | 200 |
| GCI1 | 51100 | 477100 | Advertising | FG-1004 | 800 |
| GCI1 | 51200 | 192100 | Freight | FG-2001 | 1,000 |
| GCI1 | 51200 | 192100 | Freight | FG-2002 | 1,500 |
| GCI1 | 51200 | 192100 | Freight | FG-2003 | 500 |
| GCI1 | 51200 | 477100 | Advertising | FG-2001 | 500 |
| GCI1 | 51200 | 477100 | Advertising | FG-2002 | 750 |
| GCI1 | 51200 | 477100 | Advertising | FG-2003 | 250 |

Distribution

Reference

*Figure 11.7: Example of top-down distribution*

"If you look at the top area, *Costs without product dimension*, you can see that we posted freight and advertising associated with a profit center but not with specific products. The next section shows COGS postings for specific materials, that occurred during the period. The distribution is shown in the bottom section. The percentages of the COGS posting for each material/profit center combination is applied to the freight and advertising postings for each profit center, and new postings are made with the material assigned to each new posting. For example, the freight posting for profit center 51100 totaled $5,000. This amount has been reversed and reposted to each material that was shipped. For product FG-1001, the calculated amount is $1,000, which is $5,000 multiplied by $20,000/$100,000.

$100,000 is the total COGS posting for materials assigned to profit center 51100."

"I get it now," said Alex. "Since we don't know the exact amount of freight for each material, we do the next best thing and split the costs based on the distribution rule that we used."

"That's right," replied Bob. "We only need to do that for the postings for which we can't derive the necessary characteristics that we need for attributing those costs and revenues."

"Does top-down distribution cover all of the cost allocations needed for Margin Analysis?" Alex queried.

"That's a good point, Alex," Bob responded. "No, we only use top-down distribution to assign costs that we can reliably associate with given materials. As you have seen, we also deal with non-product related costs in cost centers that are designated as SG&A, which can't be directly assigned to materials. These costs are allocated to profitability segments using rules defined in allocation cycles that we execute using the MANAGE ALLOCATIONS app during the period-end closing process. The profitability segments do not contain the full set of characteristics, including material, so these costs are reflected at a higher level, such as product line and business. Using these allocations enables us to account for all costs that affect the profitability of the business lines."

## 11.5 Flow of actual values during settlement

Production variances for cost objects can be broken down into the variance categories that were determined when the variance calculation was performed during the order settlement process. This provides a more granular view, in Margin Analysis, of the cause of production variances. Variance categories are mapped to specific accounts, and when orders are settled, the system divides the amount first assigned to the variance account into the separate category accounts.

This is enabled in configuration found via menu path TOOLS • CUSTOMIZING • IMG • SPRO EXECUTE PROJECT • FINANCIAL ACCOUNTING • GENERAL LEDGER ACCOUNTING • PERIODIC PROCESSING • INTEGRATION • MATERIALS MANAGEMENT • DEFINE ACCOUNTS FOR SPLITTING PRICE DIFFERENCES.

Accounts can be set up for the following variance categories:

- PRIV–input price variance
- RSUV–resource usage variance
- QTYV–input quantity variance
- INPV–remaining input variance
- OPPV–output price variance
- MXPV–mixed price variance
- LSFV–lot size variance
- REMV–remaining variance
- SCRP–scrap variance

This can be seen in Figure 11.8.

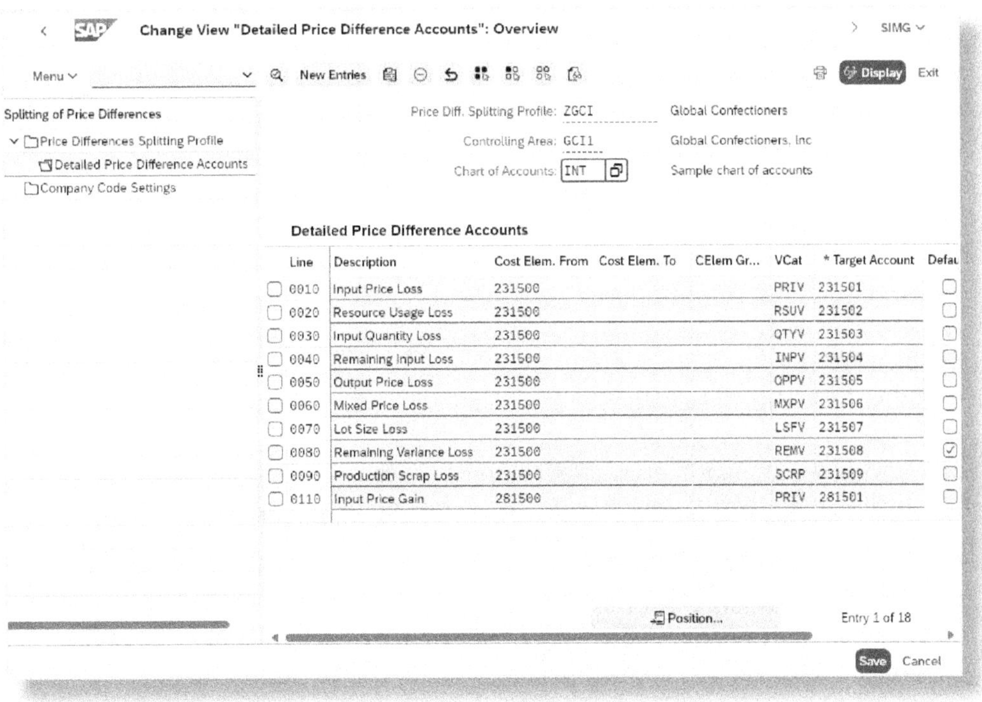


*Figure 11.8: Production variance split configuration*

The various categories are assigned to specific accounts (TARGET ACCOUNT). If you do not need to distinguish those types of variances from other more important categories, it is not necessary to assign each variance category to a separate account.

When the production variance is posted during order settlement, if variance splitting is enabled, the system first posts the amount to the main production variance account using transaction code/modifier PRD/PRF. (The order settlement accounting document is shown in Figure 11.9).

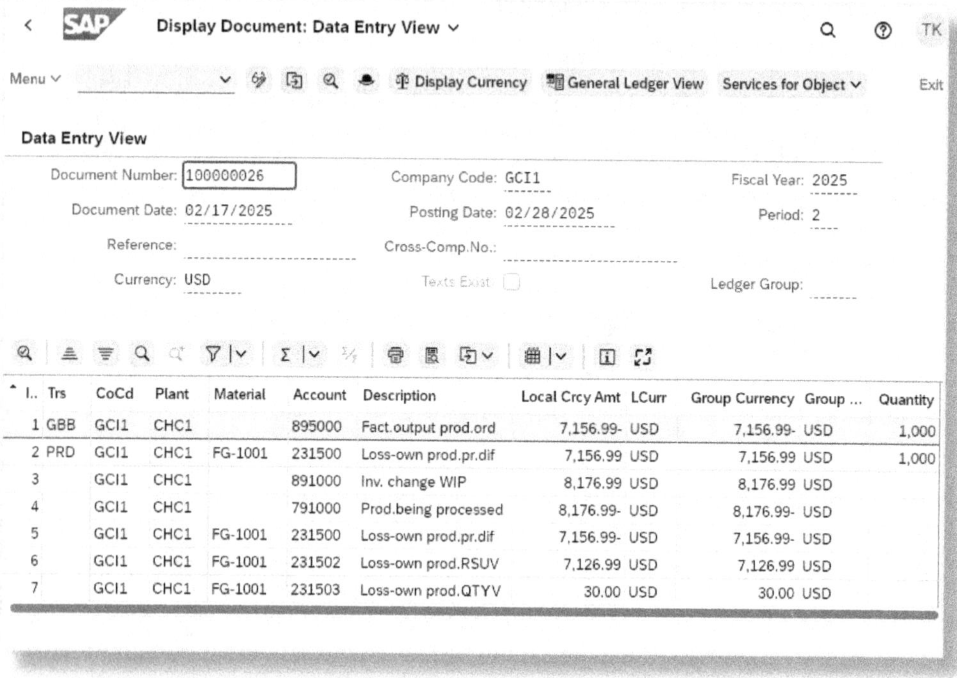


| I.. | Trs | CoCd | Plant | Material | Account | Description | Local Crcy Amt | LCurr | Group Currency | Group ... | Quantity |
|---|---|---|---|---|---|---|---|---|---|---|---|
| 1 | GBB | GCI1 | CHC1 | | 895000 | Fact.output prod.ord | 7,156.99- | USD | 7,156.99- | USD | 1,000 |
| 2 | PRD | GCI1 | CHC1 | FG-1001 | 231500 | Loss-own prod.pr.dif | 7,156.99 | USD | 7,156.99 | USD | 1,000 |
| 3 | | GCI1 | CHC1 | | 891000 | Inv. change WIP | 8,176.99 | USD | 8,176.99 | USD | |
| 4 | | GCI1 | CHC1 | | 791000 | Prod.being processed | 8,176.99- | USD | 8,176.99- | USD | |
| 5 | | GCI1 | CHC1 | FG-1001 | 231500 | Loss-own prod.pr.dif | 7,156.99- | USD | 7,156.99- | USD | |
| 6 | | GCI1 | CHC1 | FG-1001 | 231502 | Loss-own prod.RSUV | 7,126.99 | USD | 7,126.99 | USD | |
| 7 | | GCI1 | CHC1 | FG-1001 | 231503 | Loss-own prod.QTYV | 30.00 | USD | 30.00 | USD | |

*Figure 11.9: Variance categories in the settlement document*

Item 1 is the amount that updates the order to zero out its total value. Item 2 is the offset for that, which is posted to the production variance account 231500. This order settled with a WIP balance for period 1—items 3 and 4 clear the amount from the WIP clearing account. The system now needs to reverse the posting to the main variance account and distribute the values to the category accounts based on the variance calculation. Item 5 is the variance reversal, and items 6 and 7 are split to the specific variance accounts.

Figure 11.10 shows the variance calculation result for that order, broken down into the variance categories.

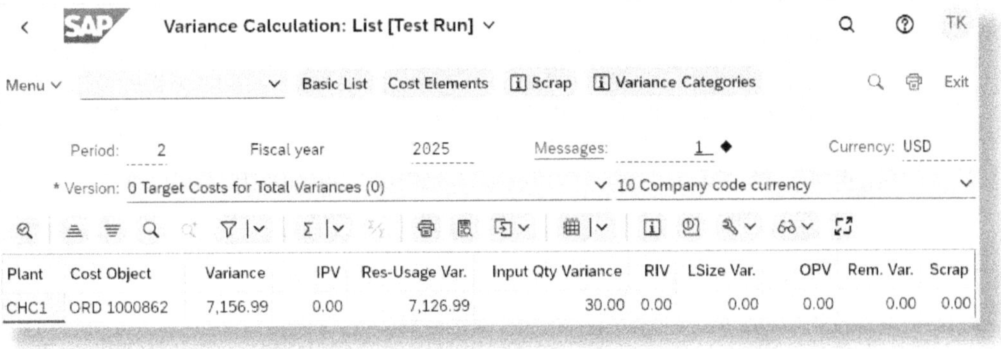


*Figure 11.10: Variance categories calculated for order 1000862*

## 11.6 Conclusion

Margin Analysis provides the data transfer and valuation of sales documents and FI/MM documents for relevant market dimensions.

In addition, it also offers a full range of allocation transactions that enable the application of overhead costs to the products, customers, and divisions that incurred them.

“So, what we’ve seen up until now,” Erin said, “is that Margin Analysis is a very powerful tool for finding out whether we are making any money or not. Corporate has information on gross sales, promotional discounts, returns, cost of goods sold, and fixed costs. They have analyzed this information for our new product line. Even though the sales and costs are in line with the expectations, the discounts are what seem to be creating noise.”

“But what about fixed costs?” Carl asked. “Our fixed costs are the same as last year. We haven’t added any capacity to manufacture this new product line—we just switched three lines from the old product line.”

“You bring up a good point,” Alex said. “Fixed costs remain fixed for the most part. Could it be that the promotional discounts are temporary in nature and if we remove them from the mix the line will be profitable? Maybe our volumes were low given the initial launch and we could have an increase in the coming months?”

“Bravo, Alex!” Bob said. “I didn’t think of that. I remember corporate telling me that they were going to check with marketing to find out how long the promotion is going to last. They spoke about having sought some special approvals and funding for this promotion, so I think it's only temporary. Let me ask if they have an update. I'll go and make few phone calls. Alex and Erin, in the meantime, can I ask you to review the data for the last week? Maybe the promotions are already phased out now? Maybe corporate has looked at the last completed month in the system, but not the latest data. Everything is in real time, so we should be able to verify quickly."

Alex and Erin looked up data from last week and found that promotions did not show up on the billing documents or in Margin Analysis reports. Bob received similar feedback from corporate and marketing. Additionally, marketing stated that the new product line had been well received in the market and that the volumes were likely to go up in the next few months. The new product line was making money after all; it was only the short-term discount and low volumes that were skewing the numbers.

"Great job, team!," Bob said. "Thanks to the details captured in the system, we were able to put our heads together and analyze what was going on. Carl, it looks like you are locked in on those three production lines for not eight, but the next twenty weeks! Let's all celebrate. Lunch is on me!" Bob thanked everyone. They all had a sense of achievement at the end of this long meeting.

# 12 "The numbers should match!"—a controller's dream...

*"Only accountants can save the world—through peace, goodwill and reconciliations."*

—the alternative accountant

**"Hey, Alex, I need your help." Dave, the inventory controller at the Chocotown facility spoke at a fast pace as he walked hurriedly into Alex's office one afternoon. "I have an e-mail from the supply chain lead at headquarters stating that the inventory numbers for the last month are off. I believe the numbers I reported are accurate and were pulled based on the same method that we have consistently used for months. I'm not sure what's going on!"**

"They might not be looking at the numbers correctly," Alex said. "Bob and I reviewed the numbers in our monthly report. Let's ask Erin if she can help solve this puzzle. I wanted to ask her a few questions about MM-FI integration anyway."

## 12.1 Material inventory values–balance summary

"I've seen this in the past," Erin said. "We had a similar issue several months back. Likely, the folks at HQ are having trouble understanding how Actual Costing updates the previous period's inventory valuation."

Dave responded, "That's possible because they're complaining that when they look at an inventory snapshot from a date in the middle of the previous period, the valuation looks to be based on the standard material price instead of the periodic unit price that they can see in the Accounting 1 tab of the material master."

"I wonder what they're looking at," Alex pondered.

"Okay, let's go step by step," Erin said. "Tell me, Dave, what do you use to view stock values on a specific day?"

"I use the MATERIAL INVENTORY VALUES – BALANCE SUMMARY app," he replied. "You can select a specific date, plant, and material or leave the selection open for all materials."

"That's just the thing," said Erin. "Let's first look at a snapshot for the end of period 1—January 31." Dave opened his laptop and ran the app. The resulting values are shown in Figure 12.1.

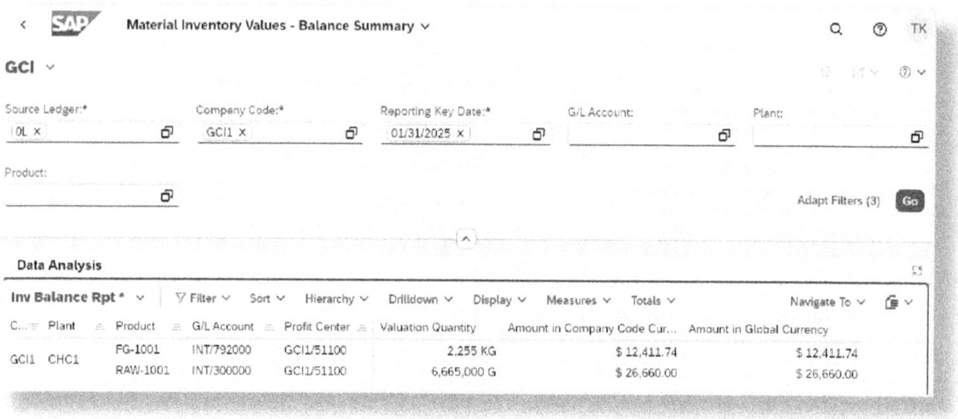


*Figure 12.1: Material inventory values for 1/31*

"We'll concentrate on material RAW-1001. This has a quantity of 6,665,000 grams with a value of $26,660.00. This works out to a value of $0.004 per gram, or $4.00 per 1000 grams, which is the standard price unit that we use for materials. Let's check to see if that matches the periodic unit price or the standard price by looking at ACCOUNTING 1 for the material."

Dave called up the DISPLAY MATERIAL app and selected the ACCOUNTING 1 tab. He then clicked on the PERIOD 001/2025 tab to show the valuation information for that period (see Figure 12.2). This showed the standard price set to $3.00 per 1,000 grams, and the periodic unit price set to $4.00 per 1,000 grams.

"That's just what I expected," said Dave. "The actual costing run of the Material Ledger calculated the periodic unit price based on price differences assigned to that material. Everything looks good to me so far!"

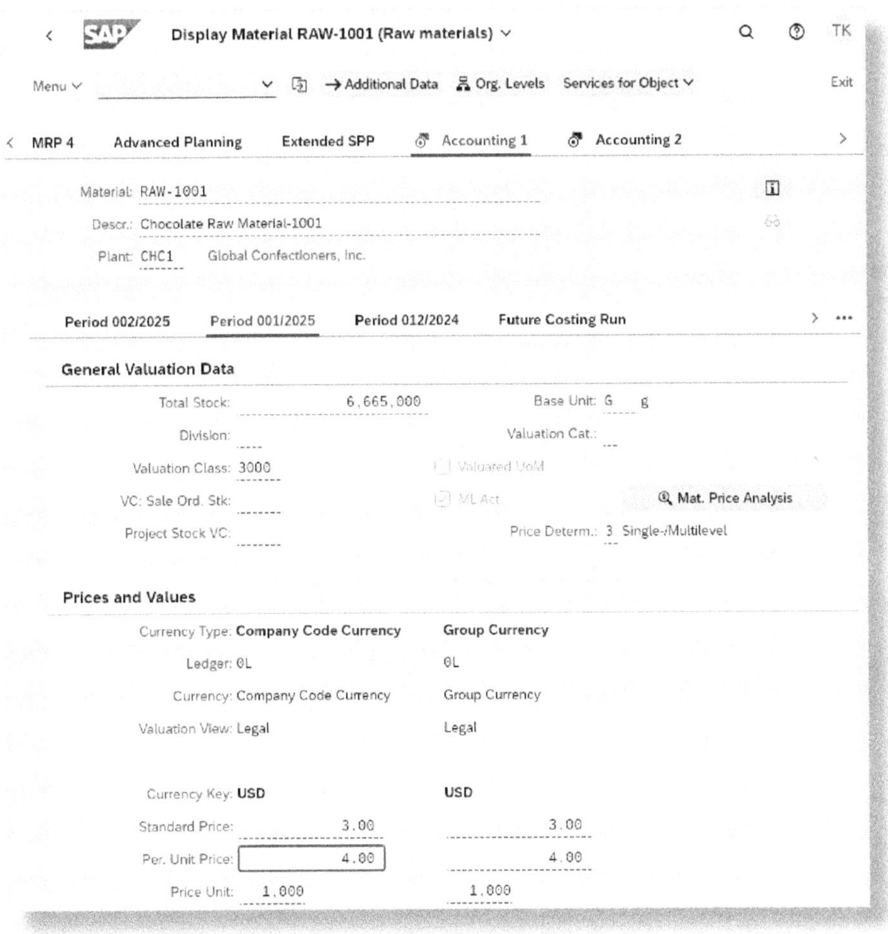

*Figure 12.2: Material RAW-1001 values for period 1*

"All right," said Erin. "Now, could you pull up the inventory balance for January 30? That should point out what HQ is complaining about."

Dave reran the MATERIAL INVENTORY VALUES – BALANCE SUMMARY app using 01/30/2025 as the snapshot date (see Figure 12.3).

Alex calculated the value per gram by dividing $20,685.00 by 6,895,000 grams. "Wait! That comes out to be $0.003 per gram or $3.00 per 1,000 grams. That is back to the standard price! I thought inventory for the previous period was supposed to be valued at the periodic unit price. The people at HQ are right, there is an issue with the valuation."

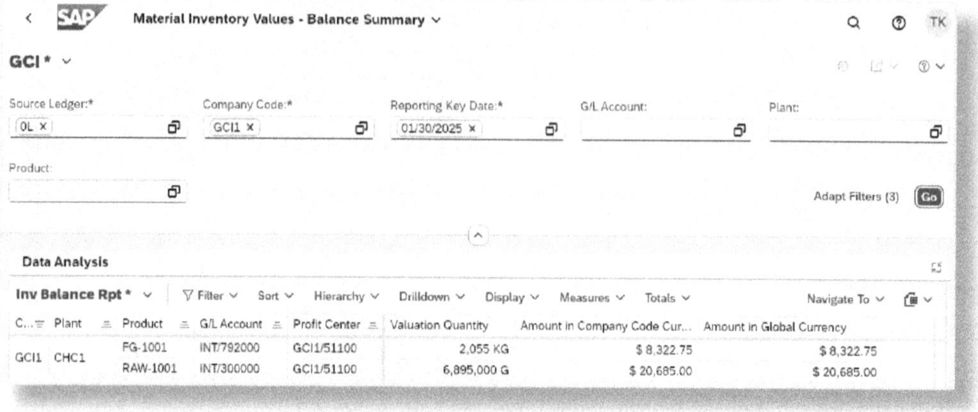


*Figure 12.3: Material inventory values from 1/30*

"Hold on," said Erin. "Don't jump to any conclusions without looking at all the evidence. Before we do any more digging, let's make sure that the valuation for the current period is based on the standard price."

Dave executed MATERIAL INVENTORY VALUES – BALANCE SUMMARY yet again using today's date as the key date (see Figure 12.4).

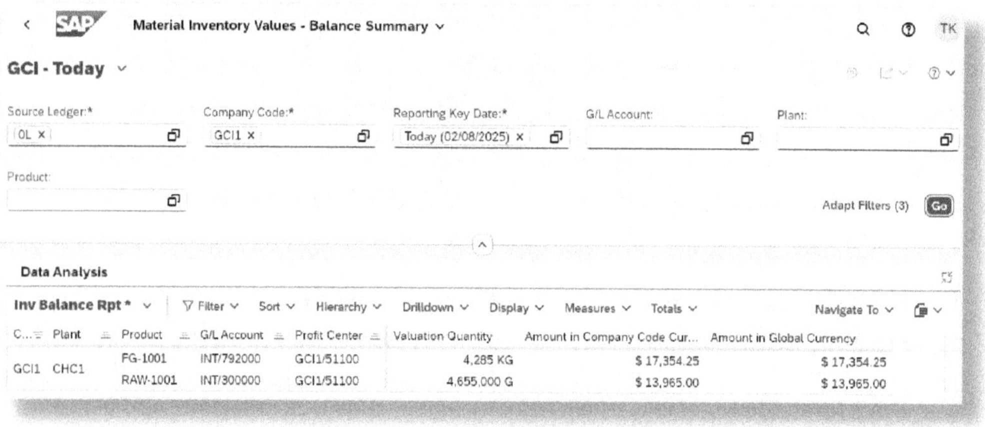


*Figure 12.4: Material inventory values for today's date*

Alex took the values reported for today for RAW-1001 ($13,965.00 and 4,655,000 grams) and calculated $3.00 per 1,000 grams, which matched the standard price.

## 12.2 Display material document list

"One thing we should probably do is to check for any goods movements for RAW-1001 from January 30 through February 1 to make sure that goods movement isn't to blame for this," suggested Dave.

"Good idea!" said Erin.

Dave called up the DISPLAY MATERIAL DOCUMENT LIST for product RAW-1001 at the Chocotown plant for the specific dates (see Figure 12.5).

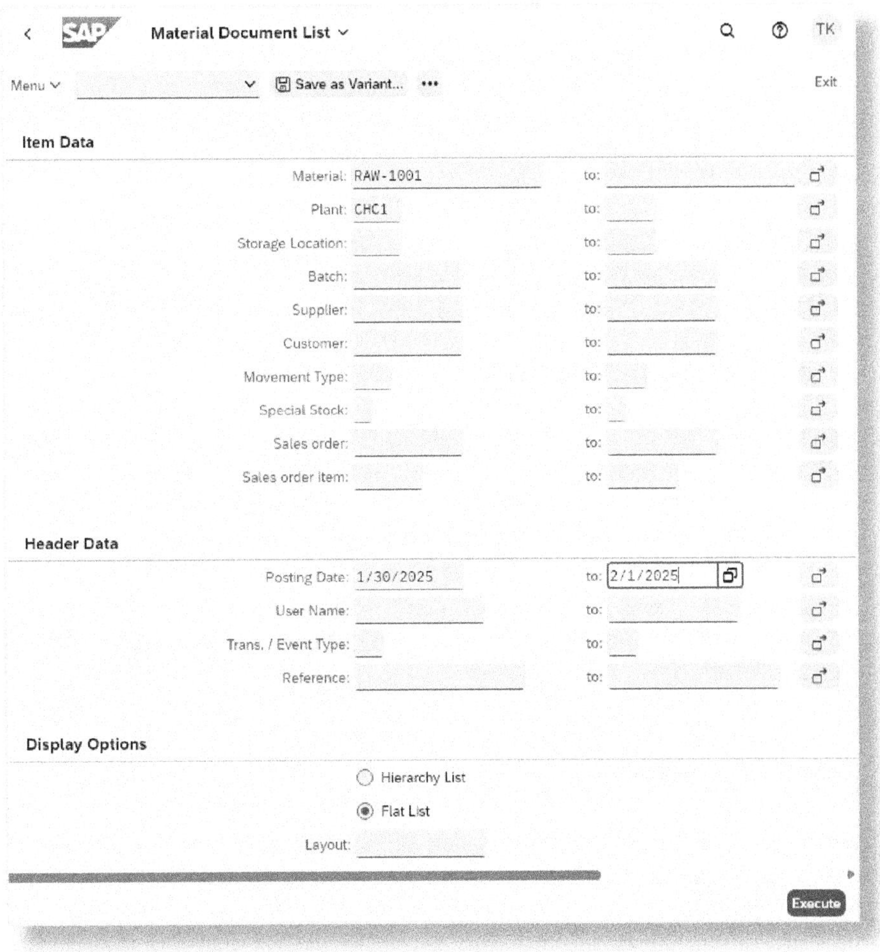


*Figure 12.5: Display material documents list selection screen*

The resulting report shows the goods movements (see Figure 12.6).

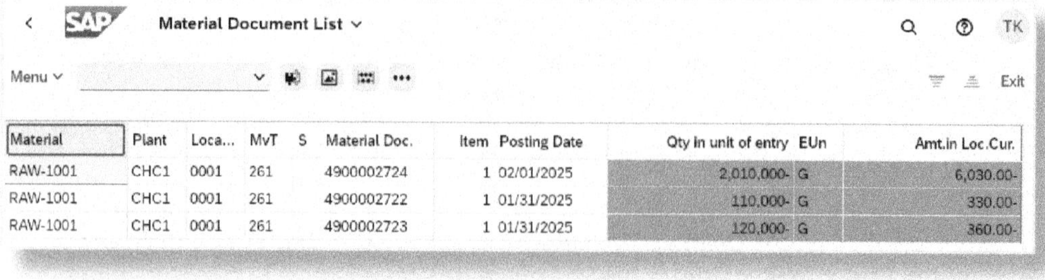


| Material | Plant | Loca... | MvT | S | Material Doc. | Item | Posting Date | Qty in unit of entry | EUn | Amt.in Loc.Cur. |
|---|---|---|---|---|---|---|---|---|---|---|
| RAW-1001 | CHC1 | 0001 | 261 | | 4900002724 | 1 | 02/01/2025 | 2,010.000- | G | 6,030.00- |
| RAW-1001 | CHC1 | 0001 | 261 | | 4900002722 | 1 | 01/31/2025 | 110.000- | G | 330.00- |
| RAW-1001 | CHC1 | 0001 | 261 | | 4900002723 | 1 | 01/31/2025 | 120.000- | G | 360.00- |

*Figure 12.6: Material document list for RAW-1001*

Alex did some quick calculations and found that the movements were all valued at $3.00 per 1,000 grams—the standard price. "Even the goods movements from January 31 are valued at the standard price. Doesn't that contradict what we saw with MATERIAL INVENTORY VALUES – BALANCE SUMMARY?"

"We're not done with our investigations yet," replied Erin.

## 12.3 Material inventory values—line items

"There is another app that enables us to view the line items, including postings that are not associated directly with goods movements," she added. "Dave, please call up the MATERIAL INVENTORY VALUES – LINE ITEMS app using the same date range we used for the MATERIAL DOCUMENT LIST."

Dave executed the app (see Figure 12.7). There were five items on the list instead of just the three goods movements shown in the MATERIAL DOCUMENT LIST report.

"Look," said Alex, "there are two items on the report with a value assigned to 0 grams! What could those refer to?"

Erin replied, "Notice that we included columns for JOURNAL ENTRY, REFERENCE DOCUMENT, and REFERENCE TRANSACTION. We use these fields to determine what is happening. Drilling into the JOURNAL ENTRY brings up the financial document generated. REFERENCE DOCUMENT points to the internal document that generated the financial document. In this case, there are two references to the same material ledger document (2000000010) and three

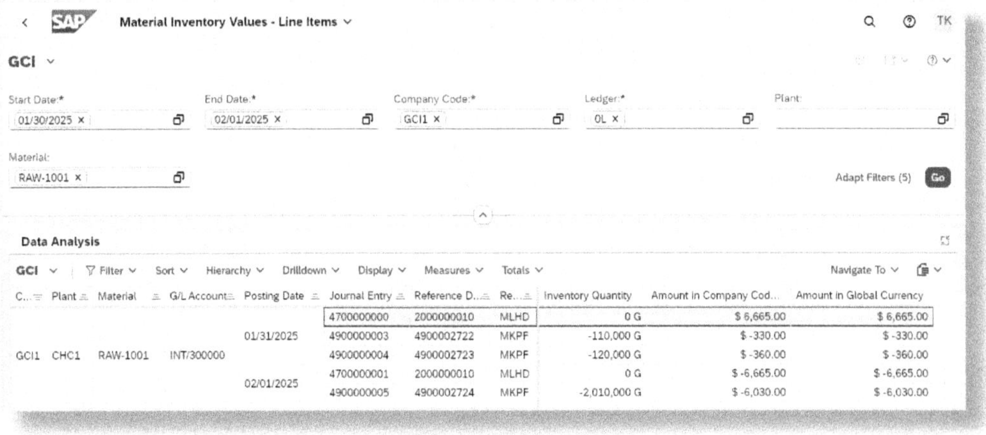


*Figure 12.7: Material inventory values—line items*

references to material documents (4900002722–4900002724). These are the same document IDs that we saw in the DISPLAY MATERIAL DOCUMENTS LIST report. I can tell what kind of documents those are by looking at the name of the internal REFERENCE TRANSACTION. Those beginning with *ML* are material ledger documents. Those starting with *MK* are material documents. Drilling into the journal entries should give us the information that we need. Dave, first click on journal entry 4900000003, and then select DISPLAY JOURNAL ENTRIES from the NAVIGATE TO dropdown menu."

Dave displayed the financial document shown in Figure 12.8.

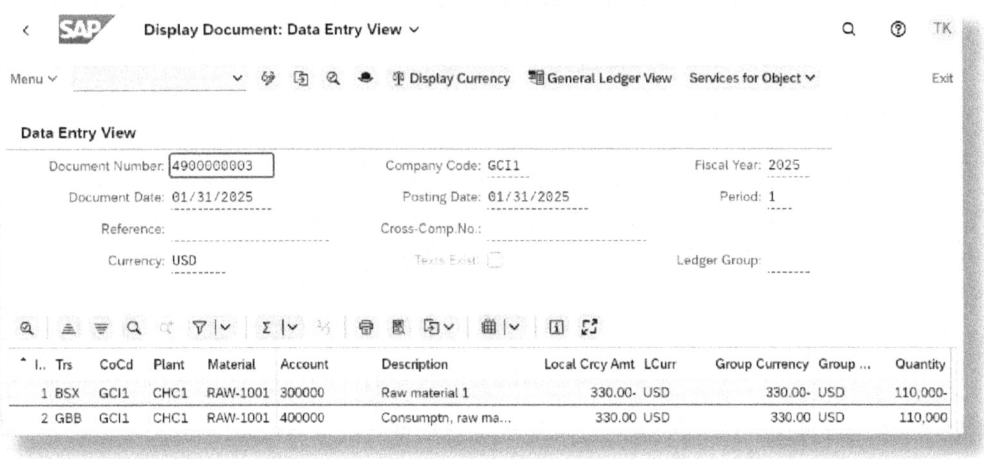


*Figure 12.8: Financial document 4900000003*

"That looks to me like a posting for a goods movement," he said. "You can see that the inventory account 300000 is credited, meaning that material was taken out of inventory, and the consumption account 400000 is debited, indicating that the material was consumed, probably in a process order. Let me click on the header button to get the header details of the posting (see Figure 12.9).

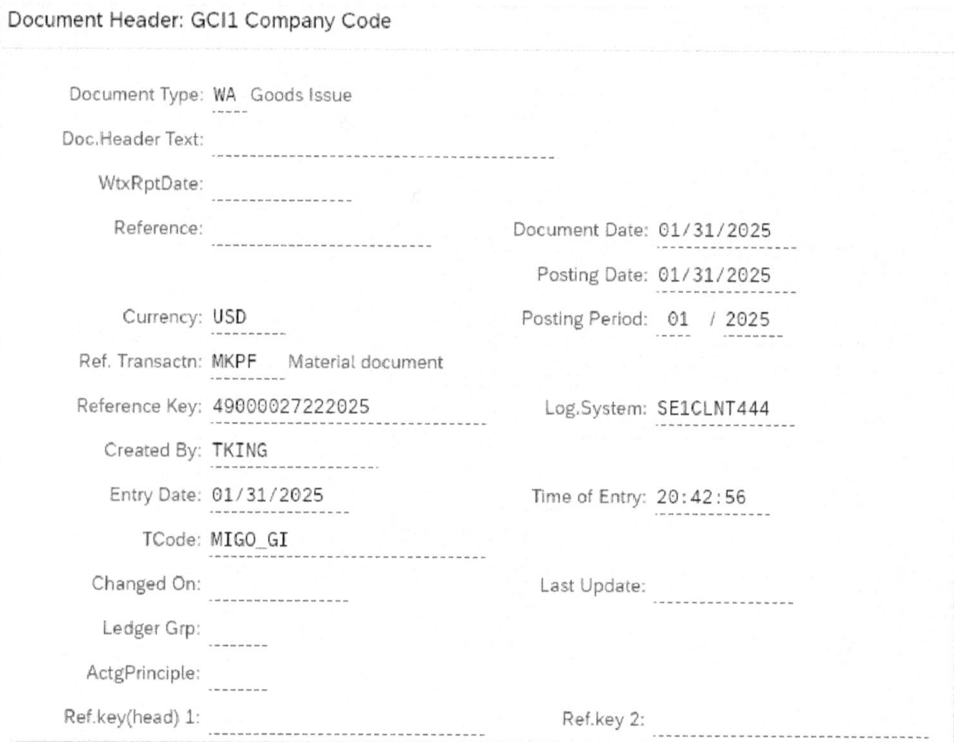
Document Header: GCI1 Company Code
Document Type: WA Goods Issue
Doc.Header Text:
WtxRptDate:
Reference:
Document Date: 01/31/2025
Posting Date: 01/31/2025
Currency: USD
Posting Period: 01 / 2025
Ref. Transactn: MKPF Material document
Reference Key: 49000027222025
Log.System: SE1CLNT444
Created By: TKING
Entry Date: 01/31/2025
Time of Entry: 20:42:56
TCode: MIGO_GI
Changed On:
Last Update:
Ledger Grp:
ActgPrinciple:
Ref.key(head) 1:
Ref.key 2:

*Figure 12.9: Document header information for entry 4900000003*

"I can see that the document type indicates that this is a goods issue and that the reference transaction is MKPF, which indicates that this was generated from producing the material document for the goods movement."

"What about the two items in the list that have an inventory quantity of 0 grams?" asked Alex.

Dave selected the first row in the list and displayed the journal entry (see Figure 12.10). "I've highlighted the line which matches material RAW-1001 and the inventory account 300000. The amount matches what we saw in the main report."

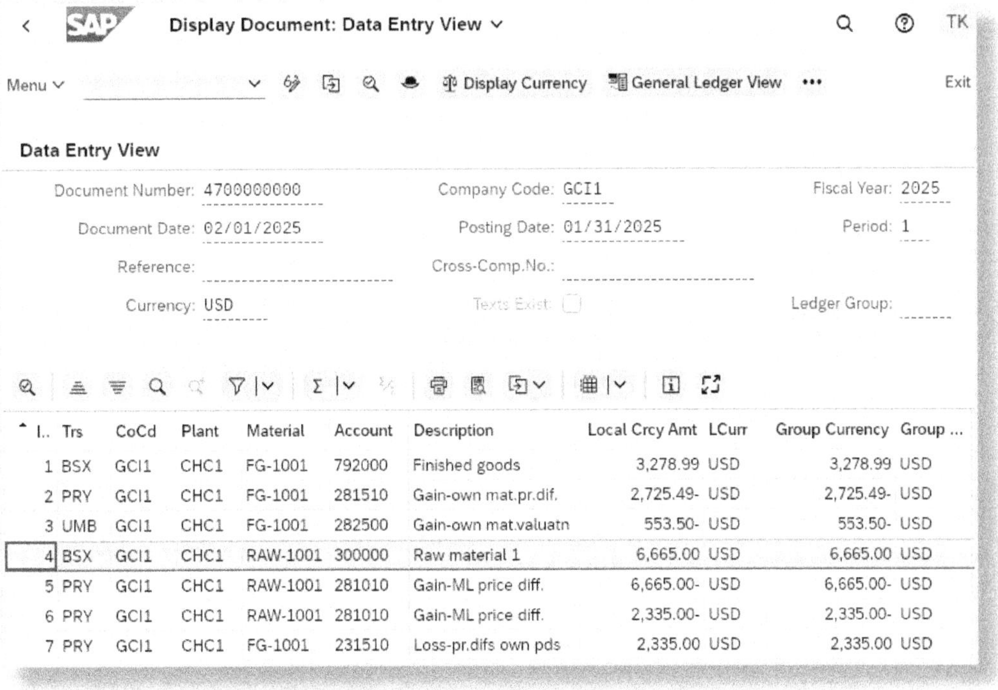


| I.. | Trs | CoCd | Plant | Material | Account | Description | Local Crcy Amt | LCurr | Group Currency | Group ... |
|---|---|---|---|---|---|---|---|---|---|---|
| 1 | BSX | GCI1 | CHC1 | FG-1001 | 792000 | Finished goods | 3,278.99 | USD | 3,278.99 | USD |
| 2 | PRY | GCI1 | CHC1 | FG-1001 | 281510 | Gain-own mat.pr.dif. | 2,725.49- | USD | 2,725.49- | USD |
| 3 | UMB | GCI1 | CHC1 | FG-1001 | 282500 | Gain-own mat.valuatn | 553.50- | USD | 553.50- | USD |
| 4 | BSX | GCI1 | CHC1 | RAW-1001 | 300000 | Raw material 1 | 6,665.00 | USD | 6,665.00 | USD |
| 5 | PRY | GCI1 | CHC1 | RAW-1001 | 281010 | Gain-ML price diff. | 6,665.00- | USD | 6,665.00- | USD |
| 6 | PRY | GCI1 | CHC1 | RAW-1001 | 281010 | Gain-ML price diff. | 2,335.00- | USD | 2,335.00- | USD |
| 7 | PRY | GCI1 | CHC1 | FG-1001 | 231510 | Loss-pr.difs own pds | 2,335.00 | USD | 2,335.00 | USD |

*Figure 12.10: Financial document 4700000000*

"I'll click on the header icon to see what else we can discover about this journal entry. As you can see, this looks to be associated with the material ledger (see Figure 12.11). You can also tell that this was a part of the post-closing step of the actual costing run by looking at the document header text. This is how the system adjusts the inventory value from standard to actual on the last day of the period."

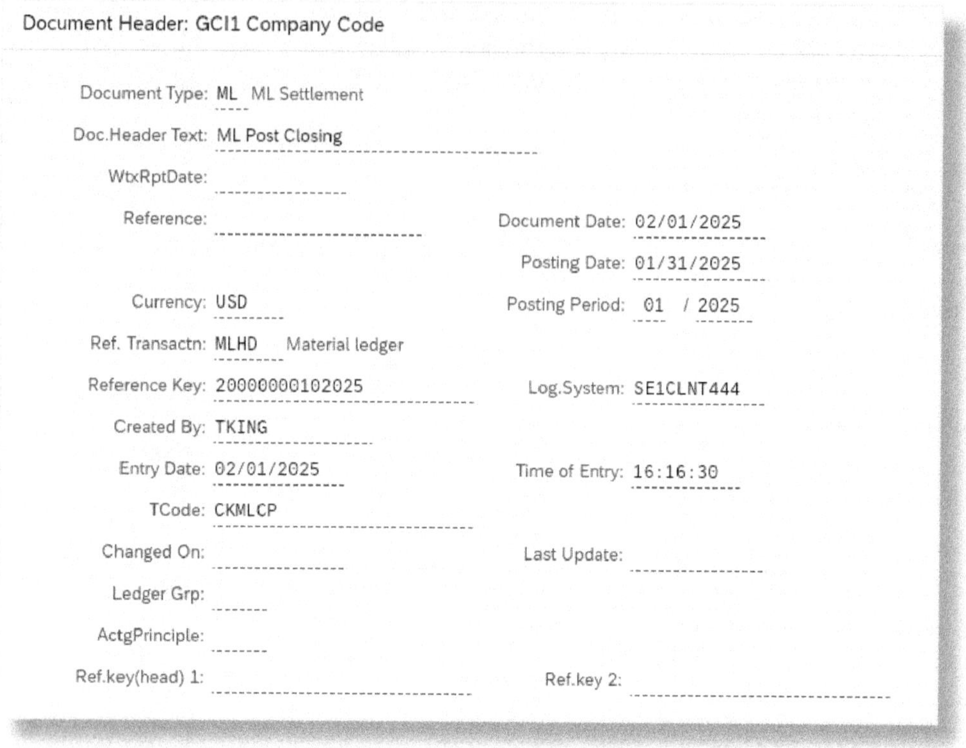
Document Header: GCI1 Company Code

| | | | |
|---|---|---|---|
| Document Type: | ML ML Settlement | | |
| Doc.Header Text: | ML Post Closing | | |
| WtxRptDate: | | | |
| Reference: | | Document Date: | 02/01/2025 |
| | | Posting Date: | 01/31/2025 |
| Currency: | USD | Posting Period: | 01 / 2025 |
| Ref. Transactn: | MLHD Material ledger | | |
| Reference Key: | 20000000102025 | Log.System: | SE1CLNT444 |
| Created By: | TKING | | |
| Entry Date: | 02/01/2025 | Time of Entry: | 16:16:30 |
| TCode: | CKMLCP | | |
| Changed On: | | Last Update: | |
| Ledger Grp: | | | |
| ActgPrinciple: | | | |
| Ref.key(head) 1: | | Ref.key 2: | |

*Figure 12.11: Document header information for entry 4700000000*

"But doesn't this mean that the inventory valuation is no longer at standard?" asked Alex.

"Yes," replied Erin. "But that's only for the last day of the period. The entry is reversed on the first day of the next period. Dave, select the report line from February 1, with quantity 0, and navigate to the journal entry for that item (see Figure 12.12). You can see that the posting amount for item 3 restores the amount in account 300000 to standard valuation. The offset to that posting is in item 4 of the list. This posts to a price difference account so that it can be included in the next period's actual costing run as part of the price differences accumulated in that period."

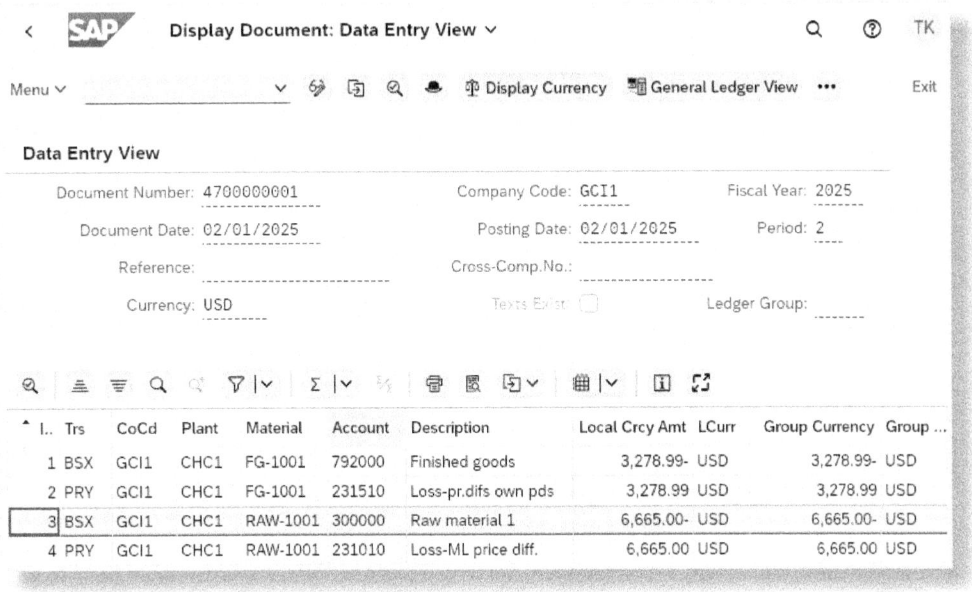


*Figure 12.12: Financial document 4700000001*

"I see," said Alex. "The lesson here is that all goods movements are processed using the standard price of the material. Adjustment to actual value from the material ledger actual costing run only applies to the last day of the period, and goods movements throughout the period are not revalued. This adjustment is backed out for the first day of the next period, bringing inventory valuation back to standard. If I look at a snapshot of inventory for any day of a previous period, except the last day, the valuation will be at standard. Only on the last day of a previous period will the actual value be seen."

"Exactly," chimed in Dave. "That makes sense. The actual valuation applies only to the final inventory quantity for the period. Thanks Erin and Alex! I can go back to HQ and help them understand what they're seeing when they look at past snapshots of inventory."

## 12.4 Display stock overview

"I'm glad we were able to work all of that out," said Alex. "Dave, I was wondering about other applications that help you manage your inventory."

"There are two that I use all the time," he replied. "DISPLAY STOCK OVERVIEW for an individual material and DISPLAY WAREHOUSE STOCK for multiple materials or the entire plant. Here, let me show you."

Dave went back to his laptop and showed two transactions to Erin and Alex.

The DISPLAY STOCK OVERVIEW screen for an individual material is shown in Figure 12.13.

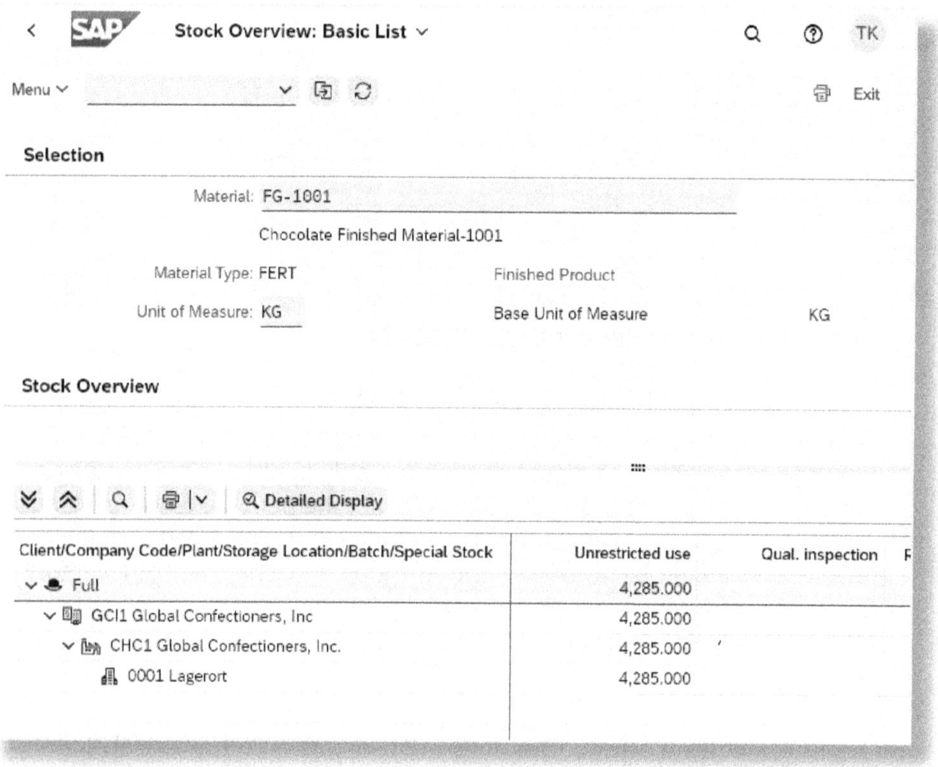


*Figure 12.13: "Display Stock Overview" app—inventory snapshot for individual material*

"This gives me a detailed understanding of the disposition of stock for a given material. It shows me information about what storage locations have inventory, batch information, how much is reserved for use in orders, how much I actually have in inventory, how much is blocked from use, and how much is on order, among other things. This is the best detailed snapshot of material inventory status that I have."

## 12.5 Display warehouse stock

"Now let me show you the DISPLAY WAREHOUSE STOCK app that I use for all my materials. I even have a layout set up so I can see the columns that I use most often."

Dave proudly showed the selection screen that he was so familiar with (see Figure 12.14).

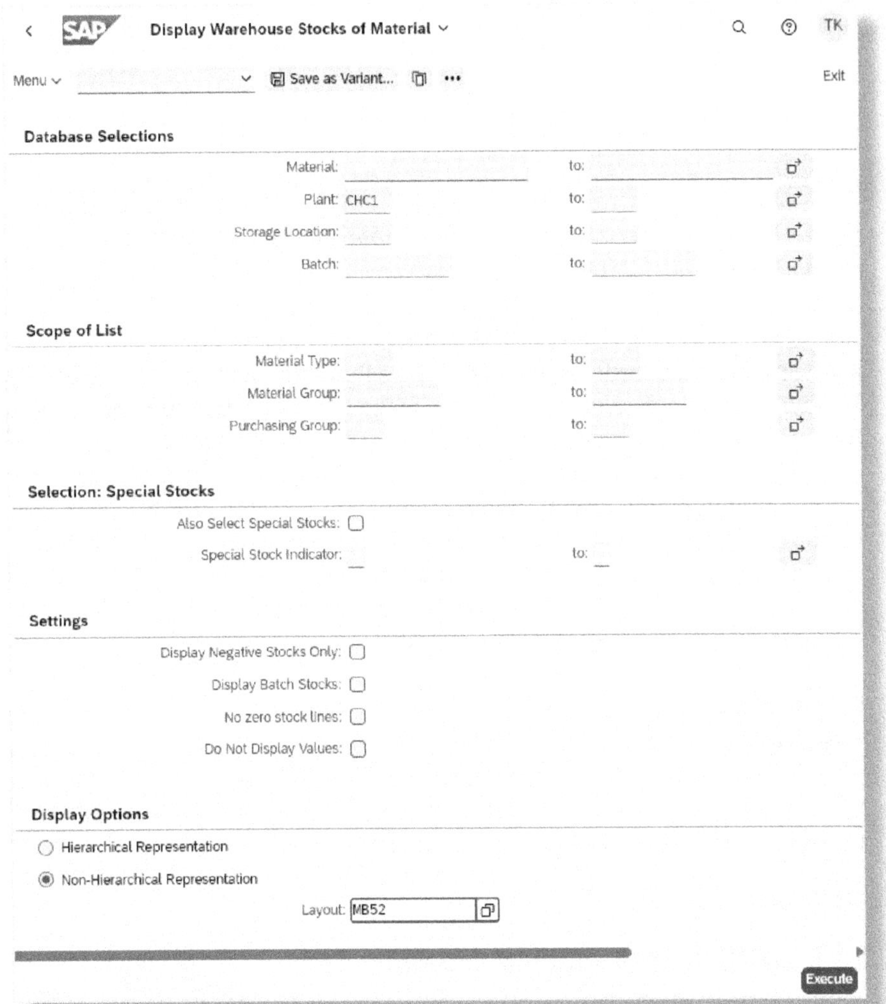


*Figure 12.14: "Display Warehouse Stock" app—inventory snapshot for multiple materials (selection)*

Dave clicked on the Execute button at the bottom right corner, and a nice report appeared, showing the current inventory levels for each of the materials. It even showed the amount of inventory held in the plant. Figure 12.15 shows the DISPLAY WAREHOUSE STOCK output screen.

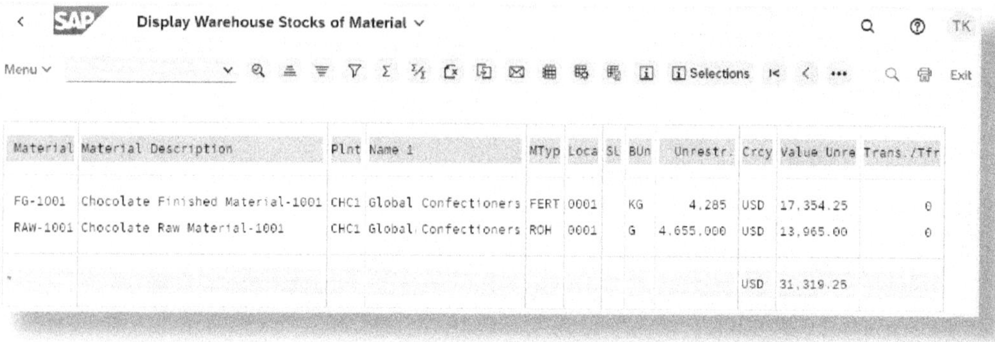


| Material | Material Description | Plnt | Name 1 | MTyp | Loca | SL | BUn | Unrestr. | Crcy | Value Unre | Trans./Tfr |
|---|---|---|---|---|---|---|---|---|---|---|---|
| FG-1001 | Chocolate Finished Material-1001 | CHC1 | Global Confectioners | FERT | 0001 | | KG | 4.285 | USD | 17,354.25 | 0 |
| RAW-1001 | Chocolate Raw Material-1001 | CHC1 | Global Confectioners | ROH | 0001 | | G | 4.655.000 | USD | 13,965.00 | 0 |
| | | | | | | | | | USD | 31,319.25 | |

*Figure 12.15: "Display Warehouse Stock" app—inventory snapshot for multiple materials (output)*

As the inventory controller of GCI's Chocotown facility, it was Dave's job to keep an eye on inventory levels and ensure that there was optimal inventory for raw materials. Too much inventory locks in a lot of working capital, and too little inventory results in production downtime. Moreover, for the previous two years, he had been given the additional responsibility of managing the finished goods inventory as well. Dave enjoyed this new role and anything that came in and went out of the plant had to pass through his team. He was proud of how the team was contributing to the operations. Each shipment that went out to a customer was something that gave Dave and his team a special sense of achievement.

"Excellent! And you know that this is the real-time inventory, as of this moment, correct?"

"Of course. This is my inventory right now as we speak. Thanks to these two apps, I am able to keep an eye on inventory levels all the time."

## 12.6 OBYC: MM-FI account determination

"It makes sense to me," Alex said. "Thanks for sharing that information. I do have a question about various movement types though. I was going through the DISPLAY MATERIAL DOCUMENTS LIST app the other day and I noticed that each material had different types of movements, and that each movement had a different accounting flow. Can you provide me an overview of movement types please?"

"Sure," Erin said. "It may be a bit on the technical side, but you seem to be interested in understanding the technical setup. Once you understand this setup, you'll be able to visualize the flow and navigate through the system efficiently. In fact, transaction OBYC *MM-FI account determination* forms the core of SAP's integration between these two modules. Thanks to this tight integration, all the materials management reports that we saw—DISPLAY STOCK OVERVIEW, DISPLAY WAREHOUSE STOCK, and DISPLAY MATERIAL DOCUMENT LIST—reflect accurately in financial accounting reports such as MATERIAL INVENTORY VALUES – BALANCE SUMMARY and MATERIAL INVENTORY VALUES – LINE ITEMS. Look at this." Erin pointed Alex to a chart which addressed movement types and accounting entries (see Figure 12.16).

The menu path for this is: TOOLS • CUSTOMIZING • IMG • SPRO EXECUTE PROJECT • MATERIALS MANAGEMENT • VALUATION AND ACCOUNT ASSIGNMENT • ACCOUNT DETERMINATION • ACCOUNT DETERMINATION WITHOUT WIZARD • CONFIGURE AUTOMATIC POSTINGS • ACCOUNT ASSIGNMENT.

| Process | Movement Type - Description | Transaction-Account Modifier | Debit GL | Debit GL Description | Transaction-Account Modifier | Credit GL | Credit GL Description |
|---|---|---|---|---|---|---|---|
| Purchase of Raw Material | 101 - Goods receipt for Purchase Order | BSX | 300000 | Inventory - Raw Material | WRX | 191100 | Goods Received / Invoice Received |
| Consumption of Raw Materials to Process Order | 261 - Goods Issue for order | GBB-VBR | 400010 | Raw materials consumed | BSX | 300000 | Inventory - Raw Material |
| Production of Semi-Finished Materials for Process Order | 101 - Goods receipt for Process Order | BSX | 790000 | Unfinished products | GBB-AUF | 895000 | Factory output of production orders |
| Consumption of Semi-Finished Materials to Process Order | 261 - Goods Issue for order | GBB-VBR | 890000 | Semi-finished products consumed | BSX | 790000 | Unfinished products |
| Production of Finished Materials for Process Order | 101 - Goods receipt for Process Order | BSX | 792000 | Finished goods inventory | GBB-AUF | 895000 | Factory output of production orders |
| Sampling for Quality Inspection | 331 - Goods Issue to sampling Quality Inspection | GBB-VQP | 237000 | Losses - consumption of quality control | BSX | 792000 | Finished goods inventory |
| Sale of Finished Material | 601 - Goods issue: delivery | GBB-VAX | 892000 | Change in finished products inventory | BSX | 792000 | Finished goods inventory |
| Scrapping of Finished Material | 551 - Goods Issue for scrapping | GBB-VNG | 890001 | Scrapped material - own production | BSX | 792000 | Finished goods inventory |
| Cycle Count (Physical Inventory) of Finished Material | 701 - Goods receipt for physical inventory adjustment | BSX | 792000 | Finished goods inventory | GBB-INV | 233000 | Losses - inventory variance |
| Initial Inventory Load of Finished Material | 561 - Initial entry of stock balances | BSX | 792000 | Finished goods inventory | GBB-BSA | 799999 | Inventory migration |
| Consumption of Raw Material from Sub-Contractor stock (special stock "O") | 543 - Goods Issue from stock at sub-contractor | GBB-VBO | 400010 | Raw materials consumed | BSX | 300000 | Inventory - Raw Material |
| Production of Finished Goods by Sub-Contractor (Production) | 101 - Goods receipt from sub-contractor | BSX | 792000 | Finished goods Inventory | BSV | 893010 | Sub-contract stock change |
| Production of Finished Goods by Sub-Contractor (Tolling Fee) | 101 - Goods receipt from sub-contractor | FRL | 417001 | Purchased services | WRX | 191100 | Goods Rcvd/Invoice Rcvd |

*Figure 12.16: Movement types and accounting entries*

"As you can see," Erin said, "we have the PROCESS listed in the column furthest to the left. MOVEMENT TYPE is in the next column, and the debit and credit postings in the subsequent columns. You can also see the TRANSACTION-ACCOUNT MODIFIER. These are SAP's terms for logically grouping similar types of transactions. The transaction-account modifier, along with the *valuation class* drive the accounting entries. Let me give you an example."

**Transaction keys and account modifier**

*Transaction keys* are used to determine general ledger accounts used by the system. *Account modifiers* are used to differentiate account determination, depending on the procedure.

A transaction key is predefined in the SAP system and cannot be changed. The transaction-account modifier and the valuation class drive the accounting entries.

The transaction key in MM-FI account determination is not the same as the transaction code. A *transaction code* is an alphanumeric code that represents a particular task in SAP. It allows users to access tasks directly without having to use menu paths.

"You may have seen an accounting entry, at the time of purchase, of a raw material as a debit to inventory and credit to GR/IR (goods receipt/invoice receipt)," Erin said. "Well, the configuration setup of transaction BSX (inventory posting) is responsible for the inventory posting and WRX (GR/IR clearing account) is responsible for GR/IR posting. So, when movement type 101 is used to record goods receipt of a raw material (valuation class 3000) for a purchase order, the system looks up the GL account for transaction BSX and WRX for valuation class 3000 and records in the accounting document.

"Similarly, when this raw material is consumed using movement type 261, the system looks up transaction GBB (offsetting entry for inventory posting) for account modifier (consumption for internal goods issues), and that reflects the GL account in the accounting document.

"The OBYC MM-FI account determination configuration is set up at the time of original implementation and once set up, these accounts are derived behind the scenes. Of course, you want to test the setup before going live to ensure that the correct accounts are being hit for the respective transactions. You can change this configuration after go-live, but the revised setup needs to be thoroughly tested, otherwise we may run the risk of impacting regular operations."

"Thank you for the explanation, Erin. I understand now," Alex said. "The other day I had an audit query where the auditors wanted me to provide GL postings for all samples consumed for quality inspection for one of our finished materials. I looked things up and saw that every material document that had movement type 331 had the same accounting impact. Now I know that the system was using GBB-VQP and BSX for the posting."

## 12.7 Conclusion

"Erin, Alex, I just got back from talking to the people at HQ" Dave said as he walked into Erin's office later that day. "They were happy with the explanation that we came up with, and they can better understand what they are looking at when they take snapshots of inventory. Thanks for all your help."

"Anytime, Dave," Erin said. "What I've always learned is that the system always behaves the right way. We just need to know where to look. It's important to understand not only how to run applications, but also what the result of running the app signifies. Without proper understanding, bad decisions can be made. What do you say, Alex?"

"I agree," Alex said. "I've always learned a lot when I go with the approach 'it is always the people and process that break things, the system always works correctly!'"

# 13 System interface—Fiori tiles and transactions

**"Erin, in looking how to access the system, there are two different interfaces in play", Alex noted when he saw her one day. "That's true," she replied. "One of the original interfaces was the graphical user interface or GUI. This was somewhat limited, and with computing power increasing over the years, a newer interface called Fiori was developed to provide a better user experience. Newer system functionality mainly uses Fiori, whereas older standard functionality still uses the GUI technology."**

## 13.1 Graphical user interface (GUI)

"What's the difference between transactions and Fiori tiles?" Alex queried.

"That's an excellent question, Alex," Erin replied. "Let's start by talking about transactions. These are programs that can execute functions in SAP based on input from the user. They're designed to run in what is known as a *graphical user interface* environment. This name for this is shortened to its initials–*GUI*. One of the features of a GUI is the ability to use your mouse to click on icons that are displayed in a window in order to let the system know what to process. SAP GUI is the earliest icon-based interface to be used by SAP systems, and it requires that a special program be installed on your computer to allow access to the SAP system. Many hundreds of transactions have been developed and added over the years. Here at GCI, however, we don't use SAP GUI. Instead, we use what's known as *Webgui*, which duplicates the functions of SAP GUI using a web browser. Webgui is also known as *SAP GUI for HTML*, which better describes how it works."

"I use the address `https://GCIhost/sap/bc/gui/sc/its/webgui` to get to the GUI login window," responded Alex. "I have saved that as a favorite site in my browser. After logging on to the system, I can use the menu to execute transactions, or I can enter a transaction ID in the field next to the MENU dropdown at the upper left of the window" (see Figure 13.1).

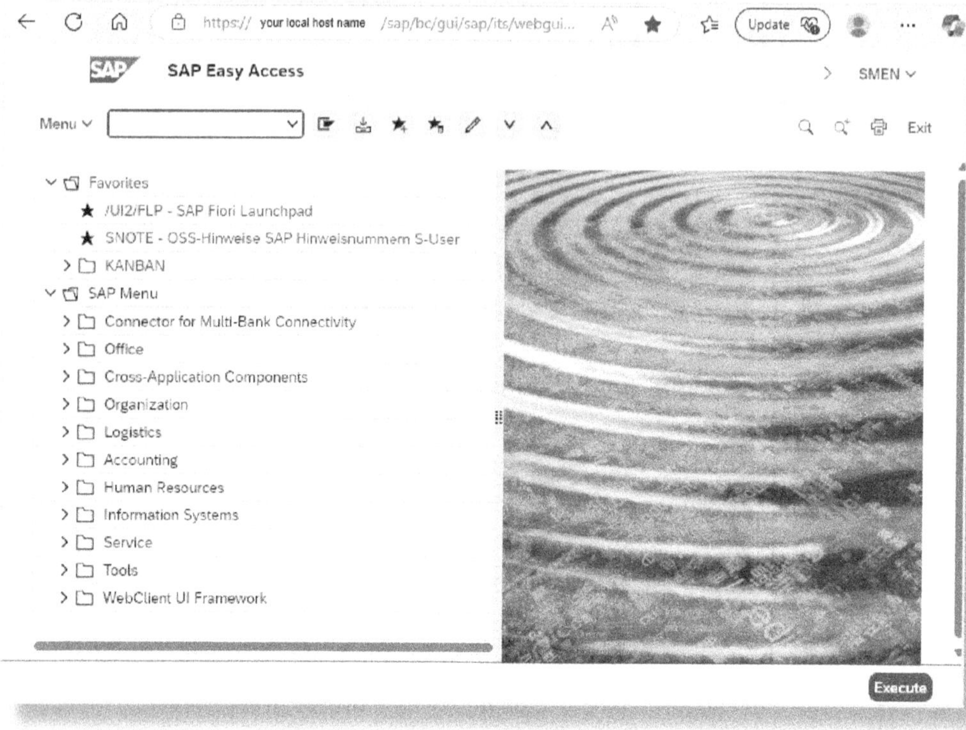


*Figure 13.1: Webgui menu with address*

## 13.2 Fiori interface

"GCI currently uses the Webgui directly for only a few transactions," continued Erin. "Almost everything is now accessed through the *Fiori* interface. With the new interface comes some new terminology. Transactions in GUI are known as applications or *apps* in Fiori. Instead of using the GUI menu structure, a special *Fiori Launchpad (FLP)* is used for "launching" (executing) apps. The apps are represented on the launchpad as *tiles* (see Figure 13.2). Clicking on a tile with your mouse starts the app."

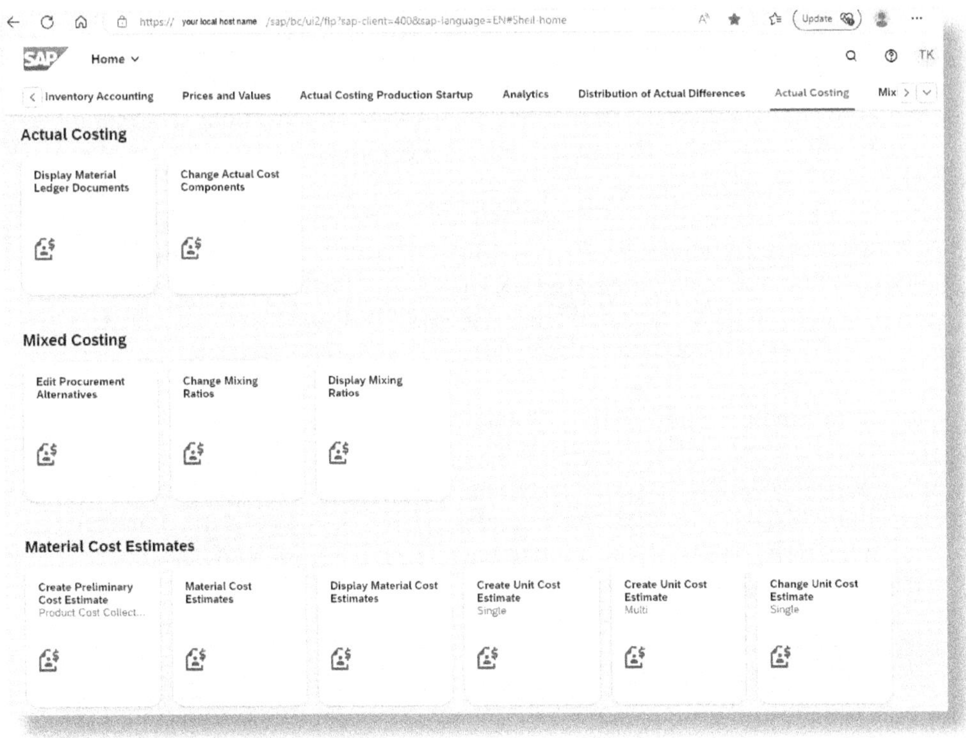


*Figure 13.2: Fiori launchpad*

"The Fiori interface is also web-based and is executed through a browser, like the Webgui interface," she went on. "You can get to it at GCI by using the address `https://GCIhost/sap/bc/ui2/flp`. *GCIhost* is the special name we use for our SAP server computer. Other companies use a different host name. If you're already logged into the GUI interface, you can also enter via transaction */n/ui2/flp*. This initiates the Fiori launchpad in your browser. You can have the Webgui and the Fiori launchpad available simultaneously as separate browser windows. That makes it easy to switch between Fiori tiles and GUI transactions."

## 13.3 GUI transactions as Fiori tiles

This discussion got Alex thinking. "Wouldn't it be a good idea to make sure that people only need one method to access data in SAP?"

Erin replied, "Actually, SAP has taken care of that. Although Fiori apps cannot be called up from the GUI menu, GUI transactions can be executed from Fiori tiles. Apps that are written from scratch to be run in the Fiori landscape have much more capabilities than the standard GUI transactions. That's the main reason SAP developed the Fiori architecture. However, SAP realized that not everything needed to have those extra capabilities, and they developed the SAP GUI for HTML web-based interface to allow transactions to be executed from the Fiori environment. In fact, a large number of GUI transactions have been delivered as Fiori tiles. However, there are a few transactions that GCI uses that are not delivered as Fiori tiles. This is due to SAP's long-term roadmap for future development of the system."

"How do I know if a transaction is assigned to a Fiori tile?" asked Alex.

"If you know the transaction ID, you can enter it in the search field of the launchpad (see Figure 13.3). As long as you have security access, if the tile is found, it will be displayed in the results. From there you can click on the tile and execute the function.

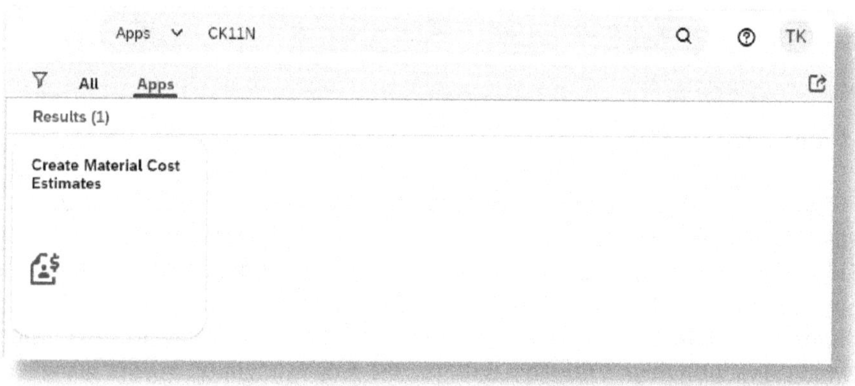


*Figure 13.3: Finding if a transaction has a Fiori tile*

"In addition, you can determine if a Fiori tile executes a transaction by going to the blue user icon at the top right of the launchpad and selecting ABOUT" (see Figure 13.4).

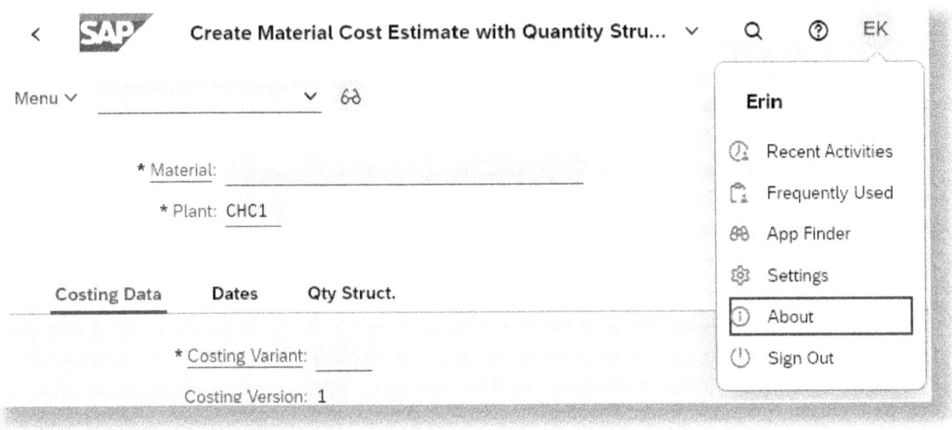


*Figure 13.4: Fiori tile—"About" menu selection*

"If the resulting window shows the FRAMEWORK ID set to GUI, then this tile calls up a GUI transaction (see Figure 13.5). These apps can be executed either as transactions in the GUI environment or as tiles in the Fiori environment.

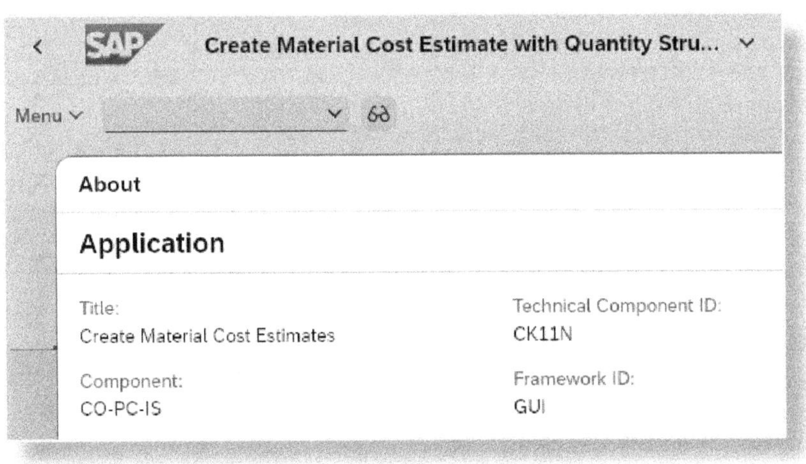


*Figure 13.5: Fiori app using SAP GUI for html interface*

"On the other hand, if the FRAMEWORK ID is set to UI5, then this is a native Fiori application (see Figure 13.6). There is usually a special app ID assigned. In this case, the app ID is F1780."

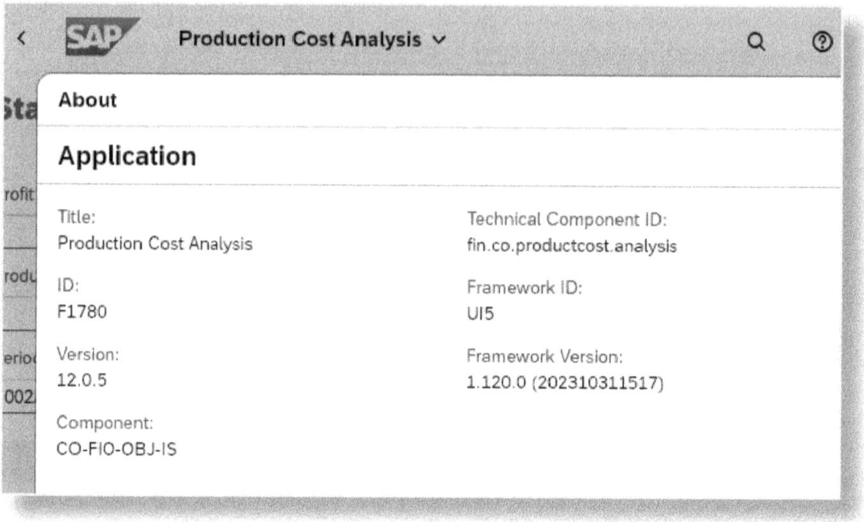


*Figure 13.6: Standard Fiori app*

"That's great information, Erin," said Alex. "But what can be done about transactions that don't have an associated Fiori tile?"

"Fortunately, SAP has enabled their customers' IT departments to create new tiles to call up those transactions. One of the notes that SAP has published about this (SAP Note 2700282–"How to create a SAP GUI for HTML(WebGUI) tile in Fiori launchpad") tells us how to do this. If you get approval, we can schedule work to create the tiles for the missing transactions. However, if this is a configuration transaction, we recommend not making a separate tile, since this work should only be performed by the technical staff."

"Thank you for all this great information, Erin!" Alex exclaimed. I'll go back through the lists that I've made to find the transactions which can be made into Fiori tiles. I'll be in touch."

Alex went back to his desk and made a list of GUI transactions that GCI used that did not have corresponding Fiori tiles, so that he could get back to Erin with the information. Figure 13.7 shows the list that he came up with.

| Transaction | Name | Transaction | Name |
|---|---|---|---|
| CON2 | Revaluation at Actual Prices | KSU5 | Execute Actual Assesment |
| CORK | Enter Process Order Confirmation | KSU7 | Create Plan Assessmnet Cycle |
| KB11N | Manual Reposting of Actual Costs | KSU8 | Change Plan Assessment Cycle |
| KKAQ | Display Work in Process: Collective | KSU9 | Display Plan Assessment Cycle |
| KKAY | Display Work in Process: Single Order | KSUA | Delete Plan Assessment Cycle |
| KP04 | Set Planner Profile | KSUB | Execute Plan Assessment |
| KP06 | Change Cost Element/Activity Planning | KSV1 | Create Actual Distribution Cycle |
| KP07 | Display Cost Element/Activity Planning | KSV2 | Change Actual Distribution Cycle |
| KP46 | Change Statistical Key Figure Planning | KSV3 | Display Actual Distribution Cycle |
| KSBL | Cost Centers: Planning Overview | KSV5 | Execute Actual Distribution |
| KSII | Actual Price Calculation | KSV7 | Create Plan Distribution Cycle |
| KSPI | Plan Price Calculation | KSV8 | Change Plan Distribution Cycle |
| KSS2 | Actual Cost Splitting | KSV9 | Display Plan Distribution Cycle |
| KSS4 | Plan Cost Splitting | KSVA | Delete Plan Distribution Cycle |
| KSU1 | Create Actual Assessment Cycle | KSVB | Execute Plan Distribution |
| KSU2 | Change Actual Assessment Cycle | MLCCSPD | Cost Components for Price |
| KSU3 | Display Actual Assessment Cycle | S_ALR_87013611 | Cost Centers: Plan/Actual/Variance |

*Figure 13.7: Transactions without delivered Fiori tiles*

Alex also noted that two programs that were run from transaction SA38 should also be processed from Fiori tiles. This required a little more work from the IT team, but making these executable from Fiori tiles would help to define them to security roles. The two programs are *R_FINS_PLAN_TRANS_CO_ERP_2_S4H* for copying the cost center plan data and *R_FINS_PLAN_TRANS_ACTY_ERP_S4H* for copying the calculated activity rates.

Alex also made a list of SAP-delivered Fiori apps, associated with Controlling, to execute GUI transactions. He knew that these could either be run from the Fiori Launchpad or from WebGUI. This is shown in Figure 13.8.

| Fiori App | Transaction | Fiori App | Transaction |
|---|---|---|---|
| Analyze Order | KKBC_ORD | Display Process Order | COR3 |
| Analyze Summarization Hierarchy | KKBC_HOE_H | Display Production Order | CO03 |
| Calculate Work in Process Collective | KKAO | Display Resource | CRC3 |
| Calculate Work in Process Order - Single | KKAX | Display Stock Overview | MMBE |
| Change Material | MM02 | Display Work Center | CR03 |
| Change Process Order | COR2 | Distribution of Inventory Differences | CKMDUVMAT |
| Change Production Order | CO02 | Edit Actual Costing Runs | CKMLCP |
| Change Resource | CRC2 | Edit Prices for Activity Types | KP26 |
| Change Work Center | CR02 | Manage Costing Runs | CK40N |
| Confirm Process Order Phase | COR6N | Manage Master Recipes | C201/C202/C203 |
| Create Material | MM01 | Material Costs and Inventory Values | S_ALR_87013181 |
| Create Material Cost Estimates | CK11N | Material Price Analysis | CKM3 |
| Create Process Order | COR1 | Material Value Flow Monitor | ML4HVFM |
| Create Production Order | CO01 | Monitor Process / Planned Orders | COOISPI |
| Create Resource | CRC1 | Monitor Produciton / Planned Orders | COOIS |
| Create Unit Cost Estimate Single | KKPAN | Post Goods Movement | MIGO |
| Create Work Center | CR01 | Release Material Cost Estimates | CK24 |
| Diplay Warehouse Stock | MB52 | Run Variance Calculation Order - Single | KKS2 |
| Display Journal Entries | FB03 | Run Variance Calculation Orders - By Lot | KKS1 |
| Display Material | MM03 | Runa Actual Settlement Order - Single | KO88 |
| Display Material Document List | MB51 | Select Orders | S_ALR_87013127 |
| Display Plan Data for Activity Types | KP27 | Settle Orders Optimized | CO88H |

*Figure 13.8: Fiori apps with associated GUI transactions*

# 14 And what if we acquire another company?

**"Alex, did you read the news on the intranet?" Bob asked Alex one day. "We're acquiring another confectionery company called National Confectioners, Limited (NCL). Headquarters is looking for suggestions on how to integrate NCL, from an operations and IT standpoint. I know by now you have a good understanding of our system setup, so can you and Erin put something together so that we can present a case to management? I'll introduce both of you to Frank, who is the plant controller at NCL. He'll explain the setup there so that you have all the facts."**

"Sure, Bob, it will be my pleasure to work on this assignment," Alex said.

After a few days, Alex met with Bob. "This is what Erin and I suggest based on our discussions with Frank," Alex said. "NCL currently uses a homegrown system for their day-to-day operations. We recommend bringing them over to our SAP system in order to leverage our system setup and harmonize our processes."

Alex proposed the following:

- **Company code**—set up NCL as a separate company code. Management wants to maintain NCL as an independent entity, while leveraging the reach of GCI's distribution network.
- **Chart of accounts**—continue to use the existing chart of accounts. This will facilitate consolidation of reporting of all the company codes. GCI will simply need to extend GL accounts to the NCL company code.
- **Operating concern, fiscal year variant, and controlling area**—NCL should use GCI's operating concern, fiscal year variant, and controlling area given that management wants a single internal reporting view of combined operations of GCI and NCL.
- **Plants**—NCL's three manufacturing facilities will be set up as three separate plants, assigned to the new company code for NCL. There is already a lot of goods movement between the three plants, and

Alex and Erin envisage a lot of movement between GCI's plants and NCL's. This will be enabled using intercompany stock transfer.

- **Sales**—NCL currently uses the distribution network of another company. They will switch over to GCI's distribution network. This will allow the combined company to use GCI's sales and distribution setup.
- **Profit centers and cost centers**—new profit centers and cost centers need to be set up for NCL. NCL's manufacturing facilities will be represented in the profit center hierarchy and cost center hierarchy, similar to GCI's current setup.
- **Activity type**—GCI's current cost drivers are direct labor and machine hours. NCL uses an additional cost driver for machine setup cost. This is a substantial cost component for NCL, and they want to retain this visibility when they move over to the GCI system. GCI could implement this additional activity type as well. However, the effort required by the production planning team to retrofit GCI's recipes needs to be reviewed.
- **Cost allocations**—apart from the plant-specific cost allocations to replicate GCI's structure in NCL, HQ cost allocations to NCL are also needed.
- **Internal orders**—since integration of NCL into GCI requires significant investment over the next eighteen months or so, the recommendation is to use internal orders for each specific function so that management can allocate budgets and track actual costs.
- **Material master**—there are a significant number of common raw materials between GCI and NCL that should be extended to NCL's plants. New material masters will be required for finished materials given that there are very few common finished products.
- **Manufacturing processes**—NCL currently uses production orders in their internal system. They do not use PI sheets. The plan is to implement process orders for NCL, which will allow harmonization of processes and also provide the benefit of using PI sheets.
- **R&D costs**—NCL has a dedicated research and development setup and there is a need to track the cost of process orders used for R&D. GCI does not have as big a focus on R&D and currently issues goods to an R&D cost center. The proposal is to use a new process order type for R&D purposes. Each R&D initiative will be created as a process order, to be settled to cost center.

"This is great. I like the recommendations," Bob said. "This is exactly what headquarters is looking for. Thanks!"

Alex and Erin had put a lot of effort into understanding NCL's requirements, as explained by Frank. Alex was especially proud of having incorporated his learning into this special assignment.

# 15 In conclusion

The SAP Controlling module consolidates the benefits of the integrated nature of SAP software.

Whereas processes in SAP Finance are very similar in most organizations, SAP Controlling offers variety, since the requirements usually differ from one company to the next. Each company's SAP installation has its own design variants, but the overall goal is to provide management with visibility of the activities within the organization.

As you may have noticed from the acquisition scenario, almost all the concepts that we explored in the previous chapters were used to arrive at the proposed design for the acquisition integration.

We hope you have enjoyed the exciting journey into this powerful, versatile tool!

# A The Authors

## Ashish Sampat

Ashish Sampat is a qualified finance and costing professional with more than two decades of industry experience in the SAP Finance and Controlling space. He has provided global clients with solutions in many areas of SAP Controlling. Born and educated in India, Ashish now lives in suburban Chicago. He is the author of several other books, all published by Espresso Tutorials: "First Steps in SAP Controlling (CO)" (English); "Vos premiers pas avec SAP Contrôle de gestion (CO)" (French); "Guia para iniciantes do SAP Controlling" (Portuguese); "First Steps in SAP Controlling (CO)" (Japanese); "Expert tips to Unleash full Potential of SAP Controlling" (English); "Customizing Changes for Controlling in S/4HANA" (English); "SAP S/4HANA Delta our la configuration CO" (French).

## Tom King

Tom King is an author, speaker, and independent CO consultant. Before retiring from a large manufacturing company, he was the lead CO analyst for over 10 years, concentrating on product costing and cost object controlling. He is also the author of five additional books published by Espresso Tutorials, covering diverse controlling topics: "Practical Guide to SAP® CO Templates", "SAP S/4HANA® Product Cost Planning Configuration and Master Data", "SAP S/4HANA® Product Cost Planning—Costing with Quantity Structure", and "Material Valuation and the Material Ledger in SAP S/4HANA®" (translated into German, French, and Spanish), and "A Practical Guide to Manufacturing Variances in SAP S/4HANA®".

# B Index

## I



## L



## M



## O



## P



## Q



## R



## S

## T



## U



## V



## W

# C Disclaimer

This publication contains references to the products of SAP SE.

SAP®, ABAP®, ExpenseIt®, Joule, OpenSAP®, SAP ActiveAttention®, SAP® Adaptive Server® Enterprise, SAP® Advantage Database Server®, SAP® AppGyver®, SAP Ariba®, SAP Business ByDesign®, SAP® Business Explorer®, SAP® Bex, SAP® BusinessObjects, SAP® BusinessObjects Explorer®, SAP® BusinessObjects Web Intelligence®, SAP Business One®, SAP Business Workflow®, SAP BW/4HANA®, SAP Concur®, SAP® Crystal Reports®, SAP EarlyWatch®, SAP® Emarsys®, SAP Fieldglass®, SAP Fiori®, SAP Garden®, SAP® Global Trade Services (SAP® GTS®), SAP HANA®, SAP® Jam, SAP Lumira®, SAP MaxAttention®, SAP® MaxDB®, SAP NetWeaver®, SAP® PartnerEdge®, SAP® Sapphire®, SAP® PowerBuilder®, SAP® PowerDesigner®, SAP® R/3®, SAP® Replication Server®, SAP® Roambi®, SAP S/4HANA®, SAP S/4HANA® Cloud, SAP Signavio®, SAP® SQL Anywhere®, SAP Strategic Enterprise Management® (SAP® SEM®), SAP SuccessFactors®, SAP Vora®, Taulia®, The Best Run SAP®, TripIt®, and other SAP products and services mentioned herein as well as their respective logos are trademarks or registered trademarks of SAP SE in Germany and other countries.

SAP SE is neither the author nor the publisher of this publication and is not responsible for its content. SAP Group shall not be liable for errors or omissions with respect to the materials. The only warranties for SAP Group products and services are those that are set forth in the express warranty statements accompanying such products and services, if any. Nothing herein should be construed as constituting an additional warranty.

# More Espresso Tutorials Books

Stefan Eifler, Christoph Theis:

**Value Flows into SAP® Margin Analysis (CO-PA) in S/4HANA®**

- Value flows based on the logistical sales and production process
- Comparison of costing-based and account-based CO-PA
- Presentation of the changes in the value flow compared to SAP ERP
- Continuous numerical example right up to closing activities

*http://5497.espresso-tutorials.com*

Tom King:

**A Practical Guide to Manufacturing Variances in SAP S/4HANA®**

- How SAP Manufacturing and Controlling modules interact
- Sources of target and actual costs used to determine variances
- How manufacturing reporting affects cost center accounting
- Strategies for interpreting and managing variances in manufacturing

*http://5646.espresso-tutorials.com*

Nora Voigt:

**Practical Guide to SAP S/4HANA® Controlling**

- New features in Controlling with SAP S/4HANA
- Overview of the functions of all subcomponents
- Effects of S/4HANA on your business processes
- Practical explanations using a continuous example

*https://es-tu.de/uXasR*

John Pringle:

**Practical Guide to SAP® Profit Center Accounting—Second Edition**

- Fundamentals of SAP Profit Center Accounting (PCA)
- Concepts, master data, actual data flow, and planning basics
- Differences between PCA in classic and new GL
- Reporting for Profit Center Accounting (PCA)

*https://es-tu.de/cYNZ*

Tanya Duncan:

**Practical Guide to SAP CO-PC (Product Cost Controlling) in SAP S/4HANA®– 2nd edition**

- Ntroduction to value flows in SAP S/4HANA Controlling
- Step-by-step examples
- Configuration for make-to- stock and make-to-order costing
- Detailed month-end closing processes

*https://es-tu.de/6wHx7q*

Janet Salmon:

**First Steps in SAP S/4HANA® Universal Parallel Accounting**

- Introduction Parallel Accounting in SAP S/4HANA
- Use Cases for Universal Parallel Accounting
- How Universal Parallel Accounting differs from Previous Approaches
- Explore key changes to asset accounting, overhead accounting, and inventory accounting

*https://es-tu.de/AbGDJ*